Jurisprudence
of international law

Melland Schill Studies in International Law
Series editor Professor Dominic McGoldrick

The Melland Schill name has a long-established reputation for high standards of scholarship. Each volume in the series addresses major public international law issues and current developments. Many of the Melland Schill volumes have become standard works of reference. Interdisciplinary and accessible, the contributions are vital reading for students, scholars and practitioners of public international law, international organisations, international relations, international politics, international economics and international development.

Jurisprudence of international law

The humanitarian dimension

Nikolaos K. Tsagourias

Juris Publishing

MANCHESTER
UNIVERSITY PRESS

Published by Manchester University Press
Oxford Road, Manchester M13 9NR, UK
http://www.man.ac.uk/mup

British Library Cataloguing-in-Publication Data
A catalogue record for this book is available from the British Library

ISBN 0 7190 5465 6 *hardback*

First published in the USA and Canada by
Juris Publishing, Inc.
Executive Park,
One Odell Plaza, NY 10701

Library of Congress Cataloging-in-Publication Data applied for

ISBN   1 929446 10 1   *hardback*

First published 2000

09 08 07 06 05 04 03 02 01 00   10 9 8 7 6 5 4 3 2 1

Typeset in 10/12pt Times
by Graphicraft Limited, Hong Kong
Printed in Great Britain
by Biddles Ltd

Contents

Contents

Series editor's foreword

As what has been called the 'century of violence' ended, humanitarian intervention was once more at the centre of legal, political and ethical discourse. Increasing recourse to such a doctrine was occasioning widespread reflection on the big questions of how and why states behave, whether there is a meaningful concept of an international community, how fundamental values are determined and how they relate to each other. This book is a challenging examination of the jurisprudence of international law on humanitarian intervention. It poses challenges to thinking and argumentation and proposes a redescription of humanitarian intervention.

Preface

This book presents the case of humanitarian intervention within a discursive theory of international law. It identifies and examines the philosophical and legal concepts which inform the case of humanitarian intervention and scrutinises the pertinent practice. It finally proposes a redescription under a discursive model where the critical parameters of any action are evaluated and accounted for.

The discursive model redirects our reflective nature towards distinguishing and de-concretising the manifold aspects which humanitarian actions contain. Instead of monolithic evaluations, we need to consider which values are at stake and how they are projected in our action. In order to do this, we need first to acquaint ourselves with the existing lego-jurisprudential discourse. Thus, there is an analysis and evaluation of the theoretical milieu and how it moulds the practice of humanitarian intervention. Also we explore how legal rules which vie to control humanitarian intervention are moulded by theory and how they inform the relevant practice in cases such as Kosovo, Rwanda or Somalia. Having exposed the constituent elements of legal discourse, we are able to proceed with a redescription under the discursive model which contains reflection, responsibility and vision.

This book is a revised study of my thesis submitted at the University of Nottingham in 1997 for the degree of Doctor of Philosophy. I am indebted to my doctoral supervisor, Professor Nigel White, for his support, guidance and encouragement and Mr. Dino Kritsiotis for his constant support. I owe a debt of gratitude to Professor Anthony Carty for his assistance and valuable comments and suggestions during the preparation of this book.

Also, I would like to thank the series editor, Professor Dominic McGoldrick, and Nicola Viinikka and Pippa Kenyon from Manchester University Press for their kindness. Finally, special thanks are owed to my family and friends.

Nikolaos K. Tsagourias

Abbreviations

AFDI	*Annuaire Français de droit international*
African JI & Comp. L	*African Journal of International and Comparative Law*
AJIL	*American Journal of International Law*
Australian YBIL	*Australian Yearbook of International Law*
BYBIL	*British Yearbook of International Law*
Cmd	United Kingdom Command Papers
Case WRJIL	*Case Western Reserve Journal of International Law*
Canadian YBIL	*Canadian Yearbook of International Law*
Cal. WILJ	*California Western International Law Journal*
CLS	Critical Legal Studies (movement)
Col. J Trans. L	*Columbia Journal of Transnational Law*
Col. L Rev	*Columbia Law Review*
Denver JIL & Pol.	*Denver Journal of International Law and Policy*
Dep't. State Bull.	*Department of State Bulletin*
ECOWAS	*Economic Community of West African States*
EJIL	*European Journal of International Law*
FRY	Federal Republic of Yugoslavia
GA	General Assembly
GAOR	General Assembly Official Records
Ga. JI & Comp. L	*Georgia Journal of International and Comparative Law*
German YBIL	*German Yearbook of International Law*
Hague YBIL	*Hague Yearbook of International Law*
Hansard	Debates of the United Kingdom Parliament
Harvard ILJ	*Harvard International Law Journal*
Harvard L Rev	*Harvard Law Review*
H. C. Deb.	House of Commons Debates
Hum. RQ	*Human Rights Quarterly*
ICJ	International Court of Justice
ICLQ	*International and Comparative Law Quarterly*
ILA	International Law Association
ILC	International Law Commission
ILM	*International Legal Materials*

Abbreviations

Indian JIL	*Indian Journal of International Law*
Israel YBHR	*Israel Yearbook on Human Rights*
JO.AN.	*Journal officiel. Débats parlementaires – Assemblée Nationale – Compte rendus*
Keesing's	Keesing's Record of World Events
LNOJ	*League of Nations Official Journal*
LNTS	*League of Nations Treaty Series*
Leiden ILJ	*Leiden International Law Journal*
Modern L Rev.	*Modern Law Review*
Neth. ILR	*Netherlands International Law Review*
Netherlands YBIL	*Netherlands Yearbook of International Law*
OAU	Organisation of African Unity
PEF	*La Politique étrangère de la France* (publication du ministère des affaires étrangères)
Proc. ASIL	*Proceedings of the American Society of International Law*
RC	*Recueil des Cours de l'Académie de Droit International*
RGDIP	*Revue générale de droit international public*
SC	Security Council
SCOR	*Security Council Official Records*
SC Res.	Security Council Resolution
UN Doc.	United Nations Document
Vanderbilt J Tran. L	*Vanderbilt Journal of Transnational Law*
Va JIL	*Virginia Journal of International Law*
YBILC	*Yearbook of the International Law Commission*
Yale JIL	*The Yale Journal of International Law*
Yale LJ	*The Yale Law Journal*
ZaöRV	*Zeitschrift für ausländisches und öffentliches Rechtund Völkerrecht*

Introduction

Humanitarian intervention entails manifold legal and theoretical constructions. The legal arguments which delineate humanitarian intervention enjoy, *per se*, inner coherence, certainty and appeal but this is eroded when one becomes acquainted with the 'opposite' reasoning which may exert an equally convincing appeal. Hence, one is faced with the dilemma of having to choose between normatively contrasting theses and there is a compulsion to singularise the trail of argument in order to reach an objective result.

The frustration experienced because of this supposedly interpretative manipulation of legal rules is precipitated by scant explication of the theoretical assumptions which inform legal arguments. Theory constructs a point of derivation which becomes the foundation of law even if mythical or notional in its premises. This foundation varied from theism to secularism, from God, nature and reason to the command of the sovereign or the will of the people. These theoretical constructions provide ideological context to the legal system, control legal reasoning and predetermine the outcome. They are external to legal argument and unific though implicit. Consequently, their acknowledgement palliates the rigidity of legal argumentation by elucidating the conditions and causes of disagreement. Their explicit demonstration remedies the sterility and simplicity of legal debate. It does not, however, conclude the debate because it refers to those presupposed foundations where agreement is hard to obtain and which taint with their subjectivity the neutrality of legal rules. Hence, legal discourse receded and reclaimed the distinction between theory and doctrine, between prescription and description, as a means of preserving the distinctive nature of law. Legal professionals feel that they should engage in the study of proper law only because theory, the extra-legal environment, jeopardises the presumed objectivity of legal norms by extending the ambit of discord to rather abstract assertions vulnerable to antagonistic constructions. This has been described graphically by A. M. Honoré: 'Decade after decade Positivist and Natural Lawyers face one another in the final of the World Cup. . . . Victory goes now to one side,

1

now to the other, but the enthusiasm of players and spectators alike ensures that the losing side will take its revenge.'[1]

At the same time, doctrinal argument has failed to provide the anticipated sense of security and clarity. There are instances where doctrinal outcomes seem either irrelevant or controversial. The area on the use of force is an example. The rule on non-intervention has been meagrely reflected in state practice or was attributed with antagonistic interpretative courses promoted as correct doctrinal answers. Those who envisage a restrictive or relative interpretation of the rule are vying to prove the accuracy of their legal position, and being unable to solve the dispute between equally valid arguments, they resort to theory as the final arbiter by employing principles such as justice, human rights, peace and sovereignty. Again, they reverberate *déjà vu* arguments and they can only 'cheer or jeer, label [the] opponent a moral leper or a disingenuous romantic'.[2]

The situation thus becomes circular. Legal theory uses abstractions which are avoided by relying exclusively on doctrine. However, the latter produces problems of definition which can be resolved by appealing to theory. Because this cannot produce clarity, we need to disentangle the debate. This is achieved by explicating the moulding of the doctrinal discourse by theoretical dispositions and their dialectical interplay. More specifically, I shall demonstrate how legal discourse appertaining to humanitarian intervention is informed by theoretical explorations, and illustrate how activity in this field emulates these legal and theoretical constructions.

What emerges as a defining point in contemporary legal discourse is a perpetual regression to monosyllabic referents which claim an objectified truth and which equip legal scholars with confidence that they possess the means to address sufficiently any situation. However, this method is inadequate to address the numerous variants involved because conditions and situations, ideals, politics and rules interweave and their significance decodes a certain incident. Humanitarian intervention has legal, political, moral, personal, human or psychological dimensions. Searching for objectivity and overlooking its multifariousness produces self-restrictive arguments. Legal discourse becomes external, lacking a sense of commitment and when *aséptisation* crumbles, we oscillate aimlessly between apology and utopia,[3] contextualisation and normativity. The missing element is the personal stigma of the discussers which is devoured by the practice and the structure. International law is portrayed as concerned only with producing structural arguments and

[1] A. M. Honoré, 'Groups, Laws and Obedience', in A. W. B. Simpson (ed.), *Oxford Essays in Jurisprudence*, Second Series (Oxford, Clarendon Press, 1973), p. 1, at pp. 1–2.
[2] A. M. Honoré, *Making Law Bind: Essays Legal and Philosophical* (Oxford, Oxford University Press, 1987), p. 33.
[3] M. Koskenniemi, *From Apology to Utopia. The Structure of International Legal Argument* (Helsinki, Finnish Lawyers' Publishing Company, 1989).

not with the significance of the argument, the responsibility of the debaters, the significance of the incidence and of its consequences.

Therefore we embrace here the dialogic knowledge contained in the value of human dignity. Human dignity as envisaged here does not rely on a previous algorithm; it is induced by our effective nature. It describes a value, the achievement of dignified life, but also a discursive process of reflection, assessment and projection. In our dialectical mode there exists deliberation, judgment and choice among manifold forms of life which should be understood and evaluated. It increases the knowledge of how things are and increases the possibilities of contemplating how they may be, expands our perceptive nature and liberates our thinking from uncritical encumbrances. Human dignity entreats appreciation, creativity, empathy, edification and multi-instructionism. It induces lawyers to encounter the phenomena, appreciate their multi-meaning, bear responsibility for their findings and imagine a new order.

Hence, human dignity redirects our envision by performing a redescription[4] through self-exploration, imagination and reflective commitment which transcends the distinction between private and public spheres and reclaims our humanity on more familiar grounds than referential anchoring. It redirects our action by acknowledging and appreciating our finitude, fears, hopes and dreams to construct a meaningful life. Inter-subjectivity materialises by appreciating our similarities as people who strive for self-creation, empowerment and happiness rather than being paralysed by our differences which emerge from diverse contextualities.

Such understanding fosters a sense of solidarity which accentuates our awareness of situations where people who strive like us are denied a meaningful life. Human dignity does not inhibit action when we notice human suffering, contrary to the paralysis which certain versions of relativism manifest. Through this imaginative identification, we expand our sense of 'we' to embrace the rest of humanity. We can also expand the level of human acquaintance to other situations by understanding human vicissitudes and appreciation of contingencies. Because this expansion is based on our understanding and realisation of ourselves, on reflecting upon our common potentialities and aspirations, humanitarian intervention becomes our practice instead of some superimposed exigency.

In the last chapter we expand on the notion of human dignity and redescribe activity in this field accordingly. This transition, the redescription, is an innate, conscious process, although its vocalisation may share similarities with more conventional discourses.[5] What is important though is this imaginative redirection emerging from understanding our human predicament. In

---

[4] R. Rorty, *Contigency, Irony and Solidarity* (Cambridge, Cambridge University Press, 1989), chs 3, 4, 9.

[5] R. Rorty, *Philosophy and the Mirror of Nature* (Oxford, Blackwell, 1979), ch. VIII.

order to do this, we need to acquaint ourselves with the existing discourse and understand the description of the world it proffers in order to reconstruct the familiar with what we propose here. We purport to show how the discourse looks and how it would look under our new idiom. Therefore, we shall present the legal and theoretical narrative and its agonising attempts to produce objective, true arguments, to introduce a modicum of morality when faced with hard cases but also to concede a leeway for moral or political relativists. For instance, humanitarian intervention within natural law appeals to modes of justification springing from theistic assumptions such as the moral standing of humans as God's mirror or Kantian ones as partakers of universal reason. On the other hand, positivism claims a distinction between facts and values which supports objective knowledge but even timidly accepts certain human values. This state of affairs, inclusive and anguishing, is contrasted with our proposal empowered by recognition of our common humanity on a more mundane basis and which positions man within the larger experience of humanity.[6]

We shall proceed then in the following chapters with developing, initially, the theoretical underpinnings for humanitarian intervention and then the legal framework which itself has been moulded by the theoretical debates and informs the state practice. Thus, we implement our purpose of acquainting ourselves with the contemporary description. However, the pluralism and even cacophony in current theoretical or legal debates does not produce a sense of despair. The theoretical and legal arguments are used as building blocks for our redescription. Having explored the aetiology for the existing debates, the axiological assumptions they make and the sources of their arguments, we are able to appreciate how this state of affairs can be re-envisioned not by substituting orthodoxies but by acknowledging our humanity. Thus we will be able to focus on our redescription under the value of human dignity.

---

[6] H. G. Gadamer, *Truth and Method* (New York, Seabury Press, 1975).

1

Natural law and humanitarian intervention

The natural law themes

Natural law is the corpus of principles, precepts, values and inquiries concerning the nature of law which are traced back to the Greek world and
transposed to modernity by the scholastic tradition.[1] Undoubtedly, within
such a time span, marked by momentous events and inexorable changes,
certain variations have surfaced. However, there are still strong identifications
and commonalities concerning inquiries and analysis on law and morality
or the continuous emphasis on humanity and human solidarity which make
this tradition distinct.

The themes whose evolution or transformation over time circumscribed
natural law have been introduced by Greek philosophy and this process
needs to be considered. A persistent philosophical quest concerns the source
of morality. Initially it was thought that morality springs from nature's
normative order. For Homeric Greeks, this is the divine order of Gods and
man satisfies his 'portion' of that order. Human and divine actions intermingle
to procure both teleology and responsibility which is understood to signify
the dawn of moral understanding.[2] Events hence acquire dual perspectives;
the normative and the real are infused for the Greeks[3] whereas their bifurcation for the medieval Christian tradition justifies the imperfections of cosmic
law against the perfect natural law. Later, the divine necessity of the normative order was replaced by rationality. The rational unity of the universe is
the basis for both spirit and matter, consequently the source of moral and

[1] As D'Entrèves has observed, it signifies the unrelenting quest of man to rise above
'the letter of the law' to the realm of the spirit. A. P. D'Entrèves, *Natural Law: An
Introduction to Legal Philosophy* (London, Hutchinson University Library, 1970), p. 127.
[2] J. Ferguson, *Moral Values in the Ancient World* (London, Methuen & Co.,
1958), pp. 15–16.
[3] H. Lloyd-Jones, *The Justice of Zeus*, 2nd edn (Berkeley and Los Angeles,
University of California Press, 1971).

physical laws.[4] Thus, reasonableness differentiates Greek from Christian ethics predicated on divine provenance.[5]

The clash between morality and human laws is central in Sophocles' *Antigone* and it is a perennial theme in the positivist-naturalist debate on the nature of law. Antigone, animated by her moral beliefs, buries her brother but eventually will be punished for defying the King's orders.[6] For Antigone, iniquitous laws are not laws whereas for others, however unjust, such laws will be enforced because they emanate from the right authority. The 'is'– 'ought' distinction has thus been introduced. The conflict between law and nature has received another twist by the Sophists who explored the theme of legal sources.[7] Protagoras argues that societies promulgate laws in their process towards civilisation and that laws are necessary for social life. Thus, they are acquired and not given by nature; they have human origin.[8] A person can achieve her or his development only within a community and only laws and customs hold a community together. This statement indicates an acknowledgement of the sociability of human nature which in its different manifestations has represented one crucial aspect for legal evolution. Law is a human creation but there exists disagreement on the nature of man. On the one hand, there were those like Socrates who presented man as a social being fulfilled only in a social context and others for whom man is an egoistic and antisocial creature, consequently might is the source for law.[9] These themes have informed international relations theory and in connection with law, they have been developed currently by the Critical Legal Studies movement. Another area which the Sophists explored is the basis for morality. Because *physis* displays permanence and encompasses reality it serves as the source for objectivity in ethics. On the other hand, Callicles denies the existence of objective moral standards in nature which 'mankind are always disputing about . . . and altering . . .'.[10]

If rationality as exhibited in nature becomes the moral and legal source, man's capacity to reason has equally inspired legal and political philosophy since antiquity. For Plato, laws are reasoned thoughts (*logismos*) embodied

[4] G. S. Kirk, J. E. Raven, M. Schofield, *The Presocratic Philosophers*, 2nd edn (Cambridge, Cambridge University Press, 1983).

[5] E. Hatch, *The Influence of Greek Ideas and Usages upon the Christian Church*, ed. A. M. Fairbairn, 7th edn (London, Williams & Nordgate, 1988), p. 158.

[6] Sophocles, 'Antigone', in D. Grene, R. Lattimore (eds), *The Complete Greek Tragedies*, vol. II (Chicago, University of Chicago Press, 1959), p. 157, at p. 174.

[7] G. B. Kerferd, *The Sophistic Movement* (Cambridge, Cambridge University Press, 1981), pp. 112–14.

[8] W. K. C. Guthrie, *A History of Greek Philosophy*, vol. III (Cambridge, Cambridge University Press, 1969), pp. 63–84.

[9] Plato, *Gorgias*, trans. R. Waterfield, *The World's Classics* (Oxford, Oxford University Press, 1994), p. 66, 483 c–d.

[10] Plato, *Laws*, 10.889–890, in B. Jowett, *The Dialogues of Plato*, vol. V, 3rd edn (Oxford, Clarendon Press, 1931), p. 274.

in convention.[11] His ethical principles derive from a normative natural order, the idea of *Forms,* which includes human and metaphysical elements.[12] The *Forms* are particularised whereas their aggregation constitutes an organic unity with the *Form* of God as the final expression. This organic system is the source and explanation of the actual world. Human things are included in the *Forms* and could reach God. The harmony of the parts and their direction towards their proper end constitutes justice in the individual as in the state.[13] Similarly, Aristotle's vision of nature is ontological and teleological but not metaphysical. Our world is the real one and its purposiveness is realised in the Form of Things. Each thing has an unchanged element, the formal element. This element which is called the essence of the object is teleological, that is, it describes the function of the object by nature. The teleological interpretation of the universe thwarts ethical relativism since principles emanating from nature are objectively valid. Aristotle in his *Rhetoric* refers to universal law, the law of nature, as 'binding on all men, even on those who have no association or covenant with each other'.[14] The moral aspiration of law in promoting the common good has become another trait of the natural law tradition. For instance, Aristotle sanctioned wars when they serve the 'good life' and are precipitated by right judgment, acting thus as a precursor of the Christian just war theory.[15]

Aristotle solved the conflict between nature and convention by distinguishing potential from actual being. Virtue, being potential or natural, is received by human beings and becomes actual only by habit, education and training. Thus, laws are the actualisation of the potential-natural virtue. The Stoics attributed the disparities between ideal and human law to human decline from the ideal world, which also informs medieval Christian thought. Seneca, for instance, justified the disharmony between institutions with the law of nature as a degeneration from an original state of innocence.[16] On the other hand, the Stoics also envisioned a process from human fallibility to an ideal future which has inspired Thomas Aquinas' natural law theory. Either way, Stoicism facilitated the integration of the ancient and the Christian world.

[11] Plato, *Laws,* 9.875, pp. 259–60.
[12] L. L. Weinreb, *Natural Law and Justice* (Cambridge, Mass., Harvard University Press, 1987), p. 32; J. P. Maguire, 'Plato's Theory of Natural Law', 10 *Yale Classical Studies* (1947), p. 151; John Wild, *Plato's Modern Enemies and the Theory of Natural Law* (Chicago, University of Chicago Press, 1953), pp. 62, 134–56.
[13] Plato, *Republic,* trans. R. Waterfield (Oxford, Oxford University Press, 1993), pp. 131–56, 427–44.
[14] W. D. Ross (ed.), *The Works of Aristotle,* 'Rhetorica', vol. XI (Oxford, Oxford University Press, 1924), 1373b.
[15] Aristotle, *The Politics,* T. Sinclair trans., revised and re-presented by T. J. Saunders (London, Penguin, [1962] 1992), Bk. VII, Ch. 2, pp. 396–7 and Bk. I, Ch. 8, p. 79.
[16] R. W. Carlyle, A. J. Carlyle, *A History of Medieval Political Theory in the West,* vol. I (Edinburgh, W. Blackwood & Sons, 1903), pp. 23–5.

The Stoics define law as 'right reason in agreement with nature; it is of universal application, unchanging and everlasting'.[17] Nature for the Stoics has descriptive and normative connotations but also a pervasive causality which reveals its teleology.[18] In such a system, moral responsibility is attained.[19] The universality of law is based upon the common nature of men. All men partake of reason and, therefore, they are equal, which is different from the Christian notion of equality based on a common progenitor. The Roman *jus gentium* as the forefather of international law signified the extent to which it applied.[20] The relation between *jus gentium* and *jus naturale* has become a matter of disagreement. Ulpian distinguished *jus gentium* from natural law.[21] Gaius[22] or Cicero, on the other hand, identified *jus gentium* with *jus naturale*. The linkage is the universality of *jus naturale* and *jus gentium*, the former referring to its source and the latter to its application.[23] Their reduction into a single concept resolves eventually the quest of their practical and theoretical existence.[24]

The Christian natural law tradition: St. Thomas Aquinas and John Finnis

As was said above, early Christian writers explained discrepancies between actual and ideal law through a dogmatic theology of the Fall.[25] St. Thomas Aquinas liberated man from the vindicatory interpretation of human fallibility

[17] Cicero, *De Re Publica*, Bk. III, XXII. 33, trans. C. W. Keyes, *Loeb Classical Library* (Cambridge, Mass., Harvard University Press, 1928), p. 211.

[18] A. A. Long, *Hellenistic Philosophy: Stoics, Epicureans, Skeptics*, 2nd edn (London, Duckworth, 1986), p. 169. A. A. Long, 'The Freedom and Determinism in the Stoic Theory of Human Action', in A. A. Long (ed.), *Problems in Stoicism* (London, Athlone Press, 1971), p. 173, at p. 178; J. M. Rist (ed.), *The Stoics* (Berkeley, University of California Press, 1978), p. 204.

[19] Long, *Hellenistic Philosophy*, p. 165.

[20] A. Nussbaum, *A Concise History of the Law of Nations* (New York, Macmillan, 1947), p. 19.

[21] 'Natural law is that which nature has taught all animals. . . . The law of nations is that law which mankind observes.' T. Mommsen, P. Krueger, A. Watson (eds), *The Digest of Justinian*, vol. 1 (Philadelphia, Pennsylvania, University of Pennsylvania Press, 1985), I, 1.

[22] Gaius, *Institutes* I.I, trans. Francis de Zulueta, *The Institutes of Gaius* (Oxford, Clarendon Press, 1946–53), pt. I, p. 3. '[I]t tacitly identifies *jus gentium* with *jus naturale*: it is the law common to all mankind as being the product of reason – common human reason or the divine reason ordering the world'. *Ibid.*, pt. II, p. 12.

[23] 'Cicero thus identifies the law of Nature with the *jus gentium*, in the sense of law common to all peoples . . .'. H. F. Jolowicz, B. Nicholas, *Historical Introduction to the Study of Roman Law*, 3rd edn (Cambridge, Cambridge University Press, 1972), pp. 104–5.

[24] W. W. Buckland, *A Textbook of Roman Law From Augustus to Justinian*, 3rd rev. edn by P. Stein (Cambridge, Cambridge University Press, 1963), pp. 54–5.

[25] E. Troeltsch, *The Social Teaching of the Christian Churches*, trans. Olive Wyon, vol. I (London, Allen & Unwin, 1931), pp. 153–5.

and by rediscovering Aristotle, delivered a theory which integrated human and ideal natural law through reason.[26] The reconciliation between faith and reason is achieved by the inclusion of *lex naturalis* into the providential order of God, the *lex aeterna*.[27] As in Aristotle everything had an essence, for St. Thomas Aquinas the essence of man is reason. Being uniquely endowed with reason, man participates actively in eternal law and reason reveals the ends towards which he may direct himself.[28] On the other hand, being subject to the same physical laws as other creatures, he also participates passively in Eternal Law.[29] Moral order thus springs from the intersection of deontological and ontological order. The two are complementary because reason leads to faith, that is, God, whereas faith recognises reason.[30]

Law is 'an ordinance of reason for the common good, made by him who has care of the community, and promulgated'.[31] This definition contains a positivistic aspect, enactment and promulgation, but also a naturalistic one, rationality and good intent. For Aquinas, positive law derives its legal appellation from natural law[32] but he was in no doubt that iniquitous laws are still laws,[33] and that reasonable calculations would enforce obedience to such laws.[34] The opposite view that it is invalid has been perpetuated by positivism[35] by misinterpreting the distinction between the morality to obey

[26] A. H. Chroust, 'The Philosophy of Law of St. Thomas Aquinas: His Fundamental Ideas and Some of his Historical Precursors', 19 *American Journal of Jurisprudence* (1974), p. 1, at p. 2.

[27] T. Aquinas, *Summa Theologia* (London, Blackfriars, 1964), 1a, 2ae, 91.1.

[28] Aquinas, *Summa*, I – II, q. 71, a.2c: 'And so whatever is contrary to the order of reason is contrary to the nature of human beings as such; and what is reasonable is in accordance with human nature as such. The good of the human being is being in accord with reason; and human evil is being outside the order of reasonableness . . .'.

[29] Aquinas, *Summa*, 1a, 2ae, 91.1, 2.

[30] 'In St. Thomas's assertion, *gratia non tollit naturam, sed perficit*, there is the recognition of the existence and dignity of a purely 'natural' sphere of rational and ethical values.' A. P. D'Entrèves, *The Medieval Contribution to Political Thought: Thomas Aquinas, Marsilius of Padua, Richard Hooker* (London, Oxford University Press, 1939), p. 21. W. Farrel, *A Companion to the Summa*, vol. II (New York, Sheed & Ward, 1945), p. 372.

[31] Aquinas, *Summa*, 1a, 2ae, 90.4.

[32] *Ibid.*, 1a, 2ae, 92.114.

[33] *Ibid.*, I – II, q. 92, a.1 ad 4.

[34] *Ibid.*, 1a, 2ae, 96.4; 2a, 2ae, 104.6. An exception is Origen who admits that the natural law of God invalidates any contrary civil law. W. A. Banner, 'Origen and the Tradition of Natural Law Concepts', 8 *Dumbarton Oaks Papers* (1954), p. 71.

[35] 'The only concept of validity is validity according to natural law, i.e., moral validity. Natural lawyers can only judge a law as morally valid, that is, just or morally invalid, i.e., wrong. They cannot say of a law that it is legally valid but morally wrong. If it is wrong and unjust, it is also invalid in the only sense of validity they recognise'. J. Raz, 'Kelsen's Theory of Basic Norm', 19 *American Journal of Jurisprudence* (1974), p. 94, at p. 100.

and the morality to promulgate or enforce the law.[36] This contention has been challenged by Finnis who, reappraising Aquinas, restates natural law in order to reconcile law and morality.[37] He distinguishes the focal from the penumbral meaning of law. The focal meaning is the ideal purpose which law should serve towards the achievement of the common good and it has a moral element. The elevation of a particular instance therein requires 'a point of view in which legal obligation is treated as at least presumptively a moral obligation'.[38] Thus, if humanitarian intervention comes to enjoy the viewpoint of a moral ideal, as was overwhelmingly claimed during the Kosovo operation,[39] whereas non-intervention does not, the latter is defective in the focal meaning.[40] Legal orders do not always satisfy the ideal order and attribute the quality of law to rules which are outside the fringes of the focal meaning. However, unjust laws are not invalid because Finnis rejects the definitional and accepts the evaluative role of natural law.[41]

For Finnis, law is an instrument for societal transformation. Its function is to promote basic goods, the self-evident principles of life, knowledge, play, aesthetic experience, sociability or friendship, practical reasonableness and religion.[42] He infers these goods by inward speculation, an intelligent practical reasoning.[43] In a similar manner, the policy school projects the

[36] H. McCoubrey, *The Development of Naturalist Legal Theory* (London, Croom Helm, 1987), p. xii.
[37] J. Finnis, *Natural Law and Natural Rights* (Oxford, Clarendon Press, 1980), pp. 276–80, 359–60.
[38] *Ibid.*, pp. 14–15.
[39] See Televised Statement by President Jacques Chirac on the Situation in Kosovo (Paris, 6 April 1999) for whom the operation is 'in the name of morality and human rights'. http://www.info-france-usa.org/news/.
[40] This reverses the statement that humanitarian intervention resides in the realm of morality whereas the law is the non-use of force. T. M. Franck and N. S. Rodley, 'After Bangladesh: The Law of Humanitarian Intervention by Military Force', 67 *AJIL* (1973), p. 275, p. 304.
[41] N. MacCormick, 'Natural Law and the Separation of Law and Morals', in R. P. George (ed.), *Natural Law Theory* (Oxford, Clarendon Press, 1992), p. 105, at p. 109: 'But the positivist theory I have in view yields just the same conclusion – the law is a valid law, but if the duties it imposes are duties in violation of the demands of justice, it will follow that the moral issue whether or not to comply is *prima facie* an open one. . . . Finnis has put it beyond denial that the mainstream of the natural law tradition . . . affirms the possible existence of such (unjust) laws, while denying or downgrading their morally compelling quality and insisting on their essential defectiveness as law.'
[42] Finnis, *Natural Law*, pp. 85–9. Similarly for the policy school, law promotes certain pre-moral values. M. S. McDougal, H. D. Lasswell, W. M. Reisman, 'The World Constitutive Process of Authoritative Decision', 19 *Journal of Legal Education* (1966), p. 253.
[43] Finnis, *Natural Law*, pp. 31–4, 85–6. For Thomas Aquinas though it is Eternal Law which attributes self-evidence to principles of natural law. Aquinas, *Summa*, I – II, q. 94, a.6c; q. 99, a. 2 ad 2; q. 100, aa. 5 ad 1, 11c. N. MacCormick, 'Natural Law Reconsidered', 1 *Oxford Journal of Legal Studies* (1981), p. 99, at p. 103. Weinreb,

basic values of human dignity as self-evident by employing in their case the methodological artifice of a framework for decision-making.[44]

Accordingly, natural law theory is 'the set of principles of practical reasonableness in ordering human life and human community'.[45] Morality is achieved through the interface of practical reasonableness with the basic goods.[46] Human rights emanate from the basic values and, therefore, they are absolute and exceptionless. 'Not to have one's life taken directly as a means to any further end'[47] is such a right. Exceptionless rights revisit Kant's Golden Rule that humans should be treated as ends and not as means[48] which is rooted in the decalogue and St. Paul's principle that evil is not to be done that good may come of it.[49] Hence the rejection of consequentialism, that one should pursue an act whose consequences are beneficial.[50]

The imbroglio though is evident. Any humanitarian disaster would create a moral impasse. Intervention to stop a human catastrophe may cause human casualties and become impermissible, whereas the situation is equally life-threatening for the intended recipients of intervention. Does the pursuit of morality warrant passivity? Does the attribution of absolute character to some rights accentuate individualistic motives?[51] Finnis excludes personal feelings or sympathy because reason requires that the basic values should be respected *in toto*. At a second level of inquiry, if action is morally reprehensible, is omission to act also morally censured? In a situation of humanitarian crisis, inaction to stop human loss may be equated with the action which provokes it. Both can be censured because they equally damage the value of

---

Natural Law, p. 115: 'Even those who agree with him on the merits may suppose that he has confused self evidence with personal conviction.'

[44] H. D. Lasswell, M. S. McDougal, 'Legal Education and Public Policy: Professional Training in the Public Interest', 52 *Yale LJ* (1943), p. 203. M. S. McDougal, 'The Ethics of Applying Systems of Authority: The Balanced Opposites of a Legal System', in H. D. Lasswell, H. Cleveland (eds), *The Ethics of Power: The Interplay of Religion, Philosophy, and Politics* (New York, Harper & Bros., 1962), p. 221, at p. 230.

[45] Finnis, *Natural Law*, p. 280.

[46] *Ibid.*, pp. 126–7. Also at p. 103: 'the requirements . . . express the "natural law method" of working out the (moral) "natural law" from the first (pre-moral) "principles of natural law"'.

[47] Finnis, *Natural Law*, p. 225.

[48] I. Kant, 'Theory of Ethics', in T. M. Greene (ed.), *Kant: Selections* (New York, Scribner's, 1957), p. 281.

[49] Karl Barth, *The Epistle to the Romans* (Oxford, Oxford University Press, 1933), p. 83, III, 7, 8.

[50] Finnis, *Natural Law*, pp. 111, 118. A. Ellis, 'Utilitarianism and International Ethics', in T. Nardin, D. R. Mapel (eds), *Traditions of International Ethics* (Cambridge, Cambridge Univeristy Press, 1992), p. 158.

[51] Thomas Aquinas has repudiated this position when he said that the captain would be moored at the port indefinitely, had the highest aim been the survival of the ship. Aquinas, *Summa*, I – II, q. 2, art. 5; L. L. Fuller, *The Morality of Law* (New Haven, Yale University Press, 1969), pp. 184–6.

life, irrespective of any beneficial effects which positive action may produce. This conclusion, if true, is illogical. Condemnation of inaction presumes affirmative action but the latter is also condemned.

In order to overcome the impasse, natural law theory introduces the concept of intention which forms part of the just war theory as promulgated by Aquinas which also includes right authority and just cause.[52] It is not merely the objective act but also the subjective element, the intention to cause harm, which is important. This refers to the Christian doctrine of 'double effect'.[53] Consequently, it is only the act which intends to harm people which is morally impermissible whereas humanitarian intervention may harm people but has no such intention. In the recent Kosovo case, the moral dilemmas encountered by the protagonists mirrored the different manifestations of natural law tradition that have been developed above. There was a humanitarian catastrophe in progress and human life was the central value to be protected. The Western powers have reaffirmed their belief in the absolute character of this right but were hesitant to act, fearing human casualties. On the other hand, inaction would entail perpetuation of killings. Both sets of possibilities were morally reprehensible. The operation cut the moral Gordian knot appealing to 'intention' and consequentialism. NATO's action may cause casualties but these are side-effects of a morally condonable action against barbarism and there would be the added benefit of the restoration of the threatened values.[54] A strong component of the Kosovo operation was also a feeling of sympathy and empathy for the victims of persecution contrary to Finnis' attempt to exclude our 'feelings, sympathy and generosity' to be implicated in the articulation of the value of life.[55]

Hugo Grotius: international law and humanitarian intervention

The decline of theological explanations which permitted the advancement of secularism and rationalism characterised Grotius' era as well. For him, law

---

[52] Aquinas, *Summa*, II – I, 12, 1; J. Finnis, 'The Ethics of War and Peace in the Catholic Natural Law Tradition', in T. Nardin (ed.), *The Ethics of War and Peace: Religious and Secular Perspectives* (Princeton, Princeton University Press, 1996), p. 15.

[53] J. Boyle, 'Towards Understanding the Principle of Double Effect', 90 *Ethics* (1980), p. 527.

[54] For instance, Lionel Jospin enumerated the exigent values which promoted the intervention as freedom, democracy and respect for human rights to which the Serb regime does not subscribe. He added 'our determination must . . . be directed towards peace that respects the human person and the rule of law'. Address by Prime Minister Lionel Jospin in Response to Questions in the National Assembly (Paris, 6 April 1999), http://www.info-france-usa.org/news/.

[55] Lionel Jospin spoke of the 'basic solidarity' and 'our duty to protect them [Kosovars]'. Address by Prime Minister Lionel Jospin in Response to Questions in the National Assembly (Paris, 6 April 1999), http://www.info-france-usa.org/news/.

is immutable because it is the product of man's reason and it would be so 'even if we should concede that . . . there is no God'.[56] Writing at the end of a tradition, Grotius makes references to God as another source of law, distinguishing, however, between the grounds for the existence and those for the knowledge of natural law. God is the creator of human creatures and, therefore, of natural law but knowing the law of nature is independent of believing in God.

Natural law is a command of good reason (*recta ratio*) 'which points out that an act, according as it is or is not in conformity with rational nature, has in it a quality of moral baseness or moral necessity; and that, in consequence, such an act is either forbidden or enjoined by the author of nature, God'.[57] The independence of human reason from God is evident. It delimits God's authority by delineating the forbidden or permitted acts according to their consonance with good reason.

Human reason is the source of this knowledge and he identifies natural law through an *a priori* and an *a posteriori* method. The former concerns the consonance of a rule with man's reason whereas the latter infers the naturalness of a principle through empirical investigation from the theorem that a universal effect should have a universal cause.[58] Only *a priori* principles as the product of human reason are true natural law principles. The *a posteriori* principles are not immutable because they belong to human will, formed by general agreement. In international law, the *a priori* principles pertain to natural law whereas the *a posteriori* to positive law.[59] The conceptual bifurcation of international law sources initiated by Grotius has been revisited by Wolff and Vattel along with Grotius' rather Aristotelian assumption of 'societas humana'. Grotius distinguished between contractual societies as the product of human will with the state being the highest contractual society and the universal society of mankind as a bond of kinship between men who have common descent.[60] Thus, the universal community of mankind embraces the inter-individual and inter-state relations in a *status naturalis*.[61] The *appetitus societatis*, the societal nature of human beings, becomes the axiom which generates the natural law principles as the mathematicians deduce propositions from axioms.

[56] H. Grotius, *De Jure Belli Ac Pacis libri tres* (Amsterdam, 1646), trans. F. W. Kelsey, A. E. R. Boak, H. A. Sanders, J. S. Reeves and H. F. Wright, J. B. Scott (ed.), *The Classics of International Law* (Buffalo, N.Y., W. S. Hein & Co. Inc., 1995), vol. 2, Bk. I, *Prolegomena*, p. 13. para. 11.

[57] Grotius, *De Jure Belli*, Bk. I, ch. I, pp. 38–9, para. X(I).

[58] *Ibid.*, Bk. I, ch. I, p. 42. para. XII(I).

[59] T. Tadashi, 'Grotius' Concept of Law', in Onuma Yasuaki (ed.), *A Normative Approach to War. Peace, War, and Justice in Hugo Grotius* (Oxford, Clarendon Press, 1993), p. 32, at pp. 41–3.

[60] Grotius, *De Jure Belli*, 'Prolegomena', p. 14, para. 14.

[61] H. van Eikema Hommes, 'Grotius on Natural and International Law', 30 *Neth. ILR* (1983), p. 61, at p. 64.

Thus Grotius attaches responsibility to humanity to punish malfeasants by waging war.[62] If a state commits a crime, it makes itself inferior to any other nation, not only to the recipient of the injury. Any nation which in this sense represents the whole society of mankind is authorised individually or collectively to punish the culprit. As Suarez put it, 'just as the sovereign prince may punish his own subjects when they offend others, so may he avenge himself on another prince or state which by reason of some offence becomes subject to him; and this vengeance cannot be sought at the hands of another judge, because the prince of whom we are speaking has no superior in temporal affairs'.[63] Thus the problem of adjudication created by equal sovereign authorities is solved by the universal society.[64]

Another issue extrapolated from Grotius' work is his obsession with peace. He disapproves of any general right to rebellion because it is disruptive and he sanctions measures against threats to public order. Grotius defends the *bellum publicum solemne* in order to prevent the extension of war.[65] War for him is 'undertaken in order to secure peace'.[66]

The modern concept of humanitarian intervention follows the same doctrinal and operational pattern either as the *societas humana* which interposes to restore the forfeited standards of humanity and to protect maltreated individuals or the need to restore peace and order threatened by human rights abuses.

Human(ity's) solidarity

Considering whether there exists just cause for undertaking war on behalf of the subjects of another ruler, Grotius says that if 'a ruler inflict[s] upon his subjects such treatment as no one is warranted in inflicting, the exercise of the right vested in human society is not precluded. . . . In conformity to this principle Constantine took up arms against Maxentius and Licinius, and other Roman emperors either took up arms against the Persians or threatened

---

[62] This is referred to as the 'Grotius' theorem'. C. Van Vollenhoven, *Grotius and Geneva*, Bibliotheca Visserianum, VI (Leyden, 1926), p. 13, at p. 21; P. H. Kooijmans, 'How to Handle the Grotian Heritage: Grotius and Van Vollenhoven', 30 *Neth. ILR* (1983), p. 81.

[63] F. Suárez, 'A Work on the Three Theological Virtues: Faith, Hope and Charity', Disputation XIII 'On Charity', Sect. II, para. 1 in *Selections from Three Works of Francisco Suárez S.J.*, in J. B. Scott (ed.), *The Classics of International Law* (Buffalo, N.Y., W. S. Hein & Co. Inc., 1995), vol. 2, p. 806.

[64] J. Finnis, 'The Ethics of War and Peace in the Catholic Natural Law Tradition', in T. Nardin (ed.), *The Ethics of War and Peace: Religious and Secular Perspectives*, pp. 22–3.

[65] Grotius, *De Jure Belli*, Bk. III, ch. IV, p. 644, para. iv.

[66] *Ibid.*, Bk. I. ch. I, p. 33, para. I.

to do so unless these should check their persecutions of the Christians on account of religion.'[67] Religious solidarity assimilated human considerations in an era when ethnicity remained an inconspicuous political force. Faith functioned as the unitary principle beyond the local jurisdiction and also as the distinctive feature among nations. In *Vindicae Contra Tyrannos*, the author defends the unity of Christianity and the unity of humanity by justifying intervention 'in behalf of neighbouring peoples who are oppressed on account of adherence to the true religion, or by any obvious tyranny'.[68]

Vattel recognises a right to intervention on the above pattern of Grotius without the religious connotations. 'If a prince, attacking the fundamental laws, gives his people a legitimate reason to resist him, if tyranny becomes so unbearable as to cause the Nation to rise, any foreign power is entitled to help an oppressed people that has requested its assistance.'[69]

Because humanitarian intervention is *prima facie* an assault on state sovereignty, it is legitimised by being integrated into a natural law theory which envisages an enveloping human society. As it is explained by Rougier, people live in a triple social organisation: national, international and the *société humaine* regulated by the *droit humain*.[70] A political society should satisfy, beyond the national and international interests of its members, those interests which are universal. Consequently, humanitarian intervention is the control of a state, 'au nom de la Société des nations', over the acts of another sovereign which are 'contraire aux lois de l'humanité'.[71] The concept of intervention to uphold minimum human standards was crystallised in the nineteenth century. Humanitarian considerations following the atrocities carried out by the Ottoman authorities justified the interventions of the Great Powers in

[67] *Ibid.*, Bk. II, ch. XXV, p. 584, para. viii (2).

[68] The *Vindiciae Contra Tyrannos* was published under the pseudonym of Stephanus Julius Brutus and written probably by either Hubert Languet or Duplessis-Mornay. W. A. Dunning, *A History of Political Theories: From Luther to Montesquieu* (New York, Macmillan, 1931), p. 47, pp. 55–6.

[69] E. de Vattel, *Le Droit des Gens ou Principes de la loi naturelle'*, *The Classics of International Law*, J. B. Scott (ed.) (Washington, Carnegie Institution of Washington, 1916), Bk. II, ch. iv, p. 298, para. 56.

[70] A. Rougier, 'La théorie de l'intervention d' humanité', 17 *RGDIP* (1910), p. 468, at pp. 489–97.

[71] Rougier, 'La théorie de l'intervention d' humanité', p. 472. A. Pillet, 'Le droit international public: ses éléments constitutifs, son domaine, son object', 1 *RGDIP* (1894), p. 1, at p. 13: 'Il existe un droit véritable en dehors des sociétés nationales et de leurs institutions juridiques, en dehors et au dessus de la société internationale et du droit qui lui correspond, droit inséparable de l'homme et qui mérite bien le nom de droit commun de l'humanité . . . un droit dont l'observation puisse être réclamée de chacun État ou individu, et imposée à chacun . . .'. 'Les divers groupes, Etat, communauté internationale ont quelque chose d'artificiel et de voulu: le bien de l'homme est leur dernier objet'. *Ibid.*, p. 19. 'Si la volonté et la force lui manquent, d'autres, de simple tiers, les rempliront à sa place dans les limites de leur intérêt'. *Ibid.*, p. 26.

Ottoman affairs.[72] Hence, France, Great Britain and Russia intervened in Greece (1827–30) when the Treaty of London (6 July 1827) for the protection of Greeks was dishonoured by Turkey.[73] In 1860, France was delegated to intervene in Syria to protect the Maronite Christians from being massacred by the Turks.[74] This intervention was approved by the Protocol of Paris (1860) which contemplated 'l'amélioration du soit des populations chrétiennes de tout rite dans l'Empire Ottoman'.[75] The European intervention in Bosnia, Herzegovina and Bulgaria (1876–78) was provoked by the harsh treatment of Christians. The Porte rejected the establishment of an International Commission whose mandate was to supervise administrative changes for the benefit of the Christian populations.[76] The Concert of Europe later signed the London Protocol (31 March 1877) according to which Turkey was required to adopt

[72] M. Ganji, *International Protection of Human Rights* (Geneva, Librairie E. Droz, 1962), ch. 1, pp. 9–45; J.-P. L. Fonteyne, 'The Customary International Law Doctrine of Humanitarian Intervention: Its Current Validity Under the UN Charter', 4 *Cal. WILJ* (1974), p. 203; T. E. Behuniak, 'The Law of Unilateral Humanitarian Intervention by Armed Force: A Legal Survey', 79 *Military Law Review* (1978), p. 157.

[73] *Treaty between Great Britain, France, and Russia, for the Pacification of Greece.* Signed at London, 6 July 1927. 14 *British and Foreign State Papers* (1826–27), p. 632, at p. 633. Under Article V of the same Treaty, they declared that they 'will not seek . . . any augmentation of Territory, any exclusive influence, or any commercial advantage for their subjects . . .'. *Ibid.*, p. 636. Turkey emphasised that 'l'affaire Grecque est une affaire interne de la Sublime Porte, et que c'est à elle seule à s'en occuper; que désormais aucune Puissance ne doit plus se mêler de cette affaire . . .'. *Manifesto of the Sublime Porte, declining the Pacification with the Greeks, proposed by the Mediating Powers.* 9 June 1827. 14 *British and Foreign State Papers* (1826–27), p. 1042, at p. 1043. See also the *Proclamation of the Ottoman Porte, declining the Mediation of the Allied Powers, and the Proposed Armistice with the Greeks.* 20 December 1827. *Ibid.*, p. 1052.

[74] I. Pogany, 'Humanitarian Intervention in International Law: The French Intervention in Syria Reexamined', 35 *ICLQ* (1986), p. 182.

[75] Rougier, 'La théorie de l'intervention d' humanité', p. 474, note 2; *Protocol of a Conference held at Paris, August 3, 1860*: 'les Puissances Contractantes n'entendent poursuivre ni ne poursuivront dans l'exécution de leurs engagements, aucun avantage territorial, aucune influence exclusive, ni aucune concession touchant le commerce de leurs sujets, et qui ne pourrait être accordé aux sujets de toutes les autres nations'. 51 *British and Foreign State Papers* (1860–61), p. 279.

[76] *General Treaty between Great Britain, Austria, France, Prussia, Russia, Sardinia, and Turkey, for the Re-establishment of Peace.* Signed at Paris, 30 March 1856. In Article VII, it guaranteed the independence and territorial integrity of the Ottoman Empire. 46 *British and Foreign State Papers* (1855–56), p. 8, at p. 12. In Article IX, it made provision for certain fundamental civil and political rights for the benefit of the Christians which would be realised by Firman. It also attached the non-intervention principle on the implementation in 'good faith' of the Firman. See *Firman and Hatti-Sherif by the Sultan, relative to Privileges and Reforms in Turkey.* February 1856. 47 *British and Foreign State Papers* (1856–57), pp. 1363–9. Due to Turkey's disregard of her obligations, the Russian government communicated to the British that: 'We seem therefore to have an undoubted right formally to intimate to the Porte that we shall not hold ourselves bound to abstain from interference till

the necessary administrative measures for the protection of Christians while the Concert retained its right to take any action should Turkey fail to uphold the minimum standards.[77] Turkey rejected the provisions of the Protocol 'en sa qualité d'Etat indépendant'.[78] The impasse ended with the declaration of war by Russia aiming 'à mettre un terme à la déplorable situation des Chrétiennes sous la domination des Turcs et aux crises permanentes qu'elle provoque'.[79] In a previous communication, the Russian government spoke of its resolution to protect 'the principles that have been recognised as equitable, human, necessary by the whole of Europe'.[80] Another incidence, this time in the twentieth century, is that of Macedonia (1903–08, 1912–13) where Greece, Bulgaria and Serbia took action in order to put an end to the Turkification of the Christian populations. In a 'Note Verbale' to the British Government, Greece explained that the three Governments 'ne pouvant plus tolérer les souffrances de leurs congérières en Turquie'.[81]

This pattern of interventions taking place in the interests of humanity antagonised sovereignty and has occasionally fallen into periods of hibernation or even disrepute. However, humanitarian interventions revived, particularly after events which shocked the conscience of mankind[82] because

---

the reforms promised by the Hatt Houmayoun are fully carried out.' *Sir H. Elliot to the Earl of Derby (Recd. Nov. 4, 1876).* 67 *British and Foreign State Papers* (1875–76), p. 289, at p. 290. Pursuant to this, a Conference in Constantinople was held between December 1876 and January 1877 which provided for the establishment of the International Commission. *Protocols of Conferences between Great Britain, Austria-Hungary, France, Germany, Italy, Russia, and Turkey, respecting the Affairs of Turkey. (Servia; Montenegro; Bulgaria; Bosnia; Herzegovina; Reforms, & c.).* Constantinople, December 1876–January 1877. 68 *British and Foreign State Papers* (1876–77), pp. 1114–1207.

[77] '... d'affirmer de nouveau ensemble l'intérêt commun qu'elles prennent à l'amélioaration du sort des populations Chrétiennes de la Turquie...'. *Protocol of Conference between the Plenipotentiaries of Great Britain, Austria, France, Germany, Italy and Russia, relative to the Affairs of Turkey. (Christian Population, Reforms in Bosnia, Herzegovina, and Bulgaria. Serbia. Montenegro, & c.).* Signed at London, 31 March 1877. 68 *British and Foreign State Papers* (1876–77), p. 823.

[78] 'La Turquie, en sa qualité d'Etat indépandant, ne saurait se reconnaître comme placée sous aucune surveillance, collective ou non.' *Turkish Note, in reply to the Protocol relative to the Affairs of Turkey, signed at London, March 31, 1877.* Constantinople, 9 April 1877. 68 *British and Foreign State Papers* (1876–77), p. 826, at p. 831.

[79] Rougier, 'La théorie de l'intervention d' humanité', p. 468, at p. 475, note 6.

[80] The Note of the Russian Government was sent on 13 November 1876. 47 *British and Foreign State Papers* (1856–57), p. 321.

[81] 106 *British and Foreign State Papers* (1913), pp. 1059–60.

[82] '... the right of humanitarian intervention in the name of the Rights of Man, trampled upon by the state in a manner offensive to the feeling of Humanity, has been recognised long ago as an integral part of the Law of Nations.' *Speeches of the Chief Prosecutors at the close of the case against the individual defendants*, Cmd 6964, p. 63.

they betray the deeply felt interests of the international community.[83] As it was perhaps said with vision, when 'the feeling of general interest in humanity increases, and with it a world-wide desire for something approaching justice and an international solidarity, interventions undertaken in the interests of humanity will also doubtless increase. We may therefore conclude that future public opinion and finally international law will sanction an ever increasing number of causes for intervention for the sake of humanity.'[84] The Kosovo operation contains those ingredients which reproduce this genre of humanitarian actions. After almost a decade of warfare, horrific atrocities and human rights abuses committed in the territory of the former Yugoslavia and the prospect of another humanitarian crisis looming menacingly in Kosovo, NATO's action was justified on grounds of morality and human society. For example, the Czech President Václav Havel wrote that the action 'happened . . . out of respect for the law, for a law that ranks higher than the law which protects the sovereignty of states . . . for human rights'.[85] And the French

---

[83] '. . . when a state renders itself guilty of cruelties against and persecution of its nationals in such a way as to deny their fundamental human rights and to shock the conscience of mankind, intervention in the interest of humanity is legally permissible.' L. Oppenheim, *International Law: A Treatise*, H. Lauterpacht (ed.), vol. I, 'Peace', 7th edn (London, Longmans, Greens & Co., 1948), p. 280, para. 137. H. Wheaton, *Elements of International Law*, 8th edn (Boston, Little, Brown & Co., 1866), p. 95, para. 69: 'The interference of the Christian powers of Europe in favour of the Greeks . . . affords a further illustration of the principles of international law authorising such an interference . . . where the general interests of humanity are infringed by the excesses of a barbarous and despotic government.' J. C. Bluntschli, *Le droit international codifié*, trans. M. C. Lardy, 4th edn (Paris, Librairie Guillaumin et Cie, 1886), p. 281, art. 478: 'On sera autorisé à intervenir pour faire respecter les droits individuels reconnus nécessaires, ansi que les principes généraux du droit international . . .'. J. Basdevant, 'Chronique des faits internationaux', 11 *RGDIP* (1904), p. 105, at p. 110: 'L'État . . . qui ne remplit par sa fonction de justice même à l'égard de ses nationaux, perd son droit au respect et les autres puissances sont . . . autorisées à substituer leur action à la sienne.' E. Borchard, *The Diplomatic Protection of Citizens Abroad* (New York, The Banks Law Pub. Co., 1915), p. 14: 'where a state under exceptional circumstances disregards certain rights of its own citizens, over whom presumably it has absolute sovereignty, the other states of the family of nations are authorised by international law to intervene on grounds of humanity.' L. Le Fur, *Intervention pour cause d'humanité* (Paris, Pedone, 1935), p. 38: 'L'intervention, a pour but d'assurer aux individus qui en sont injustement privés, les libertés consideréES aujourd'hui comme essentielles chez les peuples civilisés: liberté individuelle, liberté religieuse, droit d'usage de la langue maternelle. C'est à dire que l'oppression dont ils souffrent est en général imputable à l'Etat même dont ils sont ressortissants et que l'intervention émanera donc d'Etats tiers . . . Rejeter en principe l'intervention, serait une prime accordée à la violence et toute sécurité assurée à l'injustice.'
[84] H. G. A. Hodges, *The Doctrine of Intervention* (Princeton, The Banner Press, 1915), p. 91.
[85] V. Havel, 'Kosovo and the End of the Nation-State', XLVI *The New York Review of Books*, 10 June 1999, p. 4, at p. 6.

President Jacques Chirac spoke of 'une conscience universelle de ce que sont les Droits de l'Homme'.[86]

Peace and human rights

Grotius' other preoccupation was the maintenance of peace. He sanctions war against recalcitrant members of the international community in order to limit the effects of their actions and preserve peace. The intervention of the Great Powers in the Greek Revolution was dictated 'no less by sentiments of humanity than by the interest for tranquillity in Europe'.[87] The intervention in Bosnia, Herzegovina (1876–78) also invoked 'les intérêts de la paix générale'.[88] The modern articulation of such contingent factors urging for humanitarian actions is offered by the former British Foreign Secretary Douglas Hurd: 'If we really want a world that is truly more secure, more prosperous and more stable, then humanitarian problems may from time to time be seen not only as a moral issue but as a potential security threat as well.'[89]

Thus, according to a contemporary construction, human rights violations within a country constitute a threat to international peace and security justifying measures of redress by the international community.[90] Such violations can produce an array of complex problems such as refugee flows which may destabilise neighbouring countries, internal dislocation which may cause economic hardship, or they may also export conflict.[91] The Representative of Canada to the Security Council followed this approach in the discussions concerning Kosovo. As he said, it is 'a recognition of the human dimension of international peace and security. . . . Humanitarian and human rights

[86] Entretien du President de la Republique, M. Jacques Chirc, avec 'TF1', 10 June 1999, http://www.diplomatie.fr/actual/dossiers/kossovo/.

[87] *Treaty between Great Britain, France, and Russia, for the Pacification of Greece.* Signed at London, 6 July 1827. 14 *British and Foreign State Papers* (1826–27), p. 632, at p. 633.

[88] See *London Protocol* (31/3/1877), 68 *British and Foreign State Papers* (1876–77), p. 823, at p. 824: 'Si leur [contracting states] espoir se trouvait encore une fois déçu et si la condition des sujets Chrétiens du Sultan n'était pas améliorée . . . elles se réservent d'aviser en commun aux moyens quelles jugeront le plus propres à assurer le bien-être des populations Chrétiennes et les intérêts de la paix générale.'

[89] D. Hurd, 'The Search for a New Security System in Europe', 27 *Arms Control and Disarmament Quarterly Review* (1992), p. 33, at p. 35.

[90] G. Gaja, 'Réflexions sur le rôle du Conseil de Sécurité dans le nouvel ordre mondial', 97 *RGDIP* (1993), p. 297; P.-M. Dupuy, 'Sécurité collective et organisation de la paix', *ibid.*, p. 617.

[91] The US Permanent Representative to the Security Council stated in relation to SC Res. 794 for Somalia that 'the international community is also taking an important step in developing a strategy for dealing with the potential disorder and conflicts of the post-Cold War world'. UN Doc. S/PV. 3145, p. 36 (3 December 1992).

concerns are not just internal matters; they can and must be given new weight in the Council's definition of security and in its calculus as to when and how the Council should engage.'[92]

The assimilation of human rights violations with threats to the peace was involved in the imposition of sanctions on South Rhodesia (1968)[93] and the arms embargo on South Africa (1977).[94] A more recent demonstration of this construction is Resolution 688 (1991) responding to the Iraqi abuses against the Kurds.[95] On the basis of this resolution Western powers created safe havens in Northern Iraq.[96] Resolution 794 (1992) concerning Somalia[97] characterises internal human rights violations without international reper-cussions as a threat to international peace, whereas Resolution 688 was less explicit on this issue. According to Resolution 794, 'the magnitude of the humanitarian tragedy caused by the conflict in Somalia, further exacerbated by the obstacles being created to the distribution of humanitarian assistance, constitutes a threat to international peace and security'.

Resolutions 1199[98] and 1203[99] on Kosovo express the alarm of the inter-national community at the 'continuing grave humanitarian situation through-out Kosovo and the impeding humanitarian catastrophe' and also affirm that the unresolved situation in Kosovo 'constitutes a continuing threat to peace and security in the region'. These Resolutions are taken under Chapter VII of the UN Charter which envisages collective enforcement actions but do not contain any such authorisation. The legal basis of the operation then becomes rather opaque with France justifying the NATO action on a per-ceived mandate by these Resolutions[100] whereas NATO's Secretary General

[92] Statement by Ambassador Robert R. Fowler, Permanent Representative of Canada to the United Nations (10 June 1999), http://www.un.int/cananda/.

[93] SC Res. 253, 23 UN SCOR, Res. and Doc., at 5 (1968).

[94] SC Res. 418, 32 UN SCOR, Res. and Doc., at 5 (1977).

[95] SC Res. 688, UN SCOR, 46th Sess., 2982d mtg, UN Doc. S/RES/688 (1991): '*The Security Council, Mindful* of its duties and its responsibilities under the Charter of the United Nations for the maintenance of international peace and security, 1. *Condemns* the repression of the Iraqi civilian population in many parts of Iraq, including most recently in Kurdish populated areas, the consequences of which threaten international peace and security in the region; 2. *Demands* that Iraq, as a contribution to removing the treat to international peace and security in the region, immediately end this repression . . .'

[96] K. K. Pearse, D. P. Forsythe, 'Human Rights, Humanitarian Intervention, and World Politics', 15 *Hum. RQ* (1993), p. 290, at p. 303; J. Delbrück, 'A Fresh Look at Humanitarian Intervention under the Authority of the United Nations', 67 *Indiana Law Journal* (1992), p. 880; R. B. Lillich, 'Humanitarian Intervention through the United Nations: Towards the Development of Criteria', 53 *ZaöRV* (1993), p. 557.

[97] SC Res. 794, UN SCOR, 47th Sess., 3145th mtg, at 3, UN Doc. S/RES/794 (1992).

[98] SC Res. 1199, UN SCOR, UN Doc. S/RES/1199 (1998).

[99] SC Res. 1203, UN SCOR, UN Doc. S/RES/1203 (1998).

[100] 'L'action de l'OTAN trouve sa légitimité dans l'autorité du Conseil de sécurité. Les résolutions du Conseil concernant la situation au Kosovo ont été prises en vertu du chapitre VII . . . lequel traite des actions coercitives en cas de rupture de la paix.'

Javier Solana argued for a 'case by case' evaluation where 'it is necessary to act for humanitarian reasons, when a UN Security Council resolution will not be necessary or will not be even appropriate because the UN Charter does not contemplate humanitarian acts'.[101] His evaluation of the situation was similar to the aforementioned resolutions that 'the deterioration of the situation in Kosovo and its magnitude constitute a serious threat to peace and security in the region' with the added important caveat that following this 'there are legitimate grounds for the Alliance to threaten, and if necessary, to use force'.[102]

Social contract theories and humanitarian intervention

Related to the rationalisation and secularisation of natural law is the projection of the individual who is for Grotius the ultimate unit in national and international law.[103] States are not anthropomorphic enjoying an autonomous moral standing but are composed of individual human beings.[104] We arrive thus at those questions relating to the construct of states and their rights which influence the theory of humanitarian intervention. If man is rational and free, the formation of society is explained only through his free will implied in the social contract. The social contract was the device used to legitimise the authority of secular entities and justify the institutions deemed necessary by man's reason. It is the configuration of individualism into a political force[105] and provides a premise for evaluating social organisations and questioning their justice. Hence, the criterion for humanitarian intervention is the condition of the contract. The contractors enjoy certain natural rights which they agree to transfer to the political community. If the community forfeits these rights, humanitarian intervention, it is argued, will restore the initial contract.[106]

Ministère des Affaires Étranères, Paris, 25 march 1999, http://www.diplomatie.fr/actual/dossiers/kossovo/.

[101] Cited in I. H. Daalder, 'NATO, the UN, and the Use of Force', Brookings Institution, March 1999. http://www.unausa.org/issues/.

[102] Cited in B. Simma, 'NATO, the UN and the Use of Force: Legal Aspects', 10 *EJIL* (1999), p. 1, at p. 7.

[103] P. P. Remec, *The Position of the Individual in International Law According to Grotius and Vattel* (The Hague, Martinus Nijhoff, 1960), p. 239.

[104] H. Lauterpacht, 'The Grotian Tradition in International Law', 23 *BYBIL* (1946), p. 1, at p. 27.

[105] As Hegel said, it afforded the revision of its (state) constitution 'purely in terms of thought'. G. W. F. Hegel, *Grundlinien der Philosophie des Rechts*, in A. W. Wood (ed.), *Elements of the Philosophy of Right*, trans. H. B. Nisbet (Cambridge, Cambridge University Press, 1991), p. 277, para. 258.

[106] P. Laberge, 'Humanitarian Intervention: Three Ethical Positions', 9 *Ethics & Internatioanl Affairs* (1995), p. 15; M. J. Smith, 'Humanitarian Intervention: An Overview of the Ethical Issues', 12 *Ethics & Internatioanl Affairs* (1998), p. 63.

Modern contractarians such as Rawls follow the tradition of natural law based on equality between human beings as rational entities. Justice is for Rawls 'the first virtue of social institutions'[107] and the principles of justice are those that free and rational persons accept in an initial position of equality.[108] The participants, ignorant of their special circumstances, under the veil of ignorance[109] choose as principles of justice the Principle of Liberty[110] and the Principle of Equality.[111] The veil of ignorance thus safeguards certain deprivations for the benefit of disinterestedness and generality. By analogy, the representatives of nations in a position of ignorance, unbiased as to their historical fate,[112] choose the principle of equality which is 'analogous to the equal rights of citizens in a constitutional régime'.[113] Self-determination, that is, 'the right of a people to settle its own affairs without the interference of foreign powers', is a principle which follows from the primordial choice.[114] This accounts for sovereignty and non-intervention is its derivative. Walzer in *Just and Unjust Wars*[115] starts from these premises to proscribe interference because it will undermine the self-determination of a community. He premises his theory on a 'fit' between the government and the community based on a somewhat historical approach to political communities. The metaphorical contract he employs reflects the union among the government and the people, 'the living, the dead, and those who are yet to be born' which constitutes the state.[116] Hence, according to Walzer, a state may be illegitimate at home but its international standing is hypothesised, *as if* it were legitimate.[117] The only remedy against tyrannical regimes is revolution through the domestic process, not foreign intervention. Otherwise, the citizens' rights

[107] J. Rawls, *A Theory of Justice* (Cambridge, Mass., Harvard University Press, 1971), p. 3.

[108] *Ibid.*, p. 11.

[109] *Ibid.*, p. 12.

[110] *Ibid.*, p. 60.

[111] *Ibid.*, p. 83.

[112] 'Now at this point one may extend the interpretation of the original position and think of the parties as representatives of different nations who must choose together the fundamental principles to adjudicate conflicting claims among states . . . these representatives are deprived of various kinds of information . . . [o]nce again the contracting parties, in this case representatives of states, are allowed only enough knowledge to make a rational choice to protect their interests but not so much that the more fortunate among them can take advantage of their special situation'. Rawls, *A Theory of Justice*, p. 378.

[113] *Ibid.*

[114] *Ibid.*

[115] M. Walzer, *Just and Unjust Wars: A Moral Argument with Historical Illustrations* (New York, Basic Books, 1977).

[116] Walzer, *Just and Unjust Wars*, pp. 51–4; M. Walzer, 'The Moral Standing of States: A Response to Four Critics, 9 *Philosophy & Public Affairs* (1980)', p. 209. Also M. Walzer, *Thick and Thin: Moral Argument at Home and Abroad* (Notre Dame, Ind., University of Notre Dame Press, 1995).

[117] Walzer, *Just and Unjust Wars*, p. 89.

to rebellion and to self-determination are curbed.[118] Walzer adheres to a rather emotional notion of contract and people's consent to form political communities, which if broken, can only be restored by the same people whereas in Rawls, there is a correspondence between the causes for internal civil disobedience and external intervention which is the infringement of equal liberty. Civil resistance is a corrective action addressed to the majority and its purpose is to re-establish the shared meaning of justice. Humanitarian intervention similarly reinstates the infringed social contract.[119] It seems that Walzer's theory of social contract resembles that of Grotius' which conceptualised the existing state of affairs.[120] Grotius' social contract appears as an attempt for the philosophical rationalisation of the *status quo*,[121] whereas for the contractual philosophers it is a means for scrutinising state power. Moreover Grotius tries to minimise the political repercussions of his theory by curtailing any general right of resistance unless a ruler 'shows himself the enemy of the whole people.'[122] Intervention is permitted by Walzer only in extreme cases of enslavement or massacre where the hypothetical 'fit' seems to be lacking.[123]

On the other hand, Rawls is more permissive towards humanitarian intervention. It is only states which satisfy the principles of justice at the national level which enjoy international equal liberty, that is non-intervention.[124] Assuming that both just and unjust nations participate in the original position, its hypothetical construction will be destroyed since the parties do not share the appropriate initial position.[125] Equality is not only the promulgation but also the substantiation of the original position.[126] Parties which do not satisfy national equal liberty are excluded and may be targets of intervention. This

---

[118] *Ibid.*

[119] J. Rawls, 'The Law of Peoples', 20 *Critical Enquiry* (1993), p. 36, at p. 47; Rawls, *A Theory of Justice*, pp. 363, 372. W. G. Friedmann, 'A Theory of Justice: A Lawyer's Critique, 11 *Col. J Trans. L.* (1972), p. 369, at p. 376.

[120] Rousseau described Grotius' method as deriving 'toujours le droit par le fait'. J. J. Rousseau, *Du contrat social*, 2nd edn, (Paris, F. Rieder et Cie, 1914), Bk. I, ch. II, 'Des premières sociétés', p. 122.

[121] 'Mais Grotius, préoccupé seulement d'établir l'obligation de l'obéissance chez les sujets, attribue une valeur absolue au prétentu fait du contrat social qui, comme tel, n'existe pas. L'hypothèse du contrat n'a donc, dans son système, aucune valeur rationnelle. Elle représente uniquement un expédient, ou une fiction destinée à valoriser et ratifier le fait établi.' G. Del Vecchio, *Leçons de philosophie du droit* (Sirey, Paris, 1936), p. 64.

[122] Grotius, *De Jure Belli*, Bk. I, ch. IV, p. 157, para. xi.

[123] Walzer, 'The Moral Standing of States', at p. 217.

[124] '. . . but now they are representatives of peoples whose basic institutions satisfy the principles of justice selected at the first level'. Rawls, 'The Law of Peoples', p. 41. T. M. Franck, S. W. Hawkins, 'Justice in the International System', 10 *Michigan Journal of International Law* (1989), p. 127, at p. 144.

[125] Rawls, *A Theory of Justice*, p. 12.

[126] Rawls, 'The Law of Peoples', p. 45.

position is supported by his articulation of permissible conscription which is 'for the defence of liberty' and 'for those of persons in other societies as well'.[127] If non-intervention applies only among states which start from an original position of justice, one should be wary of situations where those principles are abandoned later. Hence, following a common trait, humanitarian intervention is permitted against a state 'if it severely frustrates the interests of its populace' since 'the contractors are concerned . . . with the well-being of persons'.[128]

In the 'Law of Peoples'[129] Rawls appears more cautious and permits humanitarian intervention exceptionally against situations of tyranny.[130] His position approximates Walzer's theory, although it is more comprehensive than the incident-specific criterion of the latter's. However, it represents a reversal from his previous position whereby persons are the ultimate moral units and units for appraising societal justice towards a cautious acknowledgement of relativism.[131] His aim in international law is peace which a comprehensive concept of justice would threaten.[132] Hence, his tolerance of less just societies. For stability and order, there is need to reduce the scope of comprehensive justice to 'certain fundamental intuitive ideas viewed as latent in the public political culture'[133] and increase the systematic adjudication of incommensurable conceptions of justice.[134] The same approach informs the positivist envision of the state which is explored in the next chapter. State sovereignty was invented as a shield against any private ideas and understandings which endanger peace with their exhibited propensity for expansion and imposition.

---

[127] Rawls, *A Theory of Justice*, p. 380.
[128] D. A. J. Richards, *A Theory of Reasons for Action* (Oxford, Clarendon Press, 1971), p. 138.
[129] Rawls, 'The Law of Peoples', p. 36.
[130] *Ibid.*, pp. 47, 67; F. Téson, 'The Kantian Theory of International Law', 92 *Col. L Rev* (1992), p. 53.
[131] R. Tesón, 'The Rawlsian Theory of International Law', 9 *Ethics & International Affairs* (1995), p. 79. T. W. Pogge, *Realising Rawls* (Ithaca, Cornell University. Press, 1989), pp. 267–73.
[132] J. Rawls, 'The Domain of the Political and Overlapping Consensus', 64 *New York University Law Review* (1989), p. 233, at p. 234.
[133] J. Rawls, 'The Priority of Right and Ideas of the Good', 17 *Philosophy & Public Affairs* (1988), p. 251, at p. 252.
[134] J. Rawls, 'The Idea of an Overlapping Consensus', 7 *Oxford Journal of Legal Studies* (1987), p. 1.

2

Positivism and humanitarian intervention

The concept of sovereignty

Grotius did not fully appreciate the role of the new political entity, the state, because his world was in a process of transformation, from medievalism, based on religious unity, to modernity, identified with secularism. Therefore, he combines in his work emerging principles with established ones, idealism with conservatism. However, following the break up of Christendom, the emergent state engendered new theoretical constructions which were encapsulated by positivism.[1] The concept of sovereignty which was introduced by Jean Bodin[2] to the political and legal lexicon appealed to national unity and allowed the state to consolidate its power. The antagonism between natural and positive law precepts to appropriate sovereignty has since then marked the legal architecture.

For Bodin sovereignty is not arbitrary but is subordinated to the law of God and nature, to the constitutional limitations or the fundamental laws and to the *Leges Imperii*.[3] Legal sovereignty is, hence, relative, epitomising

---

[1] L. Gross, 'The Peace of Westphalia 1648–1948', 42 *AJIL* (1948), p. 20; R. A. Falk, 'The Interplay of Westphalia and Charter Conceptions of the International Legal Order', in C. Black, R. A. Falk (eds), *The Future of the International Legal Order* (Princeton, Princeton University Press, 1969), p. 32.

[2] A. Gardot, 'Jean Bodin: Sa place parmi les fondateurs du droit international', 50 *RC* (1934 IV), p. 545, at pp. 580–629; F. H. Hinsley, *Sovereignty*, 2nd edn (Cambridge, Cambridge University Press, 1986); L. Wildhaber, 'Sovereignty and International Law', in R. St. J. MacDonald, D. M. Johnston (eds), *The Structure and Process of International Law: Essays in Legal Philosophy, Doctrine and Theory* (Dordrecht, Martinus Nijhoff, 1983), p. 425.

[3] J. Bodin, *Les six livres de la Republique* (Paris, 1576), Bk. I, ch. 8, p. 131: 'car si nous disons que celuy a puissance absolue, qui n'est point subiect aux lois, il n'est se trouvera Prince au monde souverain: veu que tous les Princes de la terre sont subiects aux lois de Dieu, et de la nature, et a plusieurs loix humaines communes a tous peuples.' A. Vincent, *Theories of State* (London, Blackwell, 1987), pp. 53, 59.

the medieval tradition also traced in Grotius of interface with natural law. However, in the process of consolidating state power sovereignty becomes a predominately political notion. Its alienation from the residue of legal thought transformed sovereignty into an absolute concept and interrupted its ethical content. Positive laws as man-made and emanating from the sovereign's will were gradually becoming unquestionable.[4]

A shared perception is that if sovereignty under its different guises has endowed the state with unity, order and personality, its external manifestation is to provide the same order by co-ordinating the relations between state units. International law is hence the rules extrapolated from or prognosticated by the practice of sovereignty.[5]

Wolff and Vattel became the main intellectual pioneers who conceptualised the new developments.[6] Although both writers are inspired by natural law, their methodological assumptions and conclusions differ.

For Wolff, rules are derived from a unific principle, the *civitas maxima*[7] reminiscent of the Aristotelian, Thomistic or Grotian sociability of human beings. He acknowledges that civil society, as an aggregation of individuals, imposes certain rules on its members. States are compared to individuals in their desire to form a society whose aims delineate the laws which prevail therein. Thus, methodologically, *civitas maxima* functions as a presumption which initiates and legitimises the particular laws of the civil or world society.[8] The facilitator is the fictional ruler of the great society[9] who modifies the immutable natural law. The outcome is the Voluntary Law of Nations.[10]

---

[4] Thomas Hobbes worded the new notion and identified sovereignty with might Thomas Hobbes, *Leviathan*, R. Tuck (ed.) (Cambridge, Cambridge University Press, 1991), ch. XVII, pp. 121–9.

[5] M. Forsyth, 'The Tradition of International Law', in T. Nardin, D. R. Mapel (eds), *Traditions of International Ethics* (Cambridge, Cambridge University Press, 1992), p. 23.

[6] E. de Vattel, *Le Droit Des Gens ou Principes de la Loi Naturelle, appliqués à la Conduite et aux Affaires des Nations et des Souverains*, trans. C. G. Fenwick (Washington, Carnegie Institution of Washington, 1916), in J. B. Scott (ed.), *Classics of International Law*, vol. III, 'Preface', pp. 3a–13a.

[7] 'A fixed and immovable foundation for the Voluntary Law of Nations, and there are definite principles, by force of which that law can be derived from the concept of the supreme state, so that it is not necessary to rely by blind impulse on the deeds and customs and decisions of the more civilised nations . . .'. Ch. Wolff, *Jus Gentium Methodo Scientifica Pertractatum*, trans. J. H. Drake (Oxford, Clarendon Press, 1934), in J. B. Scott (ed.), *Classics of International Law*, vol. II, p. 18, para. 22.

[8] Its function is 'for the purpose of eliciting truths as well as providing them'. Wolff, *Jus Gentium*, 'Prolegomena', p. 17, para. 21.

[9] *Ibid.*

[10] *Ibid.*, 'Prolegomena', p. 9, paras 2, 3: 'For the principles of the law of nature are one thing, but the application of them to nations another, and this produces a certain diversity in that which is inferred . . .'. Also paras 21, 22.

Viewed under another perspective, the *civitas maxima* is the device which facilitates the accommodation of 'perfect' natural law with the imperfections of human living.[11]

Vattel retains Wolff's distinction between Natural and Voluntary Law of Nations[12] but rejects the *civitas maxima*[13] and projects instead the sovereign state.[14] Vattel's sources are historical and his Voluntary Law of Nations is a systematisation of contemporary state relations reflecting the pre-eminence of sovereign states, whereas Wolff's ideational system became anachronistic, reminiscent of an old era of European political unity. As a result, Vattel introduces certain principles such as liberty, independence,[15] equality,[16] or decisional autonomy.[17] These postulates negate authority or control because '[t]he liberty of a Nation would not remain complete if other Nations presumed to inspect or control its contact; a presumption which would be contrary to the natural law, which declares every Nation free and independent of all other Nations.'[18] Hence he projected the concept of consent[19] and non-interference. As he says '[i]t clearly follows from the liberty and independence of Nations that each has the right to govern itself as it thinks proper, and that no one of them has the least right to interfere in the government of another.'[20] However, contrary to Austin's repudiation of international law in the absence of a monolithic sovereign,[21] Vattel does not reach the same conclusion because he still vacillates

[11] N. G. Onuf, 'Civitas Maxima: Wolff, Vattel and the Fate of Republicanism', 88 *AJIL* (1994), p. 280; L. Strauss, *Natural Right and History* (Chicago, University of Chicago Press, 1953), pp. 148–56.

[12] Vattel, *Le Droit Des Gens*, vol. III, p. 11a.

[13] 'But it is clear that there is by no means the same necessity for a civil society among Nations as among individuals. It cannot be said, therefore, that nature recommends it to an equal degree, far less that it prescribes it.' Vattel, *Le Droit Des Gens*, vol. III, p. 9a.

[14] Vattel, *Le Droit Des Gens*, vol. III, p. 7a, note k: 'A Nation means a sovereign State, an independent political society.'

[15] Vattel, *Le Droit Des Gens*, 'Intro.', para. 15.

[16] *Ibid.*, 'Intro.', para. 18.

[17] *Ibid.*, 'Intro.', para. 16.

[18] *Ibid.*, 'Intro.', paras 8, 9.

[19] '. . . natural law obliges Nations to consent; . . . for even if they had not given their consent, the Law of Nature supplies it, and gives it for them'. Vattel, *Le Droit Des Gens*, Bk. III, ch. XII, para. 192. S. Pufendorf, *On the Duty of Man and Citizen According to Natural Law*, J. Tully (ed.), trans. M. Silverthorne (Cambridge, Cambridge University Press, 1991), p. xvii.

[20] Vattel, *Le Droit Des Gens*, Bk. II, ch. IV, para. 54.

[21] J. Austin, *The Province of Jurisprudence Determined and the Uses of the Study of Jurisprudence* (London, Weidenfeld & Nicolson, 1955), p. 187. Also for the realists, international law does not satisfy the definition of law as 'organised force' emanating from certain authorities coupled with sanctions. H. J. Morgenthau, 'Positivism, Functionalism, and International Law', 34 *AJIL* (1940), p. 260, at pp. 273–8.

between positive consensual law and the enveloping natural law as an ethical postulate.[22]

Hence, the principle of solidarity or charity[23] betrays the conceptual interconnection between positive and natural law. Starting from the domestic analogy where individuals, guided by their sociability, construct their societies for mutual assistance and happiness,[24] individual duties to humanity are not absconded but are transferred to the state.[25] The aim of the aggregation of societies established by nature is 'mutual assistance in order to perfect themselves [states] and their condition'.[26] The duties to humanity become the *nooumental* link between civil and international society which champions a principle of humanitarian intervention. However, the question remains as to whether it is a moral or a legal duty. Vattel considers specific cases to show the difference between Voluntary and Necessary Law, that is, 'how by reason of the liberty of nations and the rules of their natural society, the external law which they must observe towards one another differs on certain points from the principles of the internal law, which however, are always binding upon the conscience'.[27] More specifically, concerning the issue of humanity, 'since every Nation is free, independent, and sovereign in its acts, it is for each to decide whether it is in a position to ask or to grant anything in that respect'.[28] According to the Necessary Law, when people defend their liberties against an oppressor, 'to give help . . . is only the part of justice and generosity. Hence, whenever such dissension reaches the state of civil war, foreign Nations may assist that one of the two parties which seems to have justice on its side. But to assist a detestable tyrant, or to come out in favour of an unjust and rebellious people would certainly be a violation of duty.'[29] However, 'since both are independent of all foreign authority, no one has the right to judge them. Hence, by virtue of the Voluntary Law of

---

[22] According to the realist school, the necessary international law contains rules indispensable for the existence of a multi-state system whereas the consensual international law is created by state agreement. H. J. Morgenthau, *Politics Among Nations. The Struggle for Power and Peace*, 6th edn, revised by K. W. Thompson (New York, McGraw-Hill, 1985), p. 297.

[23] Vattel, *Le Droit Des Gens*, 'Intro.' para. 14.

[24] *Ibid.*, Bk. II, para. 2.

[25] '. . . it devolves thenceforth upon that body, the State, and upon its rulers, to fulfil the duties of humanity towards outsiders in all matters in which individuals are no longer at liberty to act, and it peculiarly rests with the State to fulfil these duties to other States.' Vattel, *Le Droit Des Gens*, 'Intro.', para. 11.

[26] *Ibid.*, 'Intro.', para. 12. Jeremy Bentham aspires in his 'Principles of International Law' towards 'the most extended welfare of all the nations on earth'. J. Bowring (ed.), *The Collected Works of Jeremy Bentham*, vol. 2 (Edinburgh, William Tait, 1982), p. 538.

[27] Vattel, *Le Droit Des Gens*, 'Intro.', para. 27.

[28] *Ibid.*, Bk. II, para. 8.

[29] *Ibid.*, Bk. II, para. 56.

Nations, the two parties must be allowed to act as if possessed of equal right, and to be treated accordingly, until the affair is decided.'[30]

The trend explored in Vattel of ethical approbation and legal proscription has become a recurrent theme in legal discourse, expressed by the blurring between *lex lata* and *lex ferenda*. The UN Charter contains an approximation of the natural law-like principles concerning humanity but also vigorously restates *étatisme* by protecting state sovereignty.[31] Critics of humanitarian intervention rely on the principle of sovereignty and independence to uphold non-interference[32] whereas others find humanitarian actions morally, if not legally, compelling.[33]

Judge Cassese articulates this dilemma in an exemplary manner when he says in relation to Kosovo that 'from an *ethical* viewpoint resort to armed force was justified. Nevertheless, as a legal scholar I cannot avoid observing in the same breath that this moral action is *contrary to current international law (italics in original)*'.[34] Likewise, Vietnam's intervention in Kampuchea was condemned as an affront to her sovereignty and independence at the same time that Pol Pot's regime was castigated as morally pervasive. France, for example, declared that 'the notion that because a regime is detestable foreign intervention is justified and forcible overthrow is legitimate is extremely dangerous'.[35]

The above paradigms, instead of showing the antinomies of natural and positive orthodoxy, reveal their complementary character. Natural law refers to the 'substructure' whereas positive law refers to the 'superstructure' of international law.[36] This continuous process of interlacing mirrors human actuality, being informed by both spirit and facts. The process is incessant since practice expands and the realm of spirit always queries the empirical reality. Hence, the morality of sovereignty and of the rules it produces are questioned. For instance, non-intervention enjoys certain morality by defending state sovereignty and substantiating a diverse international

---

[30] *Ibid.*

[31] See Preamble, Articles 2(3), 2(4), 2(7), 55, 56 of the UN Charter.

[32] 'Cette intervention [d'humanité] est illégitime, parce qu'elle constitue une atteinte à l'indépendance des États.' P. Pradier-Fodéré, *Traité de droit international Européen et Américain*, tom. I (Paris, A. Durand & Pedone-Lauriel, 1885), p. 663, para. 430.

[33] 'It is destitute of technical legality, but it may be morally right and even praiseworthy to a high degree'. T. J. Lawrence, *The Principles of International Law*, 3rd rev. edn (Boston, D.C., Heaton & Co., 1909), p. 121.

[34] A. Cassese, *'Ex iniuria ius oritur*: Are We Moving Towards International Legitimation of Forcible Humanitarian Countermeasures in the World Community?', 10 *EJIL* (1999), p. 23, at p. 25.

[35] 34 UN SCOR, 2109th mtg, 12 January 1979, para. 36; The ASEAN Foreign Ministers 'strongly deplored the armed intervention against the independence, sovereignty and territorial integrity of Kampuchea'. UN Doc., A/13205, 12/1/1979, p. 2.

[36] M. Forsyth, 'The Tradition of International Law', in Nardin, Mapel (eds), *Traditions of International Ethics*, p. 38.

order,[37] and on the other hand, 'a coherent philosophy and practice of humanitarian intervention . . . could have the potential to save the non-intervention rule from its own absurdities and occasional inhumanities'.[38]

The Kosovo case and the legal debate it has provoked illustrates the peregrination of legal discourse between moral redemption or secular salvation. Cassese sets the scene when he says that '[f]aced with such enormous human-made tragedy . . . [s]hould one remain silent and inactive only because the existing body of international law proves incapable of remedying such a situation? Or, rather, should respect for the Rule of Law be sacrificed on the altar of human compassion?'[39] For Austinian positivists there exists no such moral dilemma because to say that 'human laws which conflict with the Divine are not binding, that is to say, are not laws, is to talk nonsense'.[40]

Cassese, however, considers the NATO operation as contributing to the crystallisation of an international rule to avert human atrocities.[41] Although the wording remains obscure and perplexing, human compassion eventually overrides the existing legal rules. This also betrays an interest in transforming world order by approximating *lex lata* with *lex ferenda*. Again Cassese pleads that international lawyers should 'pinpoint the evolving trends' which very often 'emerge as a result of a breach of *lex lata*'.[42]

Preserving the purity of law

The mystification of legal discourse emanating from the interface of substructure and superstructure has been contested within the positivist tradition

[37] C. Thomas, 'The Pragmatic Case Against Intervention', in I. Forbes, M. Hoffman (eds), *Political Theory, International Relations and the Ethics of Intervention* (London, Macmillan, 1993), p. 91, at. p. 99.

[38] A. Roberts, '"The Road to Hell": A Critique of Humanitarian Intervention', 16 *Harvard International Review* (1993), p. 10, at p. 11.

[39] Cassese, 'Ex iniuria ius oritur', p. 25.

[40] Austin, *The Province*, p. 185: 'The most pernicious laws, and therefore those which are most opposed to the will of God, have been and are continually enforced as laws by judicial tribunals. Suppose an act innocuous, or positively beneficial, be prohibited by the sovereign under the penalty of death; if I commit this act, I shall be tried and condemned, and if I object to the sentence, that it is contrary to the law of God, who has commanded that human lawgivers shall not prohibit acts which have no evil consequences, the Court of Justice will demonstrate the inconclusiveness of my reasoning by hanging me up, in pursuance of the law of which I have impugned the validity.'

[41] Cassese, 'Ex iniuria ius oritur', p. 29.

[42] *Ibid.*, p. 30. L. Vincent and P. Wilson, arguing against state morality, say that 'it turns out to be no more than a rationalisation of the existing order without any interest in its transformation'. R. Vincent and P. Wilson, 'Beyond Non-Intervention', in I. Forbes, M. Hoffman (eds), *Political Theory, International Relations and the Ethics of Intervention*, p. 122, at p. 124.

which arrives at different conclusions. For Austin, the legal character of a rule is affirmed irrespective of its contravening ethical imperatives[43] whereas in Kelsen's theory, law becomes normative and de-psychologised.[44]

Kelsen, conscious of the identified dilemmas, wants to purify law from psychological, ethical, moral, sociological or political elements.[45] His theory contains concatenated cells where valid laws are identified through the *Grundnorm* as the initial hypothesis and by imputation.[46] His theory betrays a belief in the authority of man and his capabilities to create law rather than depict nature. The *Grundnorm* as the regressive beginning of a legal system is a human 'artcraft' contrary to the inaccessibility of natural law ideals.

Methodologically though, the employment of a meta-legal device which validates a legal system resembles similar natural law tenets, the difference being that the *Grundnorm* as a mental construction provides a stable stand-ard contrary to the versatility of natural law.[47] Its introduction by legal cognition 'purifies' the legal system. Also its validity, contrary to natural law whimsicality, is presupposed 'because without this presupposition no human act could be interpreted as legal, especially as a norm-creating act'.[48] However, the purity of the model can be sustained only from the *Grundnorm* onwards because both the *Grundnorm* and the intelligible legal system which it iden-tifies exist in a dialectical relation.[49] The articulation of the *Grundnorm* entails logical deduction and abstraction, observation and departure from facts[50] and, moreover, the choice of *Grundnorm* is itself an act of volition. Hence, the *Grundnorm* in international law that 'states ought to behave as they have customarily behaved'[51] essentially implies normativisation of actualisation.

[43] Austin, *The Province*, p. 185.

[44] H. Kelsen, *General Theory of Law and State*, trans. A. Wedberg (Cambridge, Mass., Harvard University Press, 1949), pp. 33–6.

[45] H. Kelsen, *Introduction to the Problems of Legal Theory. A Translation of the First Edition of the Reine Rechtslehre or Pure Theory of Law*, trans. B. L. Paulson, S. L. Paulson (Oxford, Clarendon Press, 1992), p. 7, para. 1.

[46] H. Kelsen, *The Pure Theory of Law*, trans. Max Knight (Berkeley, Calif., Uni-versity of California Press, 1967), pp. 72, 202–03. Kelsen, *General Theory*, p. 113.

[47] Kelsen appears to admit that there is no difference: 'The reason for the validity of law is according to [natural/positive law] a hypothetical basic norm. . . . The only difference is that the validity for which the basic norm of legal positivism furnishes the reason is the validity of the positive law, its own validity.' H. Kelsen, 'What is the Reason for the Validity of Law', in D. S. Constantopoulos, C. T. Eustathiades, C. N. Fragistas (eds), *Grundprobleme Des Internationalen Rechts. Festschrift für Jean Spiropoulos* (Bon, Schimmelbusch & Co., 1957), p. 257, at p. 261.

[48] Kelsen, *General Theory*, p. 116.

[49] J. Raz, 'The Purity of the Pure Theory', *Revue Internationale de Philosophie* (1983), p. 442; S. L. Paulson, 'The Neo-Kantian Dimension of Kelsen's Pure Theory of Law', 12 *Oxford Journal of Legal Studies* (1992), p. 311; S. L. Paulson, 'Kelsen's Legal Theory: The Final Round', *ibid.*, p. 265.

[50] H. Lauterpacht, 'Kelsen's Pure Science of Law', in W. I. Jennings (ed.), *Modern Theories of Law* (London, Oxford University Press, 1933), p. 105, at p. 111.

[51] Kelsen, *General Theory*, p. 369.

Kelsen's endeavour to escape from the 'ideological fright' through the postulation of the Basic Norm stems from his belief that ideology may be used by those in power for their own purposes.[52] Such contention has been revisited by Koskenniemi who defends the formalism of the state 'against the totalitarianism inherent in a commitment to substantive values, which forces those values on people not sharing them'.[53] This position can be traced back to the concept of sovereignty which emerged in order to stabilise and incarnate a political order – national or international – against the entanglements of personal predilections and individual moralities. The extrapolated international rules, in particular the rule on the non-use of force, reflect this purpose. However, ideological neutrality which sovereignty and non-intervention presumably foster is rather an elusive target. If humanitarian intervention incarnates a destabilising form of ideological evangelism, non-intervention, extrapolated from sovereignty, is equally ideologised as promoting peace and order among a politically, economically and ethically diverse system of sovereign states. Moreover, ideological neutrality does not necessarily tame political power but may exacerbate its potential when states compete in the international arena bereft of evaluatory standards. For instance, NATO's action in Kosovo was criticised as a form of ideological imperialism which threatens international order by encroaching upon state sovereignty whereas others warned against ideological lethargy which would also cost in human lives.[54]

The issue of substantive values emerges again when Kelsen adopts effectiveness[55] as the intermediate norm between international and national law in his unitary system.[56] Effectiveness requires that a norm is applied and that it

[52] *Ibid.*, p. xvii: 'The overwhelming interest that those residing in power, as well as those craving for power, have in a theory pleasing to their wishes, that is, in a political ideology.'

[53] M. Koskenniemi, 'The Future of Statehood', 32 *Harvard ILJ* (1991), p. 397, at p. 407. M. Koskenniemi, 'Theory: Implications for the Practitioner', in P. Allott, T. Carty, M. Koskenniemi, C. Warbrick (eds), *Theory and International Law: An Introduction* (London, The British Institute of International and Comparative Law, 1991), p. 1, at p. 42: 'statehood functions as precisely that decision-process which tackles the problems of multiplicity of ideas and interpretative controversy regarding their fulfilment. Its very formality intends to operate as a safeguard so that these different (theological) ideals are not transformed into a globally enforced tyranny.'

[54] P. Avramovic, 'Cette Realpolitik qui n'ose pas dire son nom', *Le Monde*, 8 April 1999; N. Duclos, 'Oui, il fallait intervenir au Kosovo', *Le Monde*, 20 March 1999. H. A. Kissinger, 'Doing Injury to History', *Newsweek* (5 April 1999), p. 28; D. Rieff, 'A Just War is Still a War', *Newsweek* (14 June 1999), p. 39; S. P. Huntington, 'The Lonely Superpower', 75 *Foreign Affairs* (1999), p. 35.

[55] Kelsen, *The Pure Theory*, pp. 214–15; H. Kelsen, 'The Pure Theory of Law and Analytical Jurisprudence', 55 *Harvard L Rev* (1941), p. 44, at pp. 66–70.

[56] Kelsen, *The Pure Theory* (1967), pp. 345–6; J. Cohen, 'The Political Element in Legal Theory: A Look at Kelsen's Pure Theory', 88 *Yale LJ* (1978), p. 1, at p. 20; W. L. McBride, 'The Essential Role of Models and Analogies in the Philosophy of Law', 43 *New York University Law Review* (1968), p. 53, at pp. 62–72.

is obeyed but sanctions *ought to* apply.[57] Acknowledging this, one should question the premises which command effectiveness. The question is whether effectiveness, in addition to the probability of sanction, should also contain an ethical element.[58] Or rather, whether effectiveness should only reside within an authority exercised in an ethical manner.[59] For Hart, there must be a general acceptance of the rule and also an internal aspect.[60] These features may persuasively denote 'volition', that is, preferences towards certain ends.[61] By linking norms to societal commands, Hart admits the formative role of societal expectations. McDougal is explicit in his preference for effective control but also includes a multitude of parameters in its articulation.[62] He says that community expectations may produce effectiveness and detaches international law from actual sanction, thus assimilating it with Hart's acceptance of rules by the community.

The end of this argumentative web would mean that internal legitimacy would provide a criterion for intervention. The application of this reasoning in the international field can be detected in the theory of intervention against governments which do not respect human rights, provoke gross and egregious breaches of human rights as in Kosovo[63] and do not enjoy the consent of their people.[64] This reasoning corresponds to contractarian theories such as Locke's for whom the function of government is to guarantee the natural rights of people.[65] If their interests are frustrated, interference is approved.[66]

---

[57] H. Kelsen, *The Law of the United Nations* (London, Stevens & Sons, 1951), pp. 706–7; H. Kelsen, 'Théorie du Droit International Public', 84 *RC* (1953 III), p. 1, at pp. 31–50. For Austin, actual enforcement is a prerequisite, therefore, he repudiated international law. Austin, *The Province*, p. 134.

[58] T. A. Cowan, 'Law Without Force', 59 *California Law Review* (1971), p. 683.

[59] A. Verdross, 'Le fondement du droit international', 16 *RC* (1927 I), p. 245, at p. 286.

[60] H. L. A. Hart, *The Concept of Law* (Oxford, Clarendon Press, 1961), pp. 55, 84–5.

[61] N. MacCormick, *H. L. A. Hart* (Stanford, Stanford University Press, 1981), pp. 33–4; J. Finnis, *Natural Law and Natural Rights* (Oxford, Oxford University Press, 1980), chs 3–4.

[62] M. S. McDougal, W. M. Reisman, 'International Law in Policy-Oriented Perspective', in R. St. J. MacDonald, D. M. Johnston (eds), *The Structure and Process of International Law: Essays in Legal Philosophy, Doctrine and Theory* (Dordrecht, M. Nijhoff, 1983), p. 103, at pp. 104–6.

[63] Cassese, 'Ex iniuria ius oritur', p. 26.

[64] See for 'Reagan Doctrine', J. Kirkpatrick, A. Gerson, 'The Reagan Doctrine, Human Rights and International Law', in L. Henkin (ed.), *Right v. Might: International Law and the Use of Force* (New York, Council of Foreign Relations, 1991), p. 19, at p. 22.

[65] J. Locke, *Two Treatises of Civil Government* (London, Dent, 1924), Bk. 2, ch. 19, pp. 228–30.

[66] D. A. J. Richards, *A Theory of Reasons for Action* (Oxford, Clarendon Press, 1971), p. 138.

International constitutionalism and humanitarian intervention

For Kelsen, security is the common interest which federates citizens and states and shares in both national and international arenas common elements such as policing, sanctions and centralisation. Hence, international collective security[67] is a legal order guaranteed by international law whose features are the prohibition of the use of force and the collective reaction against an illegal use of force.

Collective reaction implies an institutional organ for ascertaining the delict and for determining the party responsible. It is also assisted by the rule of law which provides legal security through pre-established rules.[68] The second trait, centralisation in applying sanctions,[69] establishes 'a force monopoly of the legal community'.[70] Sanctions are executed by a centralised organ or by individual members authorised by the security organisation.[71] Interestingly, Kelsen observes that an international organisation which establishes a system of international security can request a state to sacrifice the lives of its subjects in order to guarantee international security.[72] Likewise, Bentham recognises that sovereign authority could not have 'assignable bounds',[73] in particular when 'states agree to take directions in certain specified cases, from some body or other that is distinct from all of them: consisting of members, for instance, appointed out of each'.[74]

The collective system contained in Chapter VII of the UN Charter mirrors Kelsen's or Bentham's project. The Security Council determines a situation and decides on measures which are executed institutionally and collectively or by individual members under authorisation.[75] Hence, the humanitarian crises in Rwanda or Somalia were considered to be a threat to peace and states were delegated to redeem the situation[76] whereas in Kosovo there was

---

[67] H. Kelsen, 'Collective Security under International Law', in *International Law Studies*, Naval War College, Navpapers 15031, Vol. XLIX (Washington, Government Printing Office, 1957), pp. 37–8.

[68] Kelsen, 'Collective Security under International Law', p. 16.

[69] *Ibid.*, pp. 23–6.

[70] *Ibid.*, pp. 1–6, 12–14.

[71] *Ibid.*, pp. 104–5.

[72] *Ibid.*, pp. 4–5.

[73] J. Bentham, *A Fragment on Government* (Oxford, Blackwell, 1967), ch. 4, para. 26.

[74] *Ibid.*, ch. 4, para. 23.

[75] *Ibid.*

[76] SC Res. 940, UN SCOR, 49th Sess., 3413th mtg, UN Doc. S/RES/940 (1994) (Haiti); SC Res. 794, UN SCOR, 47th Sess., 3145th mtg, UN Doc. S/RES/794 (1992) (Somalia); SC Res. 929, UN SCOR, 3393rd mtg, UN Doc. S/RES/929 (1994) (Rwanda).

no such explicit authorisation[77] although the evaluation of the situation was similarly a threat to peace.

There remains, however, the issue of the Security Council's discretionary power[78] in authorising humanitarian actions. If the Security Council enjoys wide discretion, it can introduce new law by incorporating human rights within the ambit of Chapter VII. Otherwise, it is bound by the standards contained in the Charter. These refer to the Preamble which mentions human rights or Chapter VII which does not. Consequently, the cases of Rwanda or Somalia may also be unconstitutional.

Although constitutionalism exerts its appeal to contemporary legal theorists,[79] it is equally important to consider the relational framework, the exhibited politicisation and the *ad hoc*ism of the Security Council. Kelsen's preferences lie with a judicial body that will execute the function of authoritative determination and he quite pragmatically admits that hostility stems from state interests vying to retain political influence within the security organisation.[80] Such a collective security system will be at the opposite pole to the United Nations since the judicial organ will dominate the decisional one, that is, the Security Council.[81] It will also help in depoliticising the issues. As Elihu Root advised, where issues are beclouded, 'there is but one way to make general judgement possible in such cases. That is by bringing them to the decision of a competent court which will strip away the irrelevant, reject the false, and declare what the law requires or prohibits in the particular case.'[82]

A critical issue arising for the existing system of collective security is the much advertised paralysis of the Security Council. This paralysis may be interpreted as a decision not to pursue any action,[83] probably allowing states

[77] SC Res. 1119, UN SCOR, 3930th mtg, UN Doc. S/RES/1119 (1998).

[78] R. M. Dworkin, *Taking Rights Seriously* (London, Duckworth, 1977), pp. 31–9.

[79] T. M. Franck, *Fairness in International Law and Institutions* (Oxford, Clarendon Press, 1995), pp. 272–4, 313. M. Bettati, *Le droit d'ingérence: mutation de l'ordre international* (Paris, O. Jacob, 1996).

[80] Kelsen, 'Collective Security under International Law', pp. 120–2. For Kelsen, 'the foundation of all legal organisation as of any legal community is the judicial process'. H. Kelsen, *Peace through Law* (New York, Garland Pub., [1944] 1973), p. 73. C. Tournaye, *Kelsen et la sécurité collective* (Paris, L.G.D.J., 1995). Bentham also envisages a tribunal to adjudicate among states. Its sanctions will be public opinion or military enforcement by the majority of states. J. Bentham, *Principles of International Law*, in J. Bowring (ed.), *The Collected Works of Jeremy Bentham*, vol. 2 (Edinburgh, William Tait, 1843), pp. 552–4.

[81] Kelsen criticises the discretionary power of the Security Council which prevents it from acting as a 'legal' body. H. Kelsen, *Principles of International Law*, 2nd rev. edn, R. W. Tucker (ed.) (New York, Holt, Rinehart and Winston, 1968), pp. 47–51.

[82] E. Root, 'The Outlook for International Law', *Proc. Fifth Nat'l Conf. Am. Soc'y for Jud. Settlement of Int'l Disputes* (1916), p. 30, at p. 33.

[83] T. M. Franck, *Fairness in International Law and Institutions* (Oxford, Clarendon Press, 1995), pp. 273–4.

to resort to self-help measures,[84] although in such cases Kelsen believes that the General Assembly, being more representative, is empowered to consider the matter.[85] Additionally, it has been argued that the malfunction of the collective security system has released states from their contractual obligation to refrain from the use of force. Force in international law has been viewed as a sanctioning process. For Kelsen, 'the specific sanctions provided by general international law are reprisals and war'.[86] Consequently international law enjoys the quality of law, contrary to Austin's[87] or the realist[88] repudiation based on the lack of organised sanctions; the collective system being the substitute for the unilateral use of force. It is only when the organisation fails that states assume their self-help rights and humanitarian intervention thus becomes a primitive enforcer of community policies.[89] Interestingly this point was raised by President Nyerere in relation to the intervention in Uganda, that 'when African nations find themselves collectively incapable of punishing a single country, then each country has to look after itself'.[90] It is also maintained in relation to Kosovo that the paralysis of the Security Council due to the anticipated Chinese and Russian veto released states from the institutional inhibitions and the resort to force by NATO appears

[84] A. Cassese, 'Return to Westphalia? Considerations on the Gradual Erosion of the Charter System', in A. Cassese (ed.), *The Current Legal Regulation of the Use of Force* (Dordrecht, Martinus Nijhoff, 1986), p. 505. W. M. Reisman, 'Coercion and Self-Determination: Construing Article 2(4)', 78 *AJIL* (1984), p. 642; F. R. Tesón, *Humanitarian Intervention: An Inquiry Into Law And Morality,* 2nd edn (Dobbs Ferry, N.Y., Transnational Pub., 1997), pp. 157–8.

[85] Kelsen, 'Collective Security under International Law', p. 126. See the 'Uniting for Peace' Resolution of the General Assembly concerning Korea, GA Res. 377, 5 UN GAOR, Supp. (No. 20), UN Doc. A/RES/377 (1950), p. 10; N. D. White, *Keeping the Peace* (Manchester, Manchester University Press, 1993).

[86] H. Kelsen, *The Law of the United Nations* (London, Stevens & Sons Ltd, 1951), pp. 706–7; H. Kelsen, 'Théorie du Droit International Public', 84 *RC* (1953 III), p. 1, at pp. 31–50. T. A. Walker, *The Science of International Law* (London, Stevens & Sons, 1893), pp. 1–56; J. B. Scott, 'The Legal Nature of International Law', 1 *AJIL* (1907), p. 831; R. von Jehring, *Law as a Means to an End*, I. Husic trans. (Boston, Boston Book Comp., 1913), pp. 242–4; J. W. Salmond, *Jurisprudence*, 6th edn (London, Sweet & Maxwell, 1920), p. 62.

[87] J. Austin, *The Province of Jurisprudence Determined and the Uses of the Study of Jurisprudence* (London, Weidenfeld & Nicolson, 1955), pp. 134, 141–2, 200–1.

[88] H. J. Morgenthau, 'Positivism, Functionalism, and International Law', 34 *AJIL* (1940), p. 260, at pp. 273–8; H. J. Morgenthau, *Politics Among Nations. The Struggle for Power and Peace*, 6th edn, revised by K. W. Thompson (New York, McGraw-Hill, 1985), pp. 295–6.

[89] E. C. Stowell, *Intervention in International Law* (Washington, Byrne, 1921), p. 53; W. M. Reisman, *Nullity and Revision* (New Haven, Yale University Press, 1971), p. 850; W. M. Reisman, 'Article 2(4): The Use of Force in Contemporary International Law', 78 *Proc. ASIL* (1984), p. 74, at p. 78; B. Asrat, *Prohibition of Force under the UN Charter: A Study of Art. 2(4)* (Uppsala, Justus Förlag, 1991), p. 46.

[90] *Keesing's* (1979), p. 29673.

to support community policies of enforcement when human rights viola-tions occur. NATO has acted in 'synergy' with the United Nations.[91]

Again the question remains whether constitutionalism is bereft of any ideological constituent, simply describing certain proceduralism. For Kelsen or Koskenniemi, the institutional-procedural aspect produces neutrality and obeisance if it is not tied to certain purposes.[92] State agnosticism provides the best reason for upholding statehood in the absence of a 'universally shared substantive faith'[93] whereas for others the state adopts a moral mission, becoming an emissary of higher ideas,[94] being also a subject of the interna-tional process.[95] The discussion recalls the arguments concerning the function of sovereignty. Because it is impossible to understand the essence of ideas,[96] their perception is subjective and therefore prone to antagonistic interpreta-tions. Removing the ideological substructure, international law is liberated from the pressures of parochial imperatives and allows for regulation of state interaction only. Whereas the aim is to preclude ideological imperialism, Kelsen introduces an ethical dimension to international constitutionalism which, for him, will develop into a community of human beings reminiscent of the medieval *civitas maxima*. This view coincides with Kelsen's preference for a monist and universalist legal system with international law at the apex and with an enveloping legal community. Kelsen considers the *civitas maxima* as a guarantee against the imperialism inherent in state sovereignties.[97] The conclusions one may draw from such aspirations are rather contradictory.

[91] B. Simma, 'NATO, the UN and the Use of Force: Legal Aspects', 10 *EJIL* (1999), p. 12.

[92] M. Koskenniemi, 'The Future of Statehood', 32 *Harvard ILJ* (1991), p. 405.

[93] M. Koskenniemi, 'Theory: Implications for the Practitioner', in P. Allott, T. Carty, M. Koskenniemi, C. Warbrick (eds), *Theory and International Law: An Introduction* (London, The British Institute of International and Comparative Law, 1991), p. 1, at p. 43.

[94] Bettati, *Le droit d'ingérence*, p. 37: 'promouvoir son statut [l'individu] de sujet universel'. And at p. 186: 'l'État qui intervient agit pour le compte de la société internationale défaillante'. See G. Scelle, *Droit International Public* (Paris, D. Montchrestien, 1944), p. 622.

[95] A.-M. Slaughter, 'Liberal International Relations Theory and International Economic Law', 10 *American University Journal of International Law & Policy* (1995), p. 717, at pp. 729–30.

[96] A. Gentili, *De jure Belli Libri Tres*, trans. J. C. Rolfe (New York, Oceana, 1964), p. 31.

[97] 'It is only temporary . . . that contemporary humanity is divided into states, formed in any case in more or less arbitrary fashion. Its legal unity, that is the *civitas maxima* as organisation of the world: this is the political core of the primacy of international law, which is at the same time the fundamental idea of that pacifism, in the sphere of international politics, constitues the inverted immage of imperialism.' H. Kelsen, *Das Problem der Souveränität*, quoted in D. Zolo, 'Hans Kelsen: Interna-tional Peace Through International Law', 9 *EJIL* (1998), p. 306, at p. 310. H. Bull, 'Hans Kelsen and International Law', in R. Tur, W. Twining (eds), *Essays on Kelsen* (Oxford, Clarendon Press, 1986), p. 321.

Transgressing the state and seeing human beings as components of the international society may assist us in recognising our common destiny and common humanity. On the other hand, the concept of *civitas maxima* may justify interference in the name of humanity as its medieval articulation has done.

The juxtaposition of natural and positive law

It has become already apparent that against any methodological device employed by positivism in order to disengage values, the latter persistently creep into and mould legal arguments. Hart's jurisprudence tries to bridge the legal traditions of positive and natural law by introducing an 'empirical version of natural law'.[98] Legal orders exhibit certain common forms and contingent facts which suggest why 'law and morals should include a specific content' indispensable for human survival which is reminiscent of the purposiveness of natural law.[99] The links between law and morality are only functional, not formative, thus Hart distinguishes immorality from invalidity.[100] However, it seems that the minimum content indicates which rules are incorporated into a legal system describing a rather similar function with natural law, not in pervasiveness but in procedure. Hart maintains that the minimum content is necessary for the viability of a legal system not for its existence, however eventually the two merge. When a rule does not endure, it ceases to exist. This suggests a rather longer process for rule invalidation than the instant one offered by natural law[101] but it does not specify when such a rule ceases to exist. In international law, there are persistent voices which consider the UN Charter and in particular the rules on the use of force archaic and unresponsive to human needs and concerns. For instance, during the Kosovo operation a new interventionism was hailed on the ashes of the UN Charter's old 'anti-interventionist regime' which 'has fallen out of sinc with modern notions of justice'.[102] There is no agreement though on how to revise the rules, particularly in a system such as international law which lacks formal procedures. It has been argued then that humanitarian intervention is not *ipso facto* illicit because it is not against the territorial

[98] Hart, *The Concept of Law*, p. 254.
[99] *Ibid.*, pp. 257, 189–95.
[100] *Ibid.*, pp. 194–5, 205–07. H. L. A. Hart, 'Kelsen Visited', *UCLA Law Review* (1963), p. 709; N. MacCormick, *H. L. A. Hart* (Stanford, Stanford University Press, 1981), p. 24; N. MacCormick, 'Natural Law and the Separation of Law and Morals', in R. P. George (ed.), *Natural Law Theory* (Oxford, Clarendon Press, 1992), p. 107, at p. 109.
[101] A. P. D'Entrèves, *Natural Law: An Introduction to Legal Philosophy* (London, Hutchinson University Library, 1970), p. 199.
[102] M. J. Glennon, 'The New Interventionism: The Search for a Just International Law', 78 *Foreign Affairs* (1999), p. 2.

integrity or the political independence of a state.[103] A similar argument to justify intervention because it 'threatened neither the territorial integrity nor the political independence of Albania' which 'suffered thereby neither territorial loss nor any part of its political independence' was rejected in the *Corfu Channel* case.[104] Additionally, it was said that the Kosovo operation mirrors nascent contemporary trends in rule formation concerning humanitarian actions.[105] On the other hand it was claimed that 'if a general law inhibits doing justice then it is up to each member of the community to decide whether to disobey that law' by proffering 'the most expiating explanation of the special circumstances that ordained their moral choice' and not by ridiculing the law.[106] A more advanced claim would hold that 'challenging an unjust law can reinforce the legal regime' by contributing to its reform.[107] It is interesting to note that, likewise, Kelsen drops his positivism and embraces acts which appear initially as violations of the law 'as the first steps in the development of a new law' by 'directing our views towards the future'.[108]

For Hart, the minimum content of natural law includes human vulnerability, approximate equality, limited altruism, limited resources and limited understanding. Hence, they describe the circumstances which inform the adoption of particular principles as in contractarian theories they describe the prerequisite conditions which inform the contract,[109] with the difference that Hart introduces a final end, that is human survival.[110] Human vulnerability corresponds to restrictions on violence[111] whereas limited altruism entails mutual benevolence which is more permissive to interference. Because 'human altruism is limited in range and intermittent, and the tendencies

---

[103] See submitions by the Belgian government in the *Legality of the Use of Force* case, CR 99/15, http://www.icj-cij.org. O. Schachter, 'The Right of States to Use Armed Force', 82 *Michigan Law Review* (1984), p. 1620, at p. 1633; O. Schachter, *International Law in Theory and Practice* (Dordrecht/Boston/London, Martinus Nijhoff Pub., 1991), p. 112; A. A. D'Amato, *International Law: Process and Prospect* (New York, Transnational Pub., 1987), pp. 57–73.

[104] *The Corfu Channel Case, ICJ Rep.* (1950), 'Pleadings, Oral Arguments, Documents', vol. III, p. 296; *The Corfu Channel Case, ICJ Rep.* (1949), p. 4, at p. 35.

[105] Cassese, 'Ex iniuria ius oritur', p. 29.

[106] T. M. Franck, 'Break It, Don't Fake It', 78 *Foreign Affairs* (1999), p. 116, at p. 118.

[107] Glennon, 'The New Interventionism', p. 4.

[108] H. Kelsen, *Recent Trends in the Law of the United Nations* (London, 1951), p. 912.

[109] D. Hume, *A Treatise of Human Nature* (1740), L. A. Selby Bigge (ed.), 2nd edn revised P. Nidditch (Oxford, Clarendon Press, 1978), Bk. III, pt. II, sec. ii. J. Rawls, *A Theory of Justice* (Cambridge, Mass., Harvard University Press, 1971), pp. 126–30.

[110] D. R. Mapel, 'The Contractarian Tradition and International Ethics', in T. Nardin, D. R. Mapel (eds), *Traditions of International Ethics* (Cambridge, Cambridge University Press, 1992), p. 180, at p. 185.

[111] Hart, *The Concept of Law*, p. 190.

to aggression are frequent enough to be fatal to social life',[112] a system of mutual forbearance is formed which guarantees human survival. Transmuting Hart's system into international law, mutual forbearance is equated with non-intervention which has been introduced to protect states against ideologically predatory practices. This rule secures a 'negative peace' by eliminating conflict, thus securing the survival of humankind. If we cast aside the value minimisation contained in the previous statement, the content of survival will change and adopt in addition a modicum of justice.[113] In cases of large scale human rights violations, our minimum altruism will revolt and may justify interference. The interference will secure 'positive peace', and in addition the realisation of justice.[114] Thus, human catastrophes in Kosovo or Rwanda were characterised as being threats to the peace and the ensuing actions were pursued on this basis.[115] The whole scheme resembles the UN system as it functions at the moment, expanding the concept of peace to include human rights violations.[116]

Moreover, Hart reserves forbearance only to some members of a society.[117] Consequently, certain interventions are not disclaimed. Again this argument can be identified with modern contractarian theories. Rawls derives his principles of international justice from an original position of ignorance. However, it is only just states which participate and articulate equal liberty as the most important principle.[118] Hence, equal liberty and its derivative non-intervention apply only among just states and intervention against unjust states is not precluded. During the Kosovo crisis, the British Prime Minister alluded to this when he declared a doctrine of international community in which 'democratic states would lay down rules for intervention on other countries' which perpetrate 'barbarous acts'.[119]

It becomes then evident that positivist theories are not insular and although they focus on the perennial question of law and morality, they succumb,

---

[112] *Ibid.*, p. 192.

[113] M. Krygier, 'The Concept of Law and Social Theory', 2 *Oxford Journal of Legal Studies* (1982), p. 155, at pp. 178–80.

[114] Cassese, 'Ex iniuria ius oritur', pp. 26–7.

[115] SC Res. 1199, UN SCOR, UN Doc. S/RES/1199 (1998); SC Res. 1203, UN SCOR, UN Doc. S/RES/1203 (1998); SC Res. 929, UN SCOR, 3393rd mtg, UN Doc. S/RES/929 (1994).

[116] 'The absence of war and military conflicts amongst States does not in itself ensure international peace and security. The non-military sources of instability in the economic, social, humanitarian and ecological fields have become threats to peace and security.' UN SCOR, 47th Sess., 3046 mtg, UN Doc. S/PV.3046(1992), p. 143. Société Française pour le Droit International, *Le Chapitre VII de la Charte des Nations Unies*, Colloque de Rennes (Paris, Pedone, 1995).

[117] Hart, *The Concept of Law*, p. 201.

[118] J. Rawls, *A Theory of Justice* (Cambridge, Mass., Harvard University Press, 1971), p. 378.

[119] *Keesing's* (1999), p. 42901.

even if inadvertently, to values. In the next chapter, we shall consider the policy school which stands at the opposite pillar of Kelsen's decanted theory by being invested with all these elements from which Kelsen attempted to rescue legal theory and which is more explicit in its sociological and behavioural attitudes than Hart's tepid jurisprudence.

3

The policy-oriented school in international law and humanitarian intervention

The international law premises of the policy school

Both natural law and positivism endeavour to normativise human reality through hypostatisation or abstractionism. There is an underlying fear that law will otherwise cease to function as a framework for ordering and adjudicating a whimsical reality neutrally and objectively. The realist school introduced a sociological dimension to law, emphasising its social contingency as a reaction to these flows of traditional jurisprudence.[1] Positivism is lamented for its unjustified faith in the omnipotence of rules, its dogmatism and formalism which denies any legal system, including international law, the dynamism necessary for its application. The policy school evolving from realism provides a *mélange* of realist and naturalist indices. It takes cognisance of the social context and the insights of other disciplines in the social sciences and also provides the framework for a purposive usage of law as an instrument for value optimisation.[2] Human dignity represents the ultimate and unifying value premised on natural law. The mission of international law is to promote human dignity, 'the greatest production and the widest possible sharing of all values among all human beings'[3] or in Bentham's similar terms, 'the most extended welfare of all the nations on the earth'.[4]

The legal task in a policy context extends beyond the traditional legal investigation into logical derivation and application. McDougal considers detrimental for international law its reliance on rules 'unrelated to policies,

[1] N. Duxbury, *Patterns of American Jurisprudence* (Oxford, Clarendon Press, 1995), chs 1, 2.
[2] Lung-Chu Chen, *An Introduction to Contemporary International Law: A Policy Oriented Perspective* (New Haven, Yale University Press, 1989), p. 15.
[3] M. S. McDougal, 'Perspectives for an International Law of Human Dignity', 53 *Proc. ASIL* (1959), p. 107, at p. 107.
[4] J. Bentham, *Principles of International Law*, in J. Bowring (ed.), *The Collected Works of Jeremy Bentham*, vol. 2 (Edinburgh, William Tait, 1843), p. 538.

as factors and instruments in the guiding and shaping of decisions'.[5] Kelsen is criticised for engaging the jurist in a 'syntactic clarification' of the rule.[6] For McDougal, rules are 'summary indices to relevant crystallised community expectations'.[7] They do not apply mechanically or automatically[8] because they include inherited or aspirational perspectives and values which bring about their 'normative ambiguity',[9] a belief that is shared by the Critical Legal Studies movement. What is needed is clarification of goals, description of past decisional trends, analysis of the factors which affect decisions, projection of future trends and also invention and evaluation of policy alternatives. By contrast, the sanctification of past decisions imbued in positive rules becomes incongruous in an ever-changing world, condemns creativity and conceals the subjectivity inherent in the experience of past practice.[10] As a consequence, it may elevate to law a practice which lacks community perspectives or deny the attribute of law to a pattern of expectations such as humanitarian ones.[11]

Because rules contain a penumbra of indices, indeterminacy manifests itself in imprecise terminology and complementary itinerary,[12] accentuated further in a decentralised and polymorphic system such as international law. For instance, Article 2(4) UN Charter on non-intervention can either be a descriptive statement of facts or an aspirational statement. Moreover, a factual case of aggression does not place it automatically within the framework of Article 2(4) without an evaluation of the event as aggression, self-defence, reprisals or justified intervention. Furthermore, this pattern of conduct is apprehended by exploring past practices and perspectives with

[5] M. S. McDougal, 'International Law, Power and Policy: A Contemporary Conception', 82 *RC* (1953 I), p. 133, at p. 143.
[6] M. S. McDougal, H. D. Lasswell, M. W. Reisman, 'Theories about International Law: Prologue to a Configurative Jurisprudence', 8 *Va JIL* (1968), p. 188, at p. 243.
[7] M. S. McDougal, F. P. Feliciano, *Law and Minimum World Public Order: The Legal Regulation of International Coercion* (New Haven, Yale University Press, 1961), p. 57.
[8] R. Higgins, 'Integrations of Authority and Control: Trends in the Literature of International Law and International Relations', in W. M. Reisman and B. H. Weston (eds), *Towards World Order and Human Dignity* (New York, Free Press, 1976), p. 79, at p. 85.
[9] H. D. Lasswell, M. S. McDougal, 'Legal Education and Public Policy: Professional Training in the Public Interest', 52 *Yale Law Journal* (1943), p. 203, at pp. 266–72.
[10] J. Dewey, *The Public and its Problems* (New York, Holt & Co., 1927), pp. 175–6: 'The glorification of "pure science" is a rationalisation of an escape . . .'
[11] Hart nearly admits this when he says that otherwise '[i]n so doing, one will miss out a whole dimension of the social life of those whom he is watching . . .'. H. L. A. Hart, *The Concept of Law* (Oxford, Clarendon Press, 1961), p. 87.
[12] '. . . travel in pairs of opposites', McDougal, 'International Law, Power and Policy', p. 156.

extant ones. Against this we need to intermingle law with policy for social projection whereby rules are constantly redefined and reformulated in the context of reappraised situations under their teleology of human dignity.[13] Human dignity, the *telos* of the legal system, reconciles the 'is' and the 'ought' by pulling the 'is' towards its 'ought'.

Law aquires its purposiveness[14] through identification of certain trends in humanity such as human interdependence, the demand for greater sharing of values and the realisation of an affluent, free society or the attainment of security.[15] These social factors which generate law are reminiscent of the circumstances which inform the social contract. But for the policy school there is a telos to be achieved, human dignity, which leads to value maximisation whereas for Hart and the social contract theorists the telos of survival denotes value minimisation. On the other hand, contractarians are sceptical about promoting end values mainly because agreement is not always achieved.[16] For the policy school, the choice is explicit and the decision-maker is informed of the ultimate considerations of the legal system aggregated in the value of human dignity.

In a system which pre-empts value identifications and choices, subjectivity is defied by using an intellectual framework which performs a 'neutral', scientific inquiry.[17] It facilitates the exploration of the social context by circumventing personal preferences and preventing the collusion of personal and communal perspectives which occurs in natural law.[18] Hence, the policy framework contains[19] the establishment of an observational standpoint, the formulation of problems, the delimitation of the focus of inquiry, the explicit postulation of public order goals and the performance of intellectual tasks.

Having said that, the neutrality of the method is questionable since empirical observation is not disassociated from the pursued values. Likewise, Kelsen employs cognition and abstractions[20] but again the identification of the Basic Norm is charged with the subjectivities of the social and legal

---

[13] *Ibid.*, p. 156.
[14] M. S. McDougal, 'The Law School of the Future: From Legal Realism to Policy Science in the World Community', 56 *Yale LJ* (1946–47), p. 1345, at p. 1349.
[15] McDougal, 'International Law, Power and Policy', pp. 137–91.
[16] A. Ellis, 'Utilitarianism and International Ethics', in T. Nardin, D. R. Mapel (eds), *Traditions of International Ethics* (Cambridge, Cambridge University Press, 1992), p. 158, at pp. 185–93.
[17] J. N. Moore, 'Prolegomenon to the Jurisprudence of Myres McDougal and Harold Lasswell', 54 *Virginia Law Review* (1968), p. 662, at pp. 676–7.
[18] M. S. McDougal, 'International Law and Social Science: A Mild Plea in Avoidance', 66 *AJIL* (1972), p. 77, at p. 79.
[19] M. S. McDougal, W. M. Reisman, 'International Law in Policy-Oriented Perspective', in R. St. J. MacDonald, D. M. Johnston (eds), *The Structure and Process of International Law: Essays in Legal Philosophy, Doctrine and Theory* (Dordrecht, Martinus Nijhoff, 1983), p. 103.
[20] H. Kelsen, 'The Pure Theory of Law and Analytical Jurisprudence', 55 *Harvard L Rev* (1941), p. 44, at p. 47.

context. It has been argued that the clarification of values 'objectifies' the pursued research because the participants are aware of the values which permeate the latter[21] or that observation of the aggregate trends in the world arena facilitates the extrication of 'objective' values by minimising the value references.[22] However, within a purposive system, the observer as bearer of community values and schemata is not neutral. He or she promotes through clarification, explication and commitment her or his goals[23] through a framework of inquiry which surreptitiously embeds values.[24]

The enumeration of these values as power, respect, enlightenment, wealth, well-being, skill, affection and rectitude[25] implies that reasonable people would agree in a similar way that Rawls derives the primary goods from reason[26] although they appear ensnared in Western liberal culture.[27] On the other hand, values humanise the process of authoritative decisions which in international law achieve a minimum order of restricting coercion and an optimum order of achieving human dignity.[28] What is more important is that they reinstate the individual as the focus of the system which becomes homocentric

[21] G. Myrdal, 'A Methodological Note on Facts and Valuations in Social Science', in *An American Dilemma* (New York, Harper & Bros Publ., 1944), p. 1035, at p. 1043: 'There is no other device for excluding biases in social sciences than to face the valuations and to introduce them as explicitly stated, specific and sufficiently concretised value premises.' H. L. A. Hart, *Essays in Jurisprudence and Philosophy* (Oxford, Clarendon Press, 1983), p. 132.

[22] M. S. McDougal, H. D. Lasswell, Lung-Chu Chen, *Human Rights and World Public Order: The Basic Policies of an International Law of Human Dignity* (New Haven, Yale University Press, 1980), p. 90. H. D. Lasswell, M. S. McDougal, 'Criteria for a Theory About Law', 44 *South California Law Review* (1971), p. 362, at p. 393. Stone characterises this method as 'transempirical'. J. Stone, 'A Sociological Perspective on International Law', in MacDonald and Johnston, *The Structure and Process*, p. 263, at p. 274.

[23] Hart lukewarmly acknowledges 'assumed common human objectives' through a sketchy mapping of context. H. L. A. Hart, 'Positivism and the Separation of Law and Morals', 71 *Harvard L Rev* (1958), p. 593, at p. 628.

[24] C. Taylor, *Philosophy and the Human Sciences*, vol. II (Cambridge, Cambridge University Press, 1985), pp. 75, 77–81.

[25] It is contended that they rephrase the content of existing human rights instruments and, hence, enable these values to be 'identi[fied] with the whole of humankind'. McDougal and Reisman, 'International Law in Policy-Oriented Perspective', in MacDonald and Johnston, *The Structure and Process*, pp. 117–19, 121–3; B. Rosenthal, *Étude de l'oeuvre de Myres Smith McDougal en matière de droit international public* (Paris, Librairie générale de droit et de jurisprudence, 1970), pp. 54–7.

[26] J. Rawls, *A Theory of Justice* (Cambridge, Mass., Harvard University Press, 1971), pp. 142–50.

[27] According to Dworkin, Rawls' theory entails 'choice conditions . . . constructed so as to reflect . . . principles of reasonableness suited to the political culture of Western liberal democracies'. R. Dworkin, 'What is Equality? Part 3: The Place of Liberty', 73 *Iowa Law Review* (1987), p. 1, at p. 14; P. Allott, 'Language, Method and the Nature of International Law', XLV *BYBIL* (1971), p. 79, at pp. 122–5.

[28] Chen, *An Introduction*, p. 4.

and cosmopolitan.[29] Human dignity or Bentham's happiness begins with the individual[30] but envelops humanity as a whole, contrary to realism's individual or national selfishness. As a result, there is an interest and a duty to scrutinise individual states.[31] The moral standing of states is not premised on their equation with individual autonomy. It resides in their promoting the welfare of their citizens, in Benthamite verbiage, or human dignity for McDougal, which would justify humanitarian intervention when the government fails in this regard reminiscent of the social contract theories.[32] Such cosmopolitan aspiration provides the premises for the primacy of international law, not a logical necessity as in Kelsen. McDougal believes that only an inclusive operation achieves a better apportionment of values. Certain matters are effectively enjoyed at the domestic level but they are also scrutinised by the inclusive authority. Domestic jurisdiction is a concession to national states by the general community.[33] Hence, domestic legality is predicated upon international standards. Humanitarian intervention is linked with strategies for achieving human dignity[34] when it fails in domestic arenas. As it has been maintained, the social contract theory presupposes respect for the rights of the contractors. Otherwise, it needs reinstitution and humanitarian intervention, since Grotius, has been accomplished 'in the name of a wider community of a wider body politic'.[35]

The purposiveness of McDougal's system makes it fiercely individualistic and consequentialist. The latter emphasises also its difference with natural law. The determination of what is law or the evaluation of actions is *ad hoc* according to their consequences, that is, the promotion of human dignity, as for Bentham it was the greatest happiness measured by his 'felicific calculus'.[36] Consequently, the connection 'between moral judgment and political action' materialises since the agreement on the final goal would activate action and also approximate it with the pursued goal.[37]

---

[29] M. S. McDougal, H. D. Lasswell, W. M. Reisman, 'The World Constitutive Process of Authoritative Decision', in R. A. Falk, C. E. Black (eds), *The Future of the International Legal Order*, vol. 1 (Princeton, Princeton University Press, 1969), p. 73, at p. 81.

[30] J. Bentham, *Introduction to the Principles of Morals and Legislation*, J. H. Burns, H. L. A. Hart (eds) (London, Methuen, [1789] 1970), Ch. I, para. V.

[31] Bentham, *Principles*, p. 538.

[32] C. Beitz, *Political Theory and International Relations* (Princeton, Princeton University Press, 1979), pp. 71–6.

[33] McDougal, Lasswell, Chen, *Human Rights*, p. 214.

[34] McDougal, Lasswell, Reisman, 'The World Constitutive Process of Authoritative Decision', in Falk and Black, *The Future*, p. 73, at p. 119.

[35] M. S. McDougal, 'Remarks on International Concern versus Domestic Jurisdiction', 48 *Proc. ASIL* (1954), p. 120.

[36] Bentham, *Introduction*, Ch. I, paras I, II, III.

[37] A. Ellis, 'Utilitarianism and International Ethics', in Nardin, Mapel, *Traditions of International Ethics,* p. 160.

Humanitarian intervention under the criteria of the policy school[38]

If law in a policy jurisprudence is an authoritative process, one should look to the endless process of claims, counter-claims and decisions, the underlining policies of past trends and the expectations of the wider community to achieve human dignity, in order to formulate a viable perception of the legal merits of humanitarian intervention.

The legal context under consideration is that established by the UN Charter which contains a norm on non-aggression, a collective security system and 'aspirational' norms such as human rights. These constitutive norms have frequently been disrespected.[39] As a consequence, a system of claims, counter-claims, reactions and approvals has developed which needs to be explicated in order to evaluate humanitarian actions. The most critical issue is the perspectives of the wider community for the promotion of human dignity and the refutation of parochial interests.

Any value-neutral criteria concentrating exclusively on methods and procedures for such intervention will forfeit the need for substantive evaluation. They may, on the contrary, invite and legitimise parochial actions. Moreover, such evaluation cannot be tied to value conservation, that is, peace, but should consider humanity's general aspiration to promote human dignity which alludes to value optimisation.

The homocentric perception of international law assists in diagnosing the situations which become the focus of inquiry by contemplating interests and values and how they can be approximated. The situations which command humanitarian intervention are identified by finding disparities between human values and their actualisation. They include conditions within a state where the government is not authoritative and controlling and where human rights abuses take place.[40] The interposition of states to restore the vestiges of

---

[38] N. Tsagourias, 'The Lost Innocence of Humanity: The Tragedy of Rwanda and the Doctrine of Humanitarian Intervention', 2 *International Law and Armed Conflict Commentary* (1995), p. 19.

[39] M. W. Reisman, 'Article 2(4): The Use of Force in Contemporary International Law', 78 *Proc. ASIL* (1984), p. 74, at p. 76.

[40] On 25 October 1983, US and Caribbean forces intervened in Grenada because 'the disintegration of political authority in Grenada had created a dynamic that made further violence likely and that spread uncertainty and fear.' Statement by Deputy Secretary of State, K. W. Dam before the House C/tee on Foreign Affairs, on 2 November 1983, quoted in M. N. Leich, 'Contemporary Practice of the United States Relating to International Law', 78 *AJIL* (1984), p. 200, at p. 201; President Reagan's letter to Congress on 25 October refers to 'the anarchic conditions and the serious violations of human rights and bloodshed that had occurred, and the consequent unprecedented threat to the peace and security of the region created by the vacuum of authority in Grenada'. 83 *Dep't. St. Bull.*, No. 2081, December 1983, pp. 68–9.

humanity has a long tradition stemming from social contract theories[41] and for McDougal, it also emanates from his observational point which is the citizen of humankind. Hence, in Kosovo, NATO's action was presented as a reaction to the internal abuses of human rights coupled with a sense of human compassion.[42]

Closely attached to this is the participants in such actions. Within a consequentialist theory, however, what matters is the perspectives of those involved. Thus, the argument that multilateral actions are less parochial is transparent. If unilateral intervention serves the wider community interest of safeguarding human dignity it should not be condemned whereas, on the other hand, multi-participants should not be exonerated when they pursue their own interests.[43] Hence, lacking UN authorisation would not rob the Kosovo operation of legality if the preponderant aim was to promote human dignity. It has been argued that the legitimacy of the action resides in its being authorised by the nineteen democratic states members of NATO, its humanitarian aim and the fact that it was parallel to and confirmed the UN purposes on human rights.[44]

Moreover, the prospect of abuse, the possibility of fabricating a humanitarian excuse, should not lead to a flat rejection of humanitarian actions but to a continuous evaluation in order to distinguish the spurious from the genuine humanitarian concerns and appraise the perspectives as parochial or inclusive of the world community.[45] For instance, the US intervention in

---

[41] E. C. Stowell, *Intervention in International Law* (Washington, Byrne, 1921), p. 53. C. G. Fenwick, *International Law* (New York, Century Co., 1924), pp. 287–8: 'If a sovereign abuses his sovereignty, if he perpetrates crimes against humanity, other states can lawfully use military force in protection of fundamental rights.'

[42] T. Blair, 'A New Moral Crusade', *Newsweek* (14 June 1999), p. 38.

[43] In Grenada, the humanitarian aim of the OECS intervention was 'collateral to the primary purpose of favourably resolving an internal political struggle'. C/tee on Grenada, Section of International Law and Practice, American Bar Association, *International Law and the United States Action in Grenada: A Report*, 18 *International Lawyer* (1984), p. 331, at p. 379. L. Doswald-Beck, 'The Legality of the United States Intervention in Grenada', 31 *Neth. ILR* (1984), p. 355, at p. 374. S. Davidson, *Grenada: A Study in Politics and the Limits of International Law* (Aldershot, Avebury, 1987); W. C. Gilmore, *The Grenada Intervention: Analysis and Documentation* (London, Mansell Publishing, 1984). For Somalia, see J. R. Bolton, 'Wrong Turn in Somalia', 73 *Foreign Affairs* (1994), p. 56. For Panama, see 'Agora: US Forces in Panama: Defenders, Aggressors or Human Rights Activists', 84 *AJIL* (1990), pp. 494–524.

[44] B. Simma, 'NATO, the UN and the Use of Force: Legal Aspects', 10 *EJIL* (1999), p. 12; A. Cassese, '*Ex iniuria ius oritur*: Are We Moving towards International Legitimation of Forcible Humanitarian Countermeasures in the World Community?', *ibid.*, p. 23.

[45] McDougal and Feliciano, *Law and Minimum World Public Order*, p. 416; McDougal, Lasswell, Chen, *Human Rights*, p. 242; W. M. Reisman, M. S. McDougal, 'A Humanitarian Intervention to Protect the Ibos', in R. B. Lillich (ed.), *Humanitarian Intervention and the United Nations* (Charlottesville, University Press of Virginia, 1973), p. 167, at p. 177.

Grenada was almost unanimously condemned as a pursuit by the US of its political interests in containing communism.[46] The genuine character of the humanitarian motive and appeal[47] has also been scrutinised.[48]

If the humanitarian perspective is the crucial evaluatory factor, it means that humanitarian intervention is the ultimate strategy when other methods have failed. Also its impact on the authority structures of the state is not crucial because it is triggered when there is abuse of such authority.[49] The evaluation of humanitarian actions should not be determined exclusively by the magnitude of their impact on the authoritative elite in the particular state but according to the promotion of the wider interests of human dignity. In Kosovo, there was a gradual increase in the intensity of methods adopted to prevent and terminate the human rights abuses. Following the resurgence of violence in Kosovo, an Interim Agreement for Peace and Self-Government in Kosovo was negotiated in Rambouillet by the Contact Group, the Federal Republic of Yugoslavia (FRY) and representatives from Kosovo. The agreement envisaged the introduction of administrative, judicial, constitutional and economic measures with the aim of safeguarding the Kosovar population and contributing to the democratisation and respect for the rule of law.[50] Implementation of the agreement was left with a ready-to-be-deployed NATO contingent.[51] When Yugoslavia rejected the agreement, NATO's coercive action was the final option left to reverse the human catastrophe unfolding in the region.[52] The effects on the constitutive power of the FRY were considerable, but the perspectives of the action were to secure the value of human dignity and therefore such effects become unimportant.[53] Any humanitarian

[46] GA Res. 38/7, UN GAOR, 38th Sess., Supp. No. 47, at 19, UN Doc. A/38/47 (1983), 108 votes for, 9 votes against, 27 abstentions.

[47] See Letter by the Governor-General Sir Paul Scoon addressed to the Prime Minister of Barbados, John Adams, where he seeks assistance from the United States in order to facilitate the return to democratic rule. J. N. Moore, 'Grenada and the International Double Standard', 78 *AJIL* (1984), p. 145, at p. 148.

[48] V. P. Nanda, 'The United States Armed Intervention in Grenada – Impact on World Order', 14 *Cal. WILJ* (1984), p. 395, at pp. 411–14; C. C. Joyner, 'The United States Action in Grenada: Reflections on the Lawfulness of Invasion', 78 *AJIL* (1984), p. 131, at pp. 138–9.

[49] J. N. Moore, 'Towards an Applied Theory for the Regulation of Intervention', in J. N. Moore (ed.), *Law and Civil War in the Modern World* (Baltimore, J. Hopkins University Press, 1974), p. 3, at pp. 24–6.

[50] Interim Agreement for Peace and Self-Government in Kosovo, chs 1, 2, 3, 4, http://kosovainfo.com.

[51] *Ibid.*, ch. 7.

[52] SC Res. 1160, UN SCOR, UN Doc. S/RES/1160 (1998); SC Res. 1199, UN SCOR, UN Doc. S/RES/1199 (1998); SC Res. 1203, UN SCOR, UN Doc. S/RES/1203 (1998); *Keesing's* (1999), pp. 42805–67.

[53] See Military-Technical Agreement between the International Security Force (KFOR) and the Government of the Federal Republic of Yugoslavia and the Republic of Serbia (9 June 1999), *Keesing's*, pp. 43008–9. SC Res. 1244, UN SCOR,

action, in addition to promoting the goal of human dignity, also serves as a future deterrent by increasing awareness that violations of human rights will not go unpunished and that world opinion will scrutinise domestic situations. This has a natural law residual according to which the just cause as rectification also functions as deterrent. For Victoria, 'they would only be emboldened to make a second attack if the fear of retribution did not keep them from wrongdoing'.[54] Hence, it was claimed during the Kosovo action that it may serve as a deterrent to future violations of human rights not only within the territory of the FRY but also in other parts of the world.[55]

With the policy school international law overcame its insularity and defensive mood and acquired vision and method. Its object became 'the protection of the individual in his eternal struggle for freedom of personality . . . wherever he may be and whatever his national or racial allegiance'.[56] The universal singularity of this ideal and its relentless promotion has provoked fierce reactions but was also met with recognition.[57] Leaving this aside, the policy school has opened the horizons of legal discourse by broadening the inquiries on situations, policies, values and results, thus rejecting the insistence on strict legality in international law. This involves active intellectual reasoning contrary to automatic reactions. The dichotomy between a visionary and a pragmatic view of the legal system and the employment of synthetic perspectives for the explication of legal phenomena is taken up more profoundly by the Critical Legal Studies movement, as we shall see in the next chapter.

UN Doc. S/RES/1244 (1999). Michael Walzer speaks of 'long-lasting interventions' which include trusteeship and protectorate. M. Walzer, 'The Politics of Rescue', *Dissent* (1995), p. 35, at p. 39.

[54] F. de Victoria, *De Indis et de Jure Belli Relectiones*, in *The Classics of International Law*, ed. J. B. Scott (Buffalo, N.Y., W. S. Hein & Co., 1995), p. 167, para. 420.

[55] According to Tony Blair: 'If we let an evil dictator range unchallenged we will have to spill infinitely more blood and treasure to stop him later.' *Keesing's*, p. 42901. He also stated that 'the consequences of not acting are more serious still for human life and for peace in the long term'. *The Times*, 24 March 1999.

[56] P. M. Brown, 'International Lawlessness', 32 *AJIL* (1938), p. 775, at p. 777.

[57] F. Fukuyama, *The End of History and the Last Man* (London, Hamish Hamilton, 1992), p. 338: 'the idea of a universal and directional history leading up to liberal democracy may become more plausible to people, and that the relativist impasse of modern thought will in a sense solve itself'.

4

Critical theory of international law and humanitarian intervention

Critical theory of international law

As has been seen above, realism argued against the traditional emphasis by legal systems on determinacy, objectivity and apoliticism as a means of containing the subjectivity of individual interests and sustaining legal comprehensiveness and certainty.[1] Law for the realists is a matter of choice not of discovery, hence marred with rule indeterminacy and ambiguity. The choicist character of realism is grounded on shared expectations and fundamental values. Critical Lawyers also delve into other sciences, social or political. The project of the Critical Legal Studies (CLS) movement is similarly to scrutinise the rigidity of legal-linguistic reasoning and pinpoint its contradictory character. They criticise the doctrinal falsification which upholds the neutrality and apolitical nature of rules and the reification of social discourse.[2] For them, values are co-determined with societies and legal rules reflect this.

Although they share common properties, CLS and realism have not embraced each other because CLS reacted against the predominantly individualistic liberal doctrine where individual rights and welfare are promoted. The unassumingly individualistic project of the policy school encounters the communitarian extolment of the CLS.[3] Moreover, the social inquiries of the policy school are considered to be timid because they are obsessed with the decision-making process to which they assimilate all the extra-legal perspectives.

For Critical Lawyers demonstration of legal incommensurability not only assists in demystifying law and in questioning legal complacency but also

[1] M. Sandel, *Liberalism and the Limits of Justice* (Cambridge, Cambridge University Press, 1982), pp. 116–18, 154–61; R. M. Unger, 'The Critical Legal Studies Movement', 96 *Harvard L Rev* (1983), p. 561, at pp. 564–73.
[2] C. Lévi-Strauss, *Structural Anthropology* (Harmondsworth, Penguin, 1979).
[3] M. Tushnet, 'Critical Legal Studies: A Political History', 100 *Yale LJ* (1991), p. 1515. R. Higgins, *Problems and Process: International Law and How to Use It* (Oxford, Oxford University Press, 1994).

51

strengthens the understanding of societal reality from which any vision for societal transformation springs.[4] We need therefore to understand the structure and nature of international law and its inherent tensions in order to transform it.

Traditional international law doctrine emphasises the determinacy and objectivity of its rules in order to clothe its science with legitimacy. The contention that international law represents legalisation of politics is deeply ingrained and threatening. Hence, in order to discard it, international rules should be distinguished from politics and should provide definite, detached answers to problems.[5] It is essential for the legal existence of international law to sustain this 'mystified' belief. Therefore, the CLS by presenting international law as immersed in the broader ideological struggles of life revive a perennial danger, although they emancipate legal thinking which can now embrace comprehensive modes of thinking.

More specifically, the assumption of determinacy and objectivity is formulated mainly against the arbitrariness of ideological power. Theorists such as Kelsen, Hart or Rawls have articulated frameworks which would assist in determining rules. However, such legal frameworks are eclectic because their matrix projects the boundaries within which the decisional process takes place and thus constrain choices.[6] Legal realism has also embraced rule indeterminacy but eventually opted for prediction. It blends in the study of legal rules social or political factors but in order to secure a more certain prediction.[7] Hence, the predictivist function implies the need for certainty.

Can the claim that international law is determinate be substantiated? Does it satisfy the criteria of comprehensiveness, consistency, directiveness and self-revision?[8] International law cannot cover all the factual situations which emerge from the multifarious forms of international interaction. Moreover, rules suffer from substantive inconsistency 'travelling in pairs' and allowing for exceptions. On the other hand, the systematisation of principles

---

[4] N. Duxbury, *Patterns of American Jurisprudence* (Oxford, Clarendon Press, 1995), pp. 194–5.

[5] J. Boyle, 'Ideals and Things: International Legal Scholarship and the Prison-house of Language', 26 *Harvard ILJ* (1985), p. 327, at pp. 346–9.

[6] '. . . a judicial decision is fairer if it represents the application of established standards rather than the imposition of new ones'. R. Dworkin, *Taking Rights Seriously* (London, Duckworth, 1977), pp. 5, 81–137; H. L. A. Hart, *The Concept of Law* (Oxford, Clarendon Press, 1961), pp. 132–7; J. Rawls, *A Theory of Justice* (Cambridge, Mass., Harvard University Press, 1971), pp. 4, 235.

[7] K. L. Llewellyn, *The Common Law Tradition: Deciding Appeals* (Boston, Little, Brown & Co., 1960), pp. 302–03; F. S. Cohen, 'Transcendental Nonsense and the Functional Approach', 35 *Col. L Rev* (1935), p. 809, at p. 849.

[8] J. W. Singer, 'The Player and the Cards: Nihilism and Legal Theory', 94 *Yale LJ* (1984), p. 1, at pp. 14–19.

for general application is inadequate and inconsistent.[9] Hence legal rules cannot be deduced automatically.

Actually, legal discourse is twofold. It includes both determinacy and indeterminacy, forging a compromise between the social needs for certainty and the social needs for change. Otherwise a mechanical, non-contextual application may result in arbitrariness.[10] Legal rules proffer an automatic response to 'plain, or paradigm, clear cases' but as Hart asserts, 'a large and important field is left open for the exercise of discretion'.[11] In international law, rules may denote certainty but custom alludes to change whereas the inclusion of principles such as 'justice' de-objectifies the application of 'stabilised' rules.

Additionally, rules and principles are ambiguous, their exercitation requires interpretative evaluation and they cannot determine the scope of application themselves.[12] The rule on the non-use of force is accompanied by exceptions and because the dividing line is abstruse, we need a meta-principle to diminish the discretion.[13] Hence, we use concepts such as sovereignty, self-determination and justice which either reinforce, nullify or limit the attitudinal peregrination of certain rules. The meta-principles are themselves antithetical and indeterminate. For instance, the principles of self-determination and sovereignty can be antagonistic; their application is contextual and corresponds to a plausible choice for achieving a justified solution. Self-determination as a formal quality may reinforce sovereignty and thus shield the state from foreign intervention even if gross human rights violations are committed internally whereas a substantive view of self-determination would serve as a

[9] L. Siorat, *Le problème des lacunes en droit international* (Paris, R. Pichon & R. Durand-Anzias, 1958); J. Stone, 'Non Liquet and the Function of Law in International Community', 35 *BYBIL* (1959), p. 124.

[10] D. Kennedy, 'Form and Substance in Private Law Adjudication', 89 *Harvard L Rev* (1976), p. 1685, at p. 1689: 'rigid rules require the sacrifice of precision in the achievement of the objectives lying behind the rules'. H. L. A. Hart, *The Concept of Law* (Oxford, Clarendon Press, 1961), pp. 126–7: 'We shall be forced by this technique to include in the scope of a rule cases which we would wish to exclude in order to give effect to reasonable social aims and which the open textured terms of our language would have allowed us to exclude had we left them less rigidly defined'.

[11] Hart, *The Concept of Law*, pp. 123–32. Dworkin challenges this because the 'best' interpretation of legal materials would procure determinate results. Dworkin, *Taking Rights Seriously*, pp. 14, 81–4; A. Altman, 'Legal Realism, Critical Legal Studies and Dworkin', 15 *Philosophy & Public Affairs* (1986), p. 205.

[12] J. J. A. Salmon, 'Le fait dans l'application du droit international', 175 *RC* (1982 II), p. 257, pp. 277–85; C. de Visscher, *Problèmes d'interprétation judiciaire en droit international public* (Paris, Éditions A. Pedone, 1963), p. 14; P. Winch, *The Idea of a Social Science and its Relation to Philosophy* (London, Routledge, 1958), p. 15: 'Our idea of what belongs to the realm of reality is given for us in the language we use.'

[13] Dworkin, *Taking Rights Seriously*, pp. 24–31; D. Kennedy, 'Form and Substance in Private Law Adjudication', 89 *Harvard L Rev* (1976), p. 1685, at pp. 1687–9; O. Schachter, 'International Law in Theory and Practice', 178 *RC* (1982 V), p. 9, pp. 43, 74–82.

means of evaluating the quality of sovereignty thus opening up the possibility of interference.

If rules are indeterminate and a matter of choice, then the objectivity of legal discourse is just a chimera. Objectivity refers to the quest for a rational foundation of legal rules which is a matter of knowledge not of opinion. The discovery of such legal foundation will legitimise the legal system through its inherent validity and transgress the subjectivity of human disquisition. Hence, it will become interpersonal, intersubjective and even universal. Positivism and natural law theory correspond to an external source of justificatory theory.[14] They adhere to an aprioristic assumption which involves cognition rather than judgment. The positivist command theory relied on the sovereign for its legitimisation, whereas Kelsen relied on a deductive, logical procedure. Natural law requires rational reflection on human nature and relies on mental constructions. The unreflective acceptance of the position that law is a matter of discovered truth objectifies discretionary judgments. Because the search for foundations can regress *ad infinitum*, the selection of a certain basis is unavoidably subjective. Therefore, the external source of legal argument lacks the necessary degree of neutrality.[15] On the other hand, consensus on certain values which permeate human experience promoted by theorists such as Hart, McDougal, Rawls or Finnis also gives rise to contradictions since it simultaneously embraces individualistic criteria based on rational decision but also communitarian criteria based on the negotiated wishes of particular communities.

Moreover, procedural theories fail to achieve determinacy and objectivity by creating a perspective of impartiality. Their method is deductive whereby the objectivity of a certain process dis-entrenched from our intuitions renders objective results. They are concerned more with the method than the nature of the outcomes[16] but as Rawls explains, if everyone applied the method correctly then everyone would agree.[17] This implies that predetermined results are achieved if we are all injected with the 'correct' method. Hence, judgments are made concerning the function or character of the procedure before deciding on the determinacy of certain norms. Also, procedural theories claim

[14] M. Moore, 'Moral Reality', *Wisconsin Law Review* (1982), p. 1061, at pp. 1072–5, 1106–16.

[15] R. Rorty, *Philosophy and the Mirror of Nature* (Oxford, Blackwell, 1979), pp. 334–5; R. M. Unger, *Social Theory: Its Situation and Its Task. A Critical Introduction to Politics. A Work in Constructive Social Theory* (Cambridge, Cambridge University Press, 1987), pp. 80–1.

[16] R. W. Newell, *Objectivity, Empiricism and Truth* (London, 1986), pp. 16–38: 'On the other hand, [objectivity] may also refer to the character of methods (absence of bias) in the process of knowledge production. A dispute about what one would have reason to believe tends to turn on this latter question. Here there is no question of the acceptance of "knowledge", only something that is "external". Objectivity now concerns the character of the common practices of production.'

[17] Rawls, *A Theory of Justice*, p. 21.

comparative supremacy over other relevant and competing procedures.[18] Disagreement on the procedural theories culminates in disagreement on the yielded principles and rules. Objectivity wanes whilst rival procedures, by claiming comparative or absolute supremacy, reveal alternative concepts of morality, impartial consideration of events or the objectivity of particular results. Bereft of any higher standard for adjudication, the promotion of any procedure appears arbitrary and biased. Rival claims depart from a different procedural basis which they consider as appropriate and valid. Eventually, accepting certain standards as points of reference or sources of purported results tends to integrate those standards in our interpretation of events, reproducing causative discourse. Human dignity as the major premise of the policy school is both ingrained into and a consequence of the procedure.

International law is also incomplete and inadequate to deal with the complexities of international interaction. New unanticipated events need inclusion otherwise they will remain extra-legal.[19] For instance, the argument that the Kosovo operation was humanitarian action has been rebuffed on the basis that 'the UN Charter and the corpus of modern international law do not seem specifically to incorporate such a right'.[20] On the other hand, it is claimed that the UN Charter cannot have an immutable character but should be enriched by new insights reflecting novel circumstances.[21] As it was noted, 'nothing could be more deadly than to build in uncertainty a castle of texts which did not correspond to reality'.[22] Procedural revision is, however, deficient.[23] The

[18] J. Fiskin, 'Liberal Theory and the Problem of Justification', *Nomos* XXVIII, p. 207, at p. 216.

[19] L. Husson, *Les transformations de la responsabilité. Etude sur la pensée juridique* (Paris, PUF, 1947), p. 515: 'Les catégories juridiques, comme toutes les catégories logiques, ne sont jamais que des cadres imparfaits, susceptibles de s'ouvrir à des actes ou à des situations pour lesquels ils n'ont point été faits, ou au contraire d'exlure des actes et des situations auxquelles ils devraient convenir, selon que la définition logique s'en sera tenue aux caractères communs ou, au contraire, pour introduire plus de précision, en aura fait intervenir d'autres, qu'elle aura dû envisager dans leur détermination spécifique.'

[20] *United Kingdom Materials on International Law*, ed. by G. Marston, 57 *BYBIL* (1986), p. 487, at p. 619.

[21] *Legal Consequences for States of the Continued Presence of South Africa in Namibia (South West Africa) Notwithstanding Security Council Resolution 276 (1970) (Advisory Opinion of 21 June 1971), ICJ Rep.* (1971), p. 14, at p. 31, para. 53: 'an international instrument has to be interpreted and applied within the framework of the entire legal system prevailing at the time of the interpretation'. Also Individual Opinion by Judge Alvarez in *Conditions of Admission of a State to Membership in the United Nations, ICJ Rep.* (1947–48), p. 56, at p. 68; Individual Opinion by Judge Sir P. Spender in *Certain Expenses of the United Nations (Advisory Opinion of 20 July 1962), ICJ Rep.* (1962), p. 150, at p. 186 and of Judge Jessup in *South West Africa Cases, ICJ Rep.* (1966), p. 5, at p. 439.

[22] Doc. 46, P/11 (1 May 1945), 1 UNCIOD, p. 437.

[23] J. W. Singer, 'Catcher in the Rye Jurisprudence', 35 *Rutgers Law Review* (1983), p. 275, at p. 278.

procedural function within the UN system as envisaged in Chapter VII is rather unsatisfactory. The Security Council is a body heavily politicised whose interpretation of the rules is frequently *ad hoc*, inconsistent and whimsical. Its contemporary interpretation includes issues of human rights violations within the ambit of threat to peace and security but not all such violations have been characterised accordingly and they have not led to the authorisation of appropriate measures. Moreover, advocating the involvement of international law with the international social process characterised by power makes rule determinacy adjacent thereto. This is reflected in the power inequality of the Security Council or NATO's action in Kosovo where it was claimed that 'if power is used to do justice, law will follow'.[24]

On the other hand, reified concepts such as sovereignty and non-intervention eviscerate any revisionist demand by invoking the danger of destabilisation and the threat of predatory policies. Consequently, the participants in a procedurally rigidified system are forced to alter a rule unilaterally when the circumstances change, in this way affecting rule determinacy. Humanitarian intervention is such an instance promoted often irregularly and on a case-by-case basis against the rule on the non-use of force enshrined in Article 2(4) of the UN Charter. But this gives rise to the question whether humanitarian intervention as it has been effected in Rwanda or Kosovo, rather unilaterally and against the formal legal prescription, will be accepted.[25] Moreover, it is claimed that there exists an organic connection between the unilateral abstention from the use of force contained in Article 2(4) and the collective security system. They form a sliding scale where output in one pole corresponds to input in the other pole of the scale.[26] Otherwise, the law 'which prohibits resort to force without providing a legitimate claimant with adequate alternative means of obtaining redress, contains the seeds of trouble'.[27] Lacking any other means of redressing the balance caused by the malfunction of the collective system, states reclaim the *status quo ante*, that is the unilateral use of force.[28] It has been maintained though by the

[24] M. J. Glennon, 'The New Interventionism: The Search for a Just International Law', 78 *Foreign Affairs* (1999), p. 2, at p. 7.

[25] *Ibid.*

[26] M. Virally, 'Article 2 paragraphe 4', in J. P. Cot, A. Pellet (eds), *La Charte des Nations Unies*, 2nd edn (Paris, Economica, 1991), p. 115, at p. 117: 'Réciproquement, cette règle, ne sera respectée et ne constituera une guarantie de la paix que si ses méchanismes fonctionnent de façon efficace . . .'. W. M. Reisman, 'Coercion and Self Determination: Construing Charter Article 2(4)', 78 *AJIL* (1984), p. 642.

[27] C. H. M. Waldock, 'The Regulation of the Use of Force by Individual States in International Law', 81 *RC* (1952 II), p. 455, at p. 490.

[28] A. Cassese, 'Return to Westphalia? Considerations on the Gradual Erosion of the Charter System', in A. Cassese (ed.), *The Current Legal Regulation of the Use of Force* (Dordrecht, M. Nitjhoff, 1986), p. 505; A. Cassese, *International Law in a Divided World* (Oxford, Clarendon Press, 1986), p. 223; W. M. Reisman, 'Criteria for the Lawful Use of Force in International Law', 10 *Yale JIL* (1984–85), p. 279, at p. 281.

International Court of Justice (ICJ) in the *Nicaragua* case that 'the principle of non-use of force [is] not as such conditioned by provisions relating to collective security, or to the facilities or armed contingents to be provided under Article 43 of the Charter'.[29] Lacking structures for procedural adaptation, the law remains in limbo which can be overcome only if overarching goals are allowed to guide practice.

The contradictions of the legal reasoning concerning humanitarian intervention

At this point, we need to consider the source of the inherent contradictions between 'mechanically applicable rules' and 'situation-sensitive, *ad hoc* standards', which evolves into that between individualism and altruism, culminating in liberalism and communitarism.[30] Liberal theory is reproached for keeping a suspicious silence on the issue of contradiction or denying its existence. For Critical Lawyers, individual freedom and communal restraint are viewed with equal suspicion and considered to be diametrically opposed.[31]

Rules infested with individualism produce more individualism, while altruism vies to introduce standards which underline the 'value judgments' of a certain community.[32] Standards are not determinate themselves because their apprehension and application requires choice.[33] The subsequent indeterminacy in adjudication or decision-making affects the core of legal argument which is paralysed between an individualistic and an altruistic vision. Indeterminacy is endemic in the absence of a meta-principle which would

[29] *Case Concerning Military and Paramilitary Activities in and against Nicaragua,* ICJ Rep. (1986), p. 14, at p. 100, para. 188 ('*Nicaragua Case*').

[30] D. Kennedy, 'Form and Substance in Private Law Adjudication', 89 *Harvard L Rev* (1976), p. 1685. M. Kelman, *A Guide to Critical Legal Studies* (Cambridge, Mass., Harvard University Press, 1987), p. 3: 'a system of thought [liberalism] that is simultaneously beset by internal contradiction . . . and by systematic repression of the presence of these contradictions'. The dichotomies represent an absolutist view of liberalism. See N. MacCormick, 'Reconstruction after Deconstruction: Closing In On Critique', in A. Norrie (ed.), *Closure or Critique: New Directions in Legal Theory* (Edinburgh, Edinburgh University Press, 1993), p. 142, at p. 145: 'It takes a rule to make a standard legal; it may take a standard to make a rule satisfactorily workable.'

[31] D. Kennedy, 'The Structure of Blackstone's Commentaries', 28 *Buffalo Law Review* (1979), p. 205, at pp. 211–12: 'The goal of individual freedom is at the same time dependent on and incompatible with the communal coercive action that is necessary to achieve it. . . . But at the same time that it forms and protects us, the universe of others . . . threatens us with annihilation and urges upon us forms of fusion that are quite plainly bad rather than good.'

[32] Kennedy, 'Form and Substance', p. 1752.

[33] *Ibid.*, p. 1771.

objectively assist our preference for either a standard or a rule.[34] Again, the meta-principle cannot attribute determinacy due to its own ambiguity and conflict with confluent meta-principles.

The altruistic and individualistic premises[35] pre-empt in international law the dichotomy between national egoism and communitarian morality. Individualism, identified with liberalism, insists on the regulatory function of rules which define autonomy and moderate activities located outside the spheres of individual liberty. Values are subjective and their postulation is an arbitrary exercise. Therefore, the role of the state becomes 'facilitative', it adjudicates between and accommodates diverse perceptions of values. There is a strong presumption against state intervention viewed either as a constraint on individual self-interest or as a means of pursuing parochial values. The individualistic premise is the prevalent assumption in international law. Non-intervention affirms state autonomy, asserts that the interests of a particular state take precedence over the general interests of a community and also avoids moral paternalism by extending certain values to non-consenting members. For instance, humanitarian intervention is guilty of promoting particularised interests either communal or parochial. Hence, individualism as expressed in Articles 2(4) and 2(7) on non-intervention does not define a value but interprets the value of autonomy and indifference.

The altruistic premises include a belief in shared values which are not arbitrary but the distillation of societal functions. These values are understood as being in a state of evolution towards attaining the ideal of human affiliation. Adherents to altruism attack individualism as a negative mentality. The rule obsession is identified with the regulation of the contact of the 'bad' man who needs limitations to his antisocial inclinations.[36] In international law, the rule on non-intervention purports to accomplish the function of restraining unscrupulous states. Altruism is identified with the 'good' man who promotes community values. It disputes the main argument of individualism that rules achieve certainty. Only when the 'good' man knows that the law would not criticise him when he acts in accordance with community expectations, is legal certainty secured. Individualism is also linked with a lack of concern for fellow human beings. The rules which affirm state sovereignty and enhance state autonomy create a situation whereby states function within autonomous clusters, alienated from other states and only linked horizontally on matters of their discretion. Under such a state of affairs, they become oblivious to grievous conditions existing in neighbouring states. The use of force is not excluded by altruists but the aim is to transform it into a moral force. In international law, Article 2(4) does not

[34] *Ibid.*, p. 1724; W. W. Bratton, Jr., 'Manners, Metaprinciples, Metapolitics and Kennedy's *Form and Substance*', 6 *Cardozo Law Review* (1985), p. 871, at pp. 884–6.
[35] Kennedy, 'Form and Substance', pp. 1766–77.
[36] O. W. Holmes, 'The Path of Law', 10 *Harvard L Rev* (1897), p. 457; T. Twining, 'The Bad Man Revisited', 58 *Cornell Law Review* (1973), p. 275.

secure certainty because benevolent states which resort to force in order to restore humanity are victimised by this rule. In an altruistic environment, physical coercion is justified as promoting morality.

The interlocking arguments of Critical Lawyers prove the relevance of Voltaire's observations concerning international relations.[37] Following a common trend, he views state affairs as reflecting human relations. He acknowledges the antithetical forces of *amour propre* and *bienveillance*, of egoism and benevolence which translates into the fundamental contradiction between individualism and altruism. The destructive force of egoism is alleviated by the instinct of compassion. Egoism directs human and state actions but the rule of forbearance which emanates from benevolence is stated in a negative form as equality and independence. The optimistic element is that altruism always fosters itself in the end and that nations which have attained a balance of egoistic and altruistic instincts should be able to disperse benevolence.

Altruism and individualism as the two poles of the fundamental contradiction are contained in all legal systems and the UN Charter is no exception. We discover there the tension between individualism-exclusivity and community.[38] State socialisation and participation in a community affirms their individuality but also poses a threat.[39] Collectivities impose upon their members constraints which restrict individual autonomy and it is only collective action which can transgress these constraints. The United Nations as a collective international legal order has imposed upon its members certain legal restraints, i.e. the non-use of force, which serve multiple and somewhat irreconcilable purposes: confirm state identity by excluding external interference, restrain state individuality by taming aggression and thus reaffirm state association. It is only the collectivity which can change this rule, for instance, when the United Nations Organisation initiates the use of force.

Accordingly, humanitarian intervention triggers arguments which support or negate the opposing pairs. It asserts communal values and supports the authority of the intervening state. It may also affirm the authority of the state in which it intervenes when it is accompanied by consent. On the other hand, humanitarian intervention may defeat the authority of this state, overlook equality and mutual respect and endanger other communal values, i.e. peace, which are also supported by communal will. In the contradiction between individualism and altruism, humanitarian intervention reaffirms altruism but also reaffirms the autonomy of the individual state which resorts to

[37] M. L. Perkins, 'Voltaire's Concept of International Order', *Studies on Voltaire and the Eighteenth Century*, T. Besterman (ed.), vol. XXVI (Genève, Institut et Musée Voltaire, Les Délices, 1963), p. 1291.

[38] D. Kennedy, 'Theses about International Legal Discourse', 23 *German YBIL* (1980), p. 353, at pp. 361–7.

[39] *Ibid.*, p. 361: 'individual nations find in socialisation both the source of their identity and a threat to their existence'.

action. The dilemma eventually refers to the method of choosing between individual particularism or communitarian altruism in a specific situation.

Humanitarian intervention exposes then the circularity of arguments which deny traditional theories the benefit of prediction and persuasion.[40] More specifically, Article 2(4) invokes the positivist aspect of sovereignty whereas the introduction of extra-consensual arguments such as justice and human rights invokes the natural law aspect. However, each line of argument can substitute the other or they can be mutually recombined. Hence, one may refer to the justice of keeping promises or to the order which adherence to Article 2(4) brings but also to the justice of adjusting the rule when circumstances change. Concerning the latter, separation of law from state action suffers from 'the problem of normative source', that is, the inability to determine the content of the rule. On the other hand, fusion of law with practice suffers from 'the problem of normative legitimacy'. Deviant behaviour cannot be distinguished as either 'contranormative' or 'protonormative'.[41] Article 2(4) fused with state practice fails to distinguish between mere violations of that rule or the genesis of a new rule. On the other hand, the same Article being critical of contrary state practice is reduced to irrelevance.

The ICJ encountered the dilemma between normative legitimacy and normative source in the *Nicaragua* case and solved it by choosing the former.[42] According to the Court, customary law is identified by state practice and *opinion juris.*[43] However in this case, concretisation of the non-intervention rule through state practice was dismissed[44] by the Court, which only scrutinised the sources which verify the existence of the rule. Thus the normative source lost its autonomy and determinative force by a presumption of norms.[45] On the other hand, it is claimed that the *opinio juris* is inferred from the state practice or certain modes of behavioural patterns whereas state practice cannot be deduced from the former.[46] Thus it is maintained that state

---

[40] D. Kennedy, *International Legal Structures* (Baden-Baden, Nomos Verlagsgesellschaft, 1987), ch. 1, pp. 11–107.

[41] Kennedy, 'Theses', p. 383.

[42] N. Tsagourias, 'The Nicaragua Case and the Use of Force: The Theoretical Construction of the Decision and Its Deconstruction', 1 *Journal of Armed Conflict Law* (1996), p. 81; 'Applying the Critical Jurisprudence of International Law to the *Case Concerning Military and Paramilitary Activities In and Against Nicaragua*', 71 *Virginia Law Review* (1985), p. 1183.

[43] *Nicaragua Case*, pp. 97–8, paras 183–4; *Asylum Case, ICJ Rep.* (1950), p. 265, at pp. 276–7; *North Sea Continental Shelf Cases, ICJ Rep.* (1969), p. 3, at pp. 43–4, paras 74, 77.

[44] *Nicaragua Case*, p. 98, para. 186.

[45] P. M. Eisemann, 'L'arrêt de la C.I.J. du 27 juin 1986 (fond), dans l'affaire des activités militaires et paramilitaires au Nicaragua et contre celui-ci', 32 *AFDI* (1986), p. 153, at pp. 173–4.

[46] *Case Concerning Delimitation of the Maritime Boundary in the Gulf of Maine Area, ICJ Rep.* (1984), p. 244, at p. 299, para. 111: 'together with a set of customary

practice impinges upon the corpus of a rule, modifies or crystallises a new rule. During the Kosovo operation it has been argued that state practice has contributed to the crystallisation of a rule of humanitarian intervention contrary to the presumption of absolute non-intervention contained in Article 2(4).[47]

Moreover, general principles which express values and purposes such as non-intervention and human rights also fail to contain decisions because the choice between them is irresolvable and no secondary norms exist to articulate their exercise in detail. Thus, they are stated as mutually exclusive principles which apply, if need be, without determining the inferred results. It becomes evident that we need a meta-principle which will neutralise the opposition to any particular argument by increasing the point of reference. In the particular case of humanitarian intervention, the meta-principles that may apply are those of humanism or sovereignty. Choosing between them reveals the 'right' argument but again the choice is arbitrary because there are no meta-meta-principles which would assist us in that choice.

The insistence by the CLS on deconstruction has infused legal thinking with a considerable degree of self-exploration and anticipation since it challenges us to contemplate the foundation or the substantial basis of rules and principles. A recurrent theme is the role of the state in legal theory. Critical Lawyers criticise the traditional approach of defining modernity with sovereignty and history and also criticise the traditional scholarship for revering the past.[48] Today the state encounters multiple demands and faces the forces of globalisation but also fragmentation. The reification of sovereignty as it is mirrored in international rules obscures the essence of these changes. Critical Lawyers grasp the changed situation and consider the state as a 'metaphysical entity'[49] but their response varies. It is either pessimistic because

---

rules whose presence in the *opinio juris* of States can be tested by induction based on the analysis of a sufficiently extensive and convincing practice and not by deduction from preconceived ideas'. L. Condorelli, 'La coutume', in M. Bedjaoui (réd. gén.), *Droit International. Bilan et perspectives*, tom. 1 (Paris, Editions Pedone, 1991), p. 187, at p. 197: 'En effet, ce sont les mêmes actes dont l'ensemble compose la pratique des Etats qui doivent témoigner, "par leur nature ou la manière dont ils ont accomplis", de l'existence de l'*opinio juris*.' M. Sorensen, *Les sources du droit international* (Copenhague, E. Munksgaard, 1946), p. 85; P. Haggenmacher, 'La doctrine des deux éléments du droit coutumier dans la pratique et la Cour Internationale', 90 *RGDIP* (1986), p. 5, at p. 177.

[47] A. Cassese, '*Ex iniuria ius oritur*: Are We Moving Towards International Legitimation of Forcible Humanitarian Countermeasures in the World Community?', 10 *EJIL* (1999), p. 23, at p. 29.

[48] D. Kennedy, 'A New Stream of International Law Scholarship', 7 *Wisconsin International Law Journal* (1988), p. 1, at pp. 2, 12.

[49] A. Carty, 'Critical International Law: Recent Trends in the Theory of International Law', 2 *EJIL* (1991), p. 66, at p. 94.

we cannot escape the contingency of our own world or visionary towards a world society of human beings.[50]

Koskenniemi defends the state on its formal character, being suspicious of the subjectivism inherent in a commitment to substantive values.[51] He disowns choice because it requires non-legal considerations and projects certain values which become dominant.[52] It seems that state sovereignty contrary to the claim that values are hegemonic becomes such a 'deified' value which not only obstructs other values from emerging but also over-rides them.[53] As a result, we are unable to understand the essence of the state and of the international society or respond meaningfully to the vibrations which the current forces of globalisation or fragmentation cause on the state.[54]

One the other hand, Phillip Allott attributes the anomy of the present state-structured society to the fact that the state dominates our consciousness[55] and he journeys through 'consciousness' to a new international society.[56] This international society is above the state society but behind everything lies the human being as a member of both state and international society.[57] The new international society of human beings transgresses national borders and induces our human feelings of sympathy and responsibility for other human beings. Thus, 'human societies and human beings everywhere at last begin to take moral and social responsibility for the survival and prospering

[50] P. Allot, *Eunomia: New Order for a New World* (Oxford, Oxford University Press, 1990).

[51] M. Koskenniemi, 'The Future of Statehood', 32 *Harvard ILJ* (1991), p. 397, at p. 407. M. Koskenniemi, 'Theory: Implications for the Practitioner', in P. Allott, T. Carty, M. Koskenniemi, C. Warbrick (eds), *Theory and International Law: An Introduction* (London, The British Institute of International and Comparative Law, 1991), p. 1, at p. 42: 'statehood functions as precisely that decision-process which tackles the problems of multiplicity of ideas and interpretative controversy regarding their fulfilment. Its very formality intends to operate as a safeguard so that these different (theological) ideals are not transformed into a globally enforced tyranny.'

[52] M. Koskenniemi, 'The Politics of International Law', 1 *EJIL* (1990), p. 4, at p. 32.

[53] R. Ashley, R. B. J. Walker, 'Reading Dissidence/Writing the Discipline: Crisis and the Question of Sovereignty in International Studies', 34 *International Studies Quarterly* (1990), p. 367.

[54] T. Carty, 'The Failed State and the Tradition of International Law – Towards a Renewal of Legal Humanism', Inaugural Lecture, University of Derby, 6 December 1995, pp. 5–9 (unpublished paper).

[55] Allott, *Eunomia*, paras 15.41, 16.16, 17.40, 18.18, pp. 277–8, 303, 354, 382.

[56] *Ibid.*, para. 16.17, p. 303: 'International law is a reality-forming of international society which does not recognise the reality of the total social process by which all reality is formed. It chooses to recognise only the social process of the interacting of the governments of state-societies, as if they constituted a self-contained and self-caused social process, as if they constituted the whole of the total social process of international society.' Also paras 15.26, 15.36, pp. 270, 275.

[57] *Ibid.*, para. 16.36, p. 311.

of the whole of humanity'.[58] Finally, all depends on the human spirit which is formed as 'self perfecting, self-ordering. . . . [when] humanity [acts] in love and hope'.[59]

Although the end result of their deliberations are not uniform, the employed methods are valuable in exposing the multiplicity and conflicting character of the rules or principles which compete to prevail in the field of humanitarian intervention. Having presented and explored the configuration of humanitarian intervention within the major jurisprudential schools, it is now necessary to explicate those rules of international law which are relevant in the field of humanitarian intervention. By completing this lego-jurisprudential exercise, we shall fulfil our stated aim of acquainting ourselves with the current status of the argument before we proceed with our redescription.

[58] *Ibid.*, p. xxiii.
[59] P. Allott, 'Reconstituting Humanity – New International Law', 3 *EJIL* (1992), p. 219, at p. 252, para. 41.4. 'societies are systems made by human beings for human survival and human prospering, not for human oppression and human indignity'. The Onoh Memorial Lecture 1989, (Hull, University of Hull Press, 1989), pp. 2–3.

5

Humanitarian intervention in a legal context: the prohibition on the use of force

Sovereignty – (non)intervention

The inquiry into the jurisprudence of international law has shown that legal theory influences legal reasoning and is responsible for the latter's oscillation. In this chapter and the next, we shall see how the antagonistic theoretical streams mould legal argument and how this is reflected in the UN framework and the state practice. By presenting the ideals which strive to delimit legal argumentation we can extend our perception beyond a capricious legalistic logomachy to the essence of the matter.

As was shown above, sovereignty was inferred as a principle ordering state relations from natural law analogies of individual freedom, autonomy and equality. The 'domestic analogy' is persistent in international jurisprudence. As individuals are independent and equal entities, so should states as super-individuals be independent and equal.[1]

Non-intervention is ingrained functionally in the concept of sovereignty. It is indispensable for the formation of sovereign societies and also it embodies a rule stemming from sovereignty. However, contending assumptions exist about the extent and quality of sovereignty and non-intervention. For Grotius, sovereignty and non-intervention are deduced from a conceptual perspective intersected with the natural law ideology. Because the superseded precepts of natural law apply directly to individuals as well as to states, he allows interventions for humanitarian reasons.[2] On the other hand, Vattel's principle of non-intervention is based on assessing the effects of sovereignty on state

---

[1] A. Carty, *The Decay of International Law? A Reappraisal of the Limits of Legal Imagination in International Affairs* (Manchester, Manchester University Press, 1986), p. 88.
[2] H. Bull, 'The Grotian Conception of International Society', in H. Butterfield, M. Wight (eds), *Diplomatic Investigations: Essays in the Theory of International Politics* (London, Allen & Unwin, 1966), p. 68; R. J. Vincent, *Nonintervention and International Order* (Princeton, Princeton University Press, 1974), pp. 23–4.

relations. It is not theoretical but historical. However, since state practice in his era was diverse, Vattel pronounced a principle in the form of a verisimilitude, prognosticating the effects of the concept on state interaction.[3]

Sovereignty is instrumental in installing internal order, that is, the existence of harmonious inter-social relations through respect of certain rules of conduct. The state provides institutionalisation and political or territorial stability. Similarly, international order should emulate the domestic paradigm. State sovereignty is the recognition of the exclusive sphere of order within and among societies and non-intervention becomes its legal and factual substantiation. Hence, the state as legal, political and judicial power stabilises domestic and international society.[4] Realism also subscribes to non-intervention from an instinctive preference for international order. Intervention will infringe the substance of this order, sovereignty, which emerged to shield statist political entities from individual morality and private interests. The opposing ideals are encapsulated in the exchange between the French Foreign Minister and François Mitterrand following the intervention in Central Africa: 'Intervenons-nous en Centrafrique? Alors nous sommes les gendarmes de cette Afrique, les néocolonislistes. . . . Nous abstenons-nous d'intervenir? Alors nous soutenons des régimes tyranniques, nous laissons bafouer les droits de l' homme'.[5] For similar reasons, the ICJ rejected the US contention that the human rights violations in Nicaragua justified interference and opted for sovereignty, respect for domestic jurisdiction and international peace and stability.[6]

The Court's approach acknowledges only the factual existence of sovereignty because it is feared that ideological or ethical considerations may pose a threat to its integrity and the international order it supports.[7] However, it forfeits the essence of sovereignty and conceals its *merits*. The failure of its internal aspect would affect sovereignty as a whole and this is of particular interest to humanitarian intervention. Thus, we need to consider

---

[3] P. H. Winfield, 'The History of Intervention in International Law', 3 *BYBIL* (1922–23), p. 130, at pp. 133–4; A. Carty, *The Decay of International Law? A Reappraisal of the Limits of Legal Imagination in International Affairs* (Manchester, Manchester University Press, 1986), pp. 89–90.

[4] F. Kratochwil, 'Sovereignty as *Dominium*: Is There a Right of Humanitarian Intervention?', in G. M. Lyons, M. Mastanduno (eds), *Beyond Westphalia? State Sovereignty and International Intervention* (Baltimore, J. Hopkins Press, 1995), pp. 21–42.

[5] *JO.AN.*, 6 October 1979, p. 7885.

[6] 'Every State possesses a fundamental right to choose and implement its own political, economic and social systems.' *Case Concerning Military and Paramilitary Activities in and against Nicaragua, ICJ Rep.* (1986), p. 14, p. 131, para. 258. F. R. Tesón, 'Le peuple, c'est moi! The World Court and Human Rights', 81 *AJIL* (1987), p. 173.

[7] H. Morgenthau, 'To Intervene or Not to Intervene', 45 *Foreign Affairs* (1967), p. 425; S. Huntington, 'The Clash of Civilizations?', 72 *Foreign Affairs* (1993), p. 22.

the constitution of state sovereignty and revisit the contract theories. According to Locke, the protection of people's natural rights endows the state with the political right to sovereignty.[8] Consequently, the morality invested in sovereignty reflects the morality of the individual rights. If state legitimacy is viewed in contractual terminology as protecting the basic human rights to liberty and life of its citizens, any aberration from this course may invite intervention because sovereignty is overridden through de-legitimisation.[9] Theoretical traces of internal legitimacy with external intervention can be found in Vattel who acknowledges a right of intervention when the prince derogates from his duties towards his subjects.[10] This theoretical pattern is followed by Stowell who questions the view that independence should be more sacred than the law which grants that independence, and for whom humanitarian intervention is the protection of the inhabitants of another state against treatment which 'exceeds the limits of that authority within which the sovereign is presumed to act with reason and justice'.[11] Likewise

[8] J. Locke, *Two Treatises of Government*, M. Goldie (ed.) (London, Everyman, 1993), 'The Second Treatise of Government', chs 2, 7, 8; F. H. Hinsley, *Sovereignty*, 2nd edn (Cambridge, Cambridge University Press, 1986), pp. 146–9; I. M. Wilson, 'The Influence of Hobbes and Locke in the Shaping of the Concept of Sovereignty in Eighteenth Century France', in T. Besterman (ed.), *Studies on Voltaire and the Eighteenth Century*, vol. CI (Banbury, The Voltaire Foundation, 1973), ch. II, p. 29.

[9] G. Doppelt, 'Walzer's Theory of Morality in International Relations', 8 *Philosophy & Public Affairs* (1978–79), p. 3; D. Luban, 'Just War and Human Rights', 9 *Philosophy & Public Affairs* (1980), p. 160; P. Montague, 'Two Concepts of Rights', *ibid.*, p. 372; C. R. Beitz, 'Nonintervention and Communal Integrity', *ibid.*, p. 385; G. Doppelt, 'Statism without Foundations', *ibid.*, p. 398; M. Walzer, 'The Moral Standing of States: A Response to Four Critics', *ibid.*, p. 209; M. Walzer, 'The Theory of Aggression', in S. Luper-Foy (ed.), *Problems of International Justice* (Boulder, Westview Press, 1988), p. 151.

[10] E. de Vattel, *Le Droit Des Gens ou Principes de la Loi Naturelle, appliqués à la Conduite et aux Affaires des Nations et des Souverains*, trans. C. G. Fenwick, in *Classics of International Law* (Washington, Carnegie Institution of Washington, 1916), Bk. I, chs I–IV; Bk. II, ch. IV, para. 56.

[11] E. C. Stowell, *Intervention in International Law* (Washington, Byrne, 1921), pp. 53, 59. Concerning the changing attitudes towards sovereignty and human rights, *see* Javier Pérez de Cuéllar: 'It is now increasingly felt that the principle of non-interference with the essential domestic jurisdiction of states cannot be regarded as a protective barrier behind which human rights could be massively or systematically violated with impunity. The case for not impinging on the sovereignty, territorial integrity and political independence of States is by itself indubitably strong. But it could only be weakened if it were to carry the implication that sovereignty, even in this day and age, includes the right of mass slaughter or of launching systematic campaigns of decimation or forced exodus of civilian populations in the name of controlling civil strife or insurrection. With the heightened international interest in universalising a regime of human rights, there is a marked and most welcome shift in public attitudes. To try to resist it would be politically as unwise as it is morally indefensible.' Secretary-General's Address at the University of Bordeaux, *UNDPI Press Release*, SG/SM/4560. Also former United Nations Secretary-General Boutros

66

for Tesón, 'the ultimate justification of the existence of states is the protection and enforcement of the natural rights of the citizens'; otherwise it 'forfeits not only its domestic legitimacy, but its international legitimacy as well'.[12] This aspect of contractarianism revives cosmopolitan notions of human society and solidarity[13] but is also related to issues of reciprocity which advise intervention in societies which do not satisfy the values of a polity. Non-intervention is enjoyed only by states which are on an equal footing of justice: otherwise intervention is permitted, in Mill's words, by 'civilised nations' against 'barbarians',[14] or in modern vocabulary, against unjust states.[15]

Contract theories may, on the other hand, support a view of non-intervention which protects the right to communal autonomy and self-determination. External intervention will disrupt the particularistic aspirations of a community to assert itself unless massacres and enslavement destroy communal integrity and thus invite intervention.[16] For instance, the Indian Foreign Minister in order to justify India's action in Bangladesh invoked the fact that Pakistan 'has irrevocably lost the allegiance of such a large section of its people . . . and cannot bring them under its sway . . .'.[17]

It is apparent then that different envisions of sovereignty and international society support different approaches to (non)intervention. The dilemma crystallises into the conflict between order and justice. As Tesón puts it, intervention 'opens the door for unpredictable and serious undermining of world

Boutros-Ghali: 'State sovereignty takes a new meaning in this context. Added to its dimension of rights is the dimension of responsibility, both internal and external. Violation of state sovereignty is and will remain an offence against the global order, but its misuse also may undermine human rights and jeopardise a peaceful global life . . .'. *United Nations Security Council Summit Opening Address by Members*, VP-5-2, 3, 4.

[12] F. R. Tesón, *Humanitarian Intervention: An Inquiry Into Law And Morality*, 2nd edn (Dobbs Ferry, N.Y., Transnational Pub., 1997), p. 15.

[13] '. . . the subjects of others do not seem to me to be outside that kinship of nature and society formed by the whole world. And, if you abolish that society, you will destroy the unity of the human race'. A. Gentili, *De Jure Belli Libri Tres* (1598) (New York, Oceana, 1964), p. 122.

[14] J. S. Mill, 'A Few Words on Non-Intervention', in J. S. Mill, *Dissertations: Political, Philosophical, and Historical*, vol. III (London, Longmans, 1875), pp. 153–78. 'L'intervention des *puissances civilisée* est légitime en principe, quand la population chrétienne de ces pays est exposée à des persécutions ou à des massacres. Dans ces circonstances, elle est justifiée par la communauté des intérêts religieux et par des *considérations d'humanité*, c'est-à-dire par les principes du droit naturel d'après lesquels les États civilisés se dirigent généralement dans leurs relations avec les *États barbares*.' (Italics added). F. De Martens, *Traité de droit international*, tom. 1, traduit du Russe par A. Léo (Paris, Librairie Marescq Aine, 1883), p. 398.

[15] J. Rawls, 'The Law of Peoples', 20 *Critical Enquiry* (1993), p. 36, at pp. 37, 66.

[16] M. Walzer, *Just and Unjust Wars: A Moral Argument with Historical Illustrations*, 2nd edn (New York, HarperCollins, 1991), ch. 6.

[17] UN Doc. S/PV.1611 (12 December 1971), p. 62.

order' whereas non-intervention 'entails the seemingly morally intolerable proposition that the international community ... is impotent to combat massacres, acts of genocide, mass murder and widespread torture'.[18] Legal rules are then caught within these opposing ideals.

The rule on non-intervention and the UN Charter

The legal framework to be considered here is the United Nations Charter which adheres to sovereignty and non-intervention as guarantors of international peace, order and security but also makes proclamations for justice and human rights. The interaction of the rule on non-intervention contained in Article 2(4) and the principles promoted by the UN Charter as well as their empirical substantiation has contributed to theoretical and doctrinal constructions which need to be disentangled, as well as elucidated.[19]

According to one line of argument Article 2(4) contains an all-inclusive prohibition.[20] Consequently, humanitarian intervention is illegal and located outside the premises of the Charter. This reasoning contains those theoretical ingredients which substantiate the concept of sovereignty. Stemming from a natural law tenet of moral equality among autonomous human beings, states are viewed as autonomous units which coexist in the international system. Vattel had first encapsulated in the concept of sovereignty the independent, politically and morally self-contained state units. Non-intervention is hence the substantiation of state sovereignty shielded against the onslaught of private morality or the imperialist instincts of the more powerful states. It

[18] Tesón, *Humanitarian Intervention*, p. 4; H. Bull, *The Anarchical Society*, 2nd edn (London, Macmillan, 1995), pp. 73–94.

[19] Sir F. Pollock, *A First Book of Jurisprudence*, 2nd edn (London, Macmillan, 1904), p. 3: 'We find in all human sciences that those ideas which seem to be most simple are really the most difficult to grasp with certainty and express with accuracy.' T. Kuhn, *The Structure of Scientific Revolutions*, 2nd edn (Chicago, University Press of Chicago, 1970), p. 113.

[20] See statement of the US Delegate at Committee I/1, 6 UNCIOD, p. 335: 'the intention of the authors of the original text was to state in the broadest terms an absolute all – inclusive prohibition'. C. H. M. Waldock, 'The Regulation of the Use of Force by Individual States in International Law', 81 *RC* (1952 II), p. 455, at p. 493; A. von Verdross, 'Idées directrices de l' Organisation des Nations Unies', 83 *RC* (1953 II), p. 1, at p. 14; R. Russell, J. Muther, *A History of the United Nations Charter* (Washington, D.C., The Brookings Institution, 1958), p. 456; I. Brownlie, *International Law and the Use of Force by States* (Oxford, Clarendon Press, 1963), p. 268; H. Kelsen, *Principles of International Law*, 2nd rev. edn R. W. Tucker (ed.) (New York, Holt, Rinehart and Winston, 1966), p. 45; P. de Visscher, 'Cours général de droit international public', 136 *RC* (1972 II), p. 7, at pp. 19–20; M. Lachs, 'General Course in Public International Law', 169 *RC* (1980 IV), p. 9, at p. 162; L. Henkin, 'General Course in Public International Law', 216 *RC* (1989 IV), p. 10, at p. 148.

has been argued that according to the *travaux préparatoires*, the wording of Article 2(4) was inserted upon the 'insistent behest of small states' to strengthen the guarantee against intervention.[21] Hence, as it was put by Professor Schachter, 'neither human rights, democracy or self-determination are acceptable legal grounds for waging war, nor for that matter, are traditional just causes or righting wrongs'.[22] When Vietnam overthrew the Khmer Rouge regime, the General Assembly condemned Vietnam for encroaching upon Kampuchea's sovereignty.[23] According to Greece, the violations of human rights did not justify Vietnam's intervention.[24] The pursued goal is international peace and security to which the concept of sovereignty contributes as a stabilising factor. This has been confirmed in the *Corfu Channel* case where non-intervention was connected with sovereignty, peace and order.[25]

However, intervention is a permanent feature of international relations[26] and the position which abides by the prescription contained in Article 2(4), despite its normative coherence, does not clarify the content or the validity of the non-intervention rule.[27] For this reason, verification of the correspondence between normative prescription and state reception is needed. An extreme view would consider Article 2(4) null and void considering the discrepancies in state practice.[28] A more conventional view maintains that subsequent state

[21] 6 UNCIOD, pp. 557, 720; L. M. Goodrich, E. Hambro, A. P. Simons, *Charter of the United Nations*, 3rd edn (New York, Columbia University Press, 1969), pp. 44–5; E. Giraud, 'L'interdiction du recours à la force. La théorie et la pratique des Nations Unies', 67 *RGDIP* (1963), p. 501 at pp. 512–13.

[22] O. Schachter, *International Law in Theory and Practice* (Dordrecht/Boston/London, Martinus Nijhoff, 1991), p. 128.

[23] G. A. Res. 34/22 (14 November 1979); GA Res. 35/6 (22 October 1980).

[24] 17 *United Nations Chronicle* (1980), pp. 39, 41, 44.

[25] 'Between independent States respect for territorial *sovereignty* is an essential foundation of international relations.' *The Corfu Channel Case, ICJ Rep.* (1949), p. 4, at p. 35.

[26] H. Bull (ed.), *Intervention in World Politics* (Oxford, Clarendon Press, 1984).

[27] V. Lowe, 'The Principle of Non-Intervention: Use of Force', in V. Lowe, C. Warbrick (eds), *The United Nations and the Principles of International Law* (London, Routledge, 1994), p. 66, at p. 73; For criticism of the ICJ's approach in the *Nicaragua* case where it pronounced the existence of the non-intervention rule avoiding though to indicate its content *see* A. A. D'Amato, 'Trashing Customary International Law', 81 *AJIL* (1987), p. 101; F. L. Kirgis, Jr., 'Custom on a Sliding Scale', *ibid.*, p. 146; M. H. Mendelson, 'The *Nicaragua Case* and Customary International Law', in W. E. Butler (ed.), *The Non-use of Force in International Law* (Dordrecht/Boston/London, Martinus Nijhoff, 1989), p. 85, at p. 91.

[28] E. V. Rostow, 'The Legality of the International Use of Force by and From States', 10 *Yale JIL* (1985), p. 286: 'A proposition in the form of a rule of law can be considered a legal norm even if it is not universally respected and enforced; but it cannot be characterised as a norm if respect and enforcement are the exceptions rather than the rule. By this standard, the status of Article 2(4) as law is now in doubt.' T. M. Franck, 'Who Killed Article 2(4)? or Changing Norms Governing the Use of Force by States', 64 *AJIL* (1970), p. 809; L. Henkin, 'The Reports of the Death of Article 2(4) are Greatly Exaggerated', 65 *AJIL* (1971), p. 544.

practice has modified Article 2(4) and this impinges upon the normative level. For instance, Cassese considers NATO's action in Kosovo as leading to the 'crystallisation of a general rule of international law authorising armed countermeasures for the exclusive purpose of putting an end to large-scale atrocities amounting to crimes against humanity and constituting a threat to the peace'.[29] The supposition is that in a deficient and relatively ineffective legal system *ex iniuria ius oritur*.

On the other hand, it is claimed that the normativity of the non-intervention rule remains intact despite the attempts to manipulate its application. Any conduct which is contranormative is not automatically incorporated therein.[30] Thus, if non-intervention is the principle which has been accepted formally by states, the alleged exemptions – humanitarian intervention included – should be subjected to rigorous tests in order to pass the threshold of legality. Humanitarian intervention or any intervention is multi-faceted, therefore it is illegal because it cannot be extracted as a crystallised segment of state practice.[31] For instance, in his submissions on the *Legality of the Use of Force* Professor Brownlie relied on Article 2(4) and the General Assembly Resolutions on Friendly Relations[32] and Aggression[33] which reaffirm the principle of non-intervention in order to dismiss the argument that the Kosovo operation was humanitarian intervention which, otherwise, 'would require consistent and substantial evidence'.[34] Similarly, in the *Nicaragua* case, the ICJ relied only on General Assembly Resolutions to satisfy itself that the rule on non-intervention enjoys the customary criteria of practice and *opinio juris*.[35] The Resolutions though represent what the law *ought to* be and not what the law actually *is*.[36] The Court thus opted for normative validity following

[29] A. Cassese, '*Ex iniuria ius oritur*: Are We Moving Towards International Legitimation of Forcible Humanitarian Countermeasures in the World Community?', 10 *EJIL* (1999), p. 23, at p. 29; A. Cassese, 'Return to Westphalia? Considerations on the Gradual Erosion of the Charter System', in A. Cassese (ed.), *The Current Legal Regulation of the Use of Force* (Dordrecht/Boston/Lancaster, Martinus Nijhoff, 1986), p. 505, at p. 514.

[30] 'Facts, however undisputed, which are the result of conduct violative of international law cannot claim the same right to be incorporated automatically as part of the law of nations.' H. Lauterpacht, *Recognition in International Law* (Cambridge, Cambridge University Press, 1947), p. 413.

[31] I. Brownlie, 'Humanitarian Intervention', in J. N. Moore (ed.), *Law and Civil War in the Modern World* (Princeton, Princeton University Press, 1974), pp. 227–8.

[32] *1970 Declaration on Principles of International Law Concerning Friendly Relations and Co-operation Among States in Accordance with the Charter of the United Nations.* GA Res. 2625 (XXV).

[33] *Resolution on the Definition of Aggression 1974*, GA Res. 3314 (XXIX).

[34] *Legality of Use of Force*, C 99/15, http://www.icj-cij.org.

[35] *Nicaragua* case, pp. 99–100, para. 188.

[36] G. Arangio-Ruiz, 'The Normative Role of the General Assembly of the United Nations and the Declaration of Principles of Friendly Relations', 137 *RC* (1972 III), p. 418, at pp. 471–86; C. C. Joyner, 'UN General Assembly Resolutions and International Law: Rethinking the Contemporary Dynamics of Norm-Creation', 11 *Cal.*

Kelsen's distinction between 'ought' and 'is',[37] by saying that if contrary practice appeals to exceptions or justifications, 'the significance of that attitude is to confirm rather than to weaken the rule'.[38] This position reaffirms the underlying assumptions of the non-intervention rule which in a quasi-developed system such as international law tries to distance law from power by holding the *ex iniuria ius non oritur* principle.[39]

Having said that, the question whether we should acknowledge the ethical perspectives contained in the Charter or the moral content of sovereignty remains. The dilemma between a morally but not legally condonable action has been expressed by Judge Cassese in relation to Kosovo.[40] Also in relation to the genocide committed by the Khmer Rouge in Kampuchea Senator McGovern wondered 'if any thought is being given either by our Government or at the United Nations or anywhere in the international community of sending in a force to knock this Government out of power, just on humanitarian grounds'.[41] Hence, it is maintained that since the use of force for humanitarian purposes may not impair the constitutive elements of the state and may also affirm such United Nations' purposes as justice and human rights, it escapes the prohibition of Article 2(4).[42] It was submitted for instance in the *Legality of the Use of Force* that NATO's action in Kosovo 'is an armed humanitarian intervention, compatible with Article 2, paragraph 4, of the Charter, which covers only intervention against the territorial integrity or political independence of a state'.[43]

There is in this position a strong component of an ideal human society and human solidarity which scrutinises states' behaviour towards their citizens. Additionally, it alludes to the social contract theories according to which human rights violations forfeit the internal legitimacy of the state and invite foreign intervention. If human suffering is caused by persistent violations of

---

WILJ (1981), p. 445. In a previous judgment, the ICJ discarded a certain practice because it has been 'so much influenced by considerations of political expediency'. *Asylum Case, ICJ Rep.* (1950), p. 265, at p. 277.

[37] H. Kelsen, 'The Pure Theory of Law and Analytical Jurisprudence', 55 *Harvard L Rev* (1941), p. 44, at pp. 50–7.

[38] *Nicaragua* case, p. 98, para. 186.

[39] R. W. Tucker, 'The Principle of Effectiveness in International Law', in G. A. Lipsky (ed.), *Law and Politics in the World Community* (Berkeley and Los Angeles, University of California Press, 1953), p. 31.

[40] Cassese, 'Ex iniuria ius oritur', p. 25.

[41] *Indochina: Hearings Before the Subcomm. on East-Asian and Pacific Affairs of the Senate Comm. on Foreign Relations*, 95th Cong., 2nd Sess. (1978), p. 24.

[42] W. M. Reisman, 'Criteria for the Lawful Use of Force in International Law', 10 *Yale JIL* (1984–85), p. 279, at p. 281; A. A. D'Amato, *International Law: Process and Prospect* (New York, Transnational Pub., 1987), pp. 57–73; O. Schachter, *International Law in Theory and Practice* (Dordrecht/Boston/London, Martinus Nijhoff, 1991), p. 112; Tesón, *Humanitarian Intervention*, p. 150.

[43] CR 99/15. http://www.icj-cij.org.

human rights, the rule on non-intervention does not apply, either because meaningful sovereignty needs to be reinstated or because the state has fallen outside the purview of the non-intervention rule.

Human ideals become prevalent and appraisal of state activity is not value-neutral but one has to consider the conditions, intentions and objectives of the action.[44] For instance, the Legal Advisor to the US State Department justified the intervention in the Dominican Republic on a substantive vision of international law defined by him as 'practical idealism' and on a rejection of a 'reliance on absolutes for judging and evaluating the events of our time' because this is 'artificial'.[45]

According to this position, the outcome of any intervention is evaluated according to the doctrine of double effect or the utilitarian principle. Hence, the only harmful effects on state sovereignty are those that are intended to infringe it. Humanitarian intervention does not intend to infringe it. Even if there is intentional harming of sovereignty, if the humanitarian outcome materialises it does not matter how this outcome is achieved.[46] That is, the end result compensates for the inflicted injury.

The Indian Representative to the United Nations alluded to this when he urged the Security Council members to concede some 'realities' in relation to the situation in Bangladesh: 'Refugees were a reality. Genocide and oppression were a reality. The extinction of all civil rights was a reality'.[47] He also criticised the statist paradigm, when: 'In the face of a direct violation of the Universal Declaration of Human Rights and the provisions of Articles 55 and 56 of the Charter . . . the United Nations continued to be inhibited by considerations of domestic jurisdiction.'[48] The French intervention in Central Africa was 'pour répondre aux menaces sur la sécurité des populations, compte tenu des graves atteintes aux droits de l' homme'.[49] Similarly the operation in Rwanda was 'une opération où il peut être fait usage de la force, mais avec un objectif uniquement humanitaire'[50] and which has eventually fulifilled its objectives to save lives.[51]

---

[44] W. M. Reisman, 'Criteria for the Lawful Use of Force in International Law', 10 *Yale JIL* (1984–85), p. 279, at p. 281.

[45] L. Meeker, 'The Dominican Situation in the Perspective of International Law', 53 *Dep't State Bull.* (1965), pp. 60–5.

[46] J. Boyle, 'Towards Understanding the Principle of Double Effect', 90 *Ethics* (1980), p. 527; A. Donagan, *The Theory of Morality* (Chicago, University of Chicago Press, 1977), p. 163.

[47] 9 *United Nations Monthly Chronicle* (1972), p. 25.

[48] *Ibid.*, p. 29.

[49] *J.O.A.N.*, 4 October 1979, p. 7721.

[50] Press Conference of the French Foreign Minister (5 July 1994), *PEF*, July–August, p. 30.

[51] Interview by the French Foreign Minister, 14 September 1994, *PEF*, September–October, p. 91.

Idi Amin's overthrow has been hailed as 'a singular triumph for freedom, justice and human dignity'.[52] Professor Yusuk Lule, the new leader of Uganda, challenged the Organisation of African Unity (OAU) 'not to hide behind the formula of non-intervention when human rights are blatantly violated'.[53] Following the overthrow of Bokasssa, the Central African Ambassador to the United Nations expressed his disappointment because the United Nations and the OAU remained silent in the face of massive violations of human rights, 'in the name of the sacred principle of non-intervention',[54] and added: 'These institutions, whose basic principles depend on the protection of human rights and freedoms . . . will never be able to do anything useful until they stop being a syndicate of dictatorial oppressive governments.'[55]

A third line of reasoning tries to reconcile the opposite poles of permissive and proscriptive arguments. It employs certain substantive and procedural criteria which purport to provide a consistent normative framework which would enhance the ability of the international community to evaluate the humanitarian character of interventions.[56] These criteria refer to the 'quality and quantity' of human rights violations, the necessity and proportionality of the action, the exhaustion of other available remedies, the right authorisation and the disinterestedness of the intervenor, that is, the preponderant humanitarian motive. The criteria are presented as refinements of the just war theory[57] which had assisted in resolving the dilemma of Christian pacificism and violence and here assist in solving the dilemma between sovereignty and intervention. Aquinas has spelt out the just war criteria as proper authority, just cause and right intention.[58] Consequently, the just war theory and its

---

[52] 16 *Africa Research Bull. – Political, Social and Cultural Series* (1979), p. 5223.

[53] *Keesing's* (1979), pp. 29840–1.

[54] '[France] estime, en conséquence, que tout intervention officielle de sa part auprès de ce Gouvernement au sujet de tels événements ne pourrait que constituer une immixtion dans le domaine de sa politique intérieure.' Response of the Foreign Affairs Minister, no. 12545, *JO.AN*, 15 March 1979. In the French National Assembly, the Foreign Minister responding to the accusations by François Mitterrand of neo-colonialism said: 'Intervenons-nous en Centrafrique? Alors nous sommes les gendarmes de cette Afrique, les néocolonisistes . . . Nous abstenons-nous d'intervenir? Alors nous soutenons des régimes tyranniques, nous laissons bafouer les droits de l'homme . . .'. *JO.AN*, 6 October 1979, p. 7885.

[55] 4 UN GAOR, UN Doc. A/34/PV 32 (1979), p. 32.

[56] R. B. Lillich, 'Forcible Self – Help to Protect Human Rights', 53 *Iowa Law Review* (1967), p. 325, pp. 347–51; J.-P. L. Fonteyne, 'The Customary International Law Doctrine of Humanitarian Intervention: Its Current Validity under the UN Charter', 4 *Cal. WILJ* (1974), p. 203, at pp. 258–68; R. B. Lillich, 'Humanitarian Intervention Through the United Nations: Towards the Development of Criteria', *ZaöRV* (1993), p. 557.

[57] A. J. Coates, *The Ethics of War* (Manchester, Manchester University Press, 1997).

[58] Thomas Aquinas, *Summa Theologia* (London, Blackfriars, 1964), II – I, 12, 1; Augustine, *The City of God,* trans. M. Dods (New York, Random House, 1950),

contemporary criteria belong to the natural law tradition particularly by embracing goals such as humanitarian ones and their emphasis on the intentions of the agent contrary to the utilitarian or realist consequentialism. These standards have often been recounted by political decision-makers and although they reveal a hybrid proceduralism, they are still beset with difficulties. There is, thus, no agreement on which human rights violations would trigger intervention and what would be its extent although it is admitted that humanitarian intervention is condoned against such genocidal regimes as those in Uganda[59], Kampuchea[60] or Bangladesh[61] even if the incursion may have substantial effects on the authority structures of the state.[62]

The intention criterion is also crucial but is impossible to quantify. For instance, the Indian delegate to the UN Security Council said in relation to the Bangladesh operation that 'we . . . have in this particular occasion nothing but the purest of motives and the purest of intentions: to rescue the people of East Bengal from what they are suffering'.[63] On the other hand, the role of humanitarian motives in Vietnam's intervention[64] in Kampuchea casts some doubt as to its sincerity. It appears that intention is measured *ex post facto*, relapsing into sheer consequentialism.

The intention, disinterestedness and right authority criteria intermingle in betraying a preference for collective action under the authorisation of the UN. For instance, the French operation in Rwanda had 'un objectif

---

pp. 86, 683; National Conference of Catholic Bishops, *The Challenge of Peace: God's Promise and Our Response* (Washington, D.C., US Catholic Conference, 1983).

[59] *Uganda: The Human Rights Situation: Hearings Before the Subc/tee on Foreign Economic Policy of the Senate C/tee on Foreign Relations*, 95th Cong., 2nd Sess. 11 (1978). *Amnesty International, Annual Report* (1980), p. 38.

[60] M. J. Bazyler, 'Re-examining the Doctrine of Humanitarian Intervention in Light of the Atrocities in Kampuchea and Ethiopia', 23 *Stanford Journal of International Law* (1987), p. 547. The issue of humanitarian intervention was raised by Senator McGovern who wondered 'if any thought is being given either by our Government or at the United Nations or anywhere in the international community of sending in a force to knock this Government out of power, just on humanitarian grounds'. *Indochina: Hearings Before the Subcomm. on East-Asian and Pacific Affairs of the Senate Comm. on Foreign Relations*, 95th Cong., 2nd Sess. (1978), p. 24.

[61] *The Events in East Pakistan, 1971, A Legal Study by the Secretariat of the International Commission of Jurists* (Geneva, 1972). T. M. Franck, N. S. Rodley, 'After Bangladesh: The Law of Humanitarian Intervention by Military Force', 67 *AJIL* (1973), p. 275.

[62] N. D. White, 'Humanitarian Intervention', 1 *International Law and Armed Conflict Commentary* (1994), p. 13, at p. 21.

[63] 26 UN SCOR, 1606th mtg, UN Doc. S/PV. 1606 (1971), p. 18.

[64] According to the Lawyer's Committee for Human Rights: 'The primary purpose of the [Vietnamese] invasion has been to bring about the replacement of Pol Pot's regime, which had been unremittingly violent in its hostility towards the Socialist Republic of Vietnam (SRV) since 1977, by one that could be relied upon to be friendly to it.' *Kampuchea: After the Worst* (1985), p. 17.

uniquement humanitaire' and it was undertaken by 'un mandat du Conseil de Sécurité des Nations Unies' because it was felt that 'une action de ce type, qui répond à un devoir humanitaire, devrait être, malgré l'urgence, autorisée par la communauté internationale'.[65] 'Opération Turquoise' was condoned by the Security Council in Resolution 929.[66] The disinterestedness of the intervenor is not, however, unblemished. Military intervention by France was on the agenda before Resolution 929 was adopted.[67] Moreover, the execution of the operation was national[68] and this has been recognised by the UN Secretary-General.[69]

The Kosovo operation reveals the weaknesses of such criteria to bridle intervention legally. Repression, human right violations and the humanitarian crisis were serious although they may not have constituted acts of genocide. However, we can only pontificate on whether the mass exodus of refugees was the result of NATO's action or whether NATO just reversed the execution of a premeditated policy. Moreover, the Security Council did not explicitly authorise the action.[70] Concerning intention, humanitarian ones were invoked together with the strategic interest in regional stability.[71] Finally, the issue of proportionality and necessity is interconnected with the intention criterion. If humanitarian interests intermingle with other interests such as regional security or NATO's identity, the action tries to addresses them simultaneously and may go beyond the humanitarian purview.[72]

In order to recapitulate, the above argumentation contains a medley of natural and positive law premises mirrored in the antagonism between

---

[65] *JO.AN.*, 23 June 1994, p. 3339. Also Communiqué conjoint du palais de l'Elysée et de l'hôtel Matignon, 18 June 1994, *PEF*, May–June, 1994, p. 296.

[66] SC Res. 929, UN SCOR, 3393rd mtg, UN Doc. S/RES/929 (1994). China, Brazil, New Zealand, Pakistan and Nigeria abstained.

[67] 'La France serait prête à monter ... une intervention sur le terrain visant à protéger les groupes menacés d'extermination.' Point de presse précité du M.A.E. le 15 juin 1994, *PEF*, p. 271; Interview du M.A.E. le 27 juin 1994, *PEF*, May–June, p. 342: 'j'ai proposé au Premier ministre, de prendre une initiative et d'intervenir'. *AFDI* (1994), p. 1030.

[68] J.-D. Mouton, 'La crise Rwandaise de 1994 et les Nations Unies', *AFDI* (1994), p. 214, at p. 222: 'Car il est claire que l'opération turquoise a été nationale de bout en bout et que de ce point de vue, le contrôle onusien a été réduit au strict minimum.'

[69] 'Dès l'instant qu'ils utilisent des forces qui ne sont pas des forces onusiennes à proprement parler, je suis partisan de sous-traiter à des États membres les opérations de maintien de la paix impliquant l'emploi de la force.' *Le Monde*, 26 July 1994; 'Croniques des faits internationaux', 98 *RGDIP* (1994), p. 991, at p. 992.

[70] SC Res. 1199, UN SCOR, UN Doc. S/RES/1199 (1998); SC Res. 1203, UN SCOR, UN Doc. S/RES/1203 (1998).

[71] See Statement on Kosovo by Prime Minister Tony Blair: 'We do so primarily to avert what would otherwise be a humanitarian disaster in Kosovo. ... Strategic interests for the whole of Europe are at stake. ... To walk away now would not merely destroy NATO's credibility ...'. *Hansard*, 23 March 1999, columns 161–3.

[72] See submissions by Professor Brownlie in the case concerning *Legality of Use of Force*, CR 99/14.

sovereignty, order, justice, non-intervention and human rights. The argument which relies on Article 2(4) invokes the consensual aspect of positive international law and the role of sovereignty whereas that which relies on notions of justice and human rights invokes extra-consensual, naturalistic, aspects.[73] The demarcation is not clear because the rhetoric can switch freely between the two poles, substituting or recombining them. As was said, the vast literature on the subject 'has wrestled with the difficulty of reconciling a state's supposedly absolute sovereignty with even more fundamental rights which may be held to justify intervention on behalf of oppressed nationals of another state'.[74]

This framework of antithesis and synthesis is accommodated by interlacing the human rights dimension in the polymorphous concept of peace.[75] Following the humanitarian catastrophe in Liberia, the Liberian Representative to the Security Council pleaded to 'review and perhaps reinterpret the Charter, particularly its provisions which calls for non-interference in the internal affairs of Member States' and said in connection with the Charter that its 'strict application . . . has hampered the effectiveness of the Council and its principal objective of maintaining international peace and security. As a result, millions of innocent men, women and children have continued to be victimised by conflicts throughout the world and this world body, which has the moral obligation and authority, has been prevented from averting these human tragedies.'[76] The new approach to peace and security includes then 'non-military sources of instability in the economic, social, humanitarian and ecological fields'.[77] Thus, although peace and order for years monopolised the political and legal reasoning, humanitarian concerns emerged as complementary indices when evaluating a situation as 'a threat to or breach of peace'.[78] This

[73] D. Kennedy, *International Legal Structures* (Baden-Baden, Nomos Verlagsgesellschaft, 1987), ch. 1, pp. 11–108.
[74] *United Kingdom Materials on International Law*, ed. G. Marston, 57 *BYBIL* (1986), p. 487, at p. 618.
[75] P.-M. Dupuy, 'Sécurité collective et organisation de la paix', 97 *RGDIP* (1993), p. 617, at pp. 622–7.
[76] Statement of Mr. Bull, UN SCOR, 2974th mtg, UN Doc. S/PV 2974 (1991).
[77] UN SCOR, 47th Sess., 3046 mtg, UN Doc. S/PV.3046 (1992); *An Agenda For Peace: Preventive Diplomacy, Peacemaking and Peace-Keeping*, UN SCOR, 47th Sess., Agenda Item 10, para. 13, UN Doc. A/47/277, S/24111(1992).
[78] 'The primary place ascribed to international peace and security is natural, since the fulfillment of the other purposes will be dependent upon the attainment of that basic condition.' *Certain Expenses of the United Nations (Advisory Opinion of 20 July 1962), ICJ Rep.* (1962), p. 150, at p. 168; L. Henkin, 'Use of Force: Law and US Policy', in L. Henkin (ed.), *Right v. Might: International Law and the Use of Force* (New York, Council on Foreign Relations Press, 1991), p. 37, at pp. 38–9: 'Peace was more important than progress and more important than justice. War was inherently unjust.' O. Schachter, 'In Defence of International Rules on the Use of Force', 53 *University of Chicago Law Review* (1986), p. 113, at pp. 126–8; W. V. O'Brien,

approach recognises their instrumental relation[79] but also reveals the compromise contained in the UN Charter which recognises sovereignty to such an extent that it does not threaten the order it implies.

According to Resolution 688 the repression of Kurds by Iraq 'led to a massive flow of refugees towards and across international frontiers and to cross-border incursions, which threaten international peace and security.'[80] These are the two elements which sketch the limits of sovereignty and non-intervention under Chapter VII of the UN Charter. It is debatable whether the statist concept of international order would not have prevailed had there been no repercussions to neighbouring countries. Actually, Turkey and Iran, the neighbouring countries more affected by the flow of refugees, had invoked before the Security Council the dangers to regional peace and security.[81] Those who opposed the Resolution challenged the view that humanitarian issues can justify interference or constitute threat to the peace.[82] However, there were also those who acknowledged that when human right violations 'assume the dimension of a crime against humanity', they become an issue of international concern.[83] Resolution 794[84] which authorised Operation 'Restore Hope' in Somalia, is also indicative. Whereas the effects of the humanitarian disaster were felt in the region[85] the resolution characterises internal issues such as the magnitude of the human tragedy and the obstacles in the distribution of humanitarian assistance as a threat to peace, vowing also 'respect for the territorial integrity, the political independence and the principle of non-intervention'.[86] Resolution 929 considers that 'the magnitude

---

The Conduct of Just and Limited War (New York, Praeger Publ., 1981), p. 23: 'Modern international law has sacrificed justice in its attempt virtually to eliminate the competence of the state to engage in war unilaterally'. H. McCoubrey, N. D. White, *International Law and Armed Conflict* (Aldershot, Dartmouth, 1992), p. 129.

[79] M. Koskenniemi, 'The Police in the Temple, Order, Justice and the UN: A Dialectical View', 6 *EJIL* (1995), p. 325. Société Française pour le Droit International, *Le Chapitre VII de la Charte des Nations Unies*, Colloque de Rennes (Paris, Pedone, 1995).

[80] SC Res. 688, UN SCOR, 46th Sess., 2982d mtg, UN Doc. S/RES/688 (1991), p. 2.

[81] *Letter Dated 2 April 1991 from Turkey to the President of the Security Council*, UN Doc. S/22435 (1991); *Letter Dated 4 April 1991 from Iran to the Secretary-General*, UN Doc. S/22447 (1991).

[82] See Statements by Yemen, Cuba, Zimbabwe or Iraq in UN Doc. S/PV.2982 (1991), pp. 17, 27, 31, 46.

[83] See Statement by France, UN Doc. S/PV.2982 (1991), pp. 53–5.

[84] SC Res. 794, UN SCOR, 47th Sess., 3145th mtg, UN Doc. S/RES/794 (1992), p. 7.

[85] The Secretary-General Boutros Boutros-Ghali urged the Security Council 'to make a determination under Article 39 of the Charter that a threat to the peace exists, as a result of the repercussions of the Somali conflict on the entire region' because: 'At present no government exists in Somalia.' *Letter Dated 29 November 1992 from the Secretary-General to the President of the Security Council*, UN SCOR, 47th Sess., UN Doc. S/24868 (1992).

[86] *Memorandum of Understanding signed on 18 April 1991*, 30 *ILM* (1991), p. 860.

of the humanitarian crisis in Rwanda constitutes a threat to peace and security in the region'.[87] Resolution 940 which authorised the intervention in Haiti had expressed its concern for the 'further deterioration of the humanitarian situation in Haiti, in particular the continuing escalation . . . of systematic violations of civil liberties' which was characterised as a threat to peace and security.[88]

In Kosovo, Resolution 1203 refers to the internal humanitarian situation as a threat to peace and security[89] and in Resolution 1264 for East Timor it is again the internal systematic and flagrant violations of human rights and humanitarian law which constitutes a threat to peace and security.[90]

The scheme described above betrays the internal relation of order and justice as ideological premises in the United Nations. Its intriguing aspect is the conceptual amalgamation of justice within the comprehensive norm of order. Order is not legitimised autonomously but only by containing an element of justice. However, its pre-eminence may singularise our perception and evaluation of events. Additionally, in the instrumental relation between justice and order, the former may be reinterpreted wantonly so as to satisfy the latter. For instance, although the Pol Pot regime was notorious, the Vietnamese action was condemned as an affront to sovereignty and the General Assembly asserted that non-intervention would facilitate 'just and lasting resolution of the Kampuchean problem'.[91] This argument is rather unconvincing and becomes even more so when the notorious Pol Pot regime was considered to be the legitimate representative for United Nations purposes.[92] Concerning the question of representation, General Assembly Resolution 396 provides that 'the question should be considered in the light of the Purposes and Principles of the Charter and the circumstances of each case'.[93] It could be maintained that the introduction of a value element in determining representation alludes to legitimisation standards and, in particular, the human rights considerations contained in the Charter. However, the end result conformed to the statist international mode of peace and order. It is best captured by France's statement before the Security Council: 'The notion that because a regime is detestable, foreign intervention is justified and forcible overthrow is legitimate is extremely dangerous. That could ultimately jeopardise the very maintenance of international law and order

[87] SC Res. 929, UN SCOR, 3393rd mtg, UN Doc. S/RES/929 (1994).

[88] SC Res. 940, UN SCOR, 3134th mtg, UN Doc. S/RES/940 (1994).

[89] SC Res. 1203, UN SCOR, 53rd Sess., 3937th mtg, UN Doc. S/RES/1203.

[90] SC Res. 1264, UN SCOR, 54th Sess., 4045th mtg, UN Doc. S/RES/1264.

[91] GA Res. 41/6 (21 October 1986); GA Res. 34/22 (14 November 1979), para. 9.

[92] GA Res. 34/2 (22 September 1979); GA Res. 35/3 (13 October 1980); 25 *AFDI* (1979), p. 461; 26 *AFDI* (1980), p. 408; 27 *AFDI* (1981), pp. 400–1.

[93] GA Res. 396(V), UN GAOR (1950), p. 675. For a contrary view dismissing extraneous considerations see *Conditions of Admission of a State to Membership in the United Nations*, *ICJ Rep.* (1947–48), p. 57, at p. 62.

and make the continued existence of various regimes dependent on the judgement of their neighbours.'[94]

In conclusion, humanitarian intervention is performed by invoking arguments concerning the morality of the internal order and principles of solidarity or institutionally by extenuating the circumstances which amount to a threat to peace or security. The modification relates to the changing jurisdiction of the Security Council which acknowledges the incorporation of evaluative truisms but does not emancipate justice from the constraints of order.[95] The interpretative articulations of Article 2(4) affirm the intermingling of theoretical and legal positions and by presenting the background deliberations, the uneasy truce between these arguments has been revealed.

[94] 34 UN SCOR, 2109th mtg (12 January 1979), para. 36. See the official position of France, 26 *AFDI* (1980), pp. 888–9. The position of New Zealand was: 'the misdeeds of one State do not . . . justify the invasion of its territory by another'. UN Doc. S/PV. 2110 (13 January 1979), pp. 23–5.

[95] Concerning the changing attitudes regarding the relationship between sovereignty and human rights, *see Document of the Copenhagen Meeting of the Conference on the Human Dimension of the CSCE*, 29 *ILM* (1990), p. 1312. *Charter of Paris for a New Europe*, 30 *ILM* (1991), p. 190: 'Human rights and fundamental freedoms are the birthright of all human beings, are inalienable and are guaranteed by law. . . . Their observance and full exercise are the foundation of freedom, justice and peace.'

6

The protection of nationals as humanitarian action

The protection of nationals as self-defence

In international practice there exists another instance of forcible action which raises the same issues as humanitarian intervention. It is the protection of nationals abroad which traditionally has been treated as a self-defence measure under the formula that an attack on a national is an attack on the state.[1] Our aim here is to address the legal, philosophical and empirical enquiries which the protection of nationals entails and which would justify its assimilation into a concept of humanitarian intervention *lato sensu*. Prior to this, it is necessary to explore the legal and theoretical structure of the self-defence argument.

The origins of self-defence are traced back in the world of nature where self-defence is recognised as inherent to human beings as their instantaneous reaction to injury. For Gentili, 'even the brutes are given the right of defence by nature, and we are persuaded and convinced of this right not by argument but by some innate power.'[2] Likewise for Grotius, 'self-defence . . . has its

[1] C. H. M. Waldock, 'The Regulation of the Use of Force by Individual States in International Law', 81 *RC* (1952 II), p. 455, at pp. 495–505; J. Stone, *Aggression and World Order: A Critique of the United Nations Theories of Aggression* (London, Stevens & Sons, 1958), pp. 43–4; D. W. Bowett, *Self-defence in International Law* (Manchester, Manchester University Press, 1958), ch. IX, p. 182; M. S. McDougal, F. P. Feliciano, *Law and Minimum World Public Order: The Legal Regulation of International Coercion* (New Haven, Yale University Press, 1961), p. 232; S. M. Schwebel, 'Aggression, Intervention and Self-defence', 136 *RC* (1972 II), p. 411, at pp. 479–83.

[2] A. Gentili, *De Jure Belli Libri Tres* (1588–89), J. B. Scott (ed.), *The Classics of International Law*, vol. II (Oxford, Clarendon Press, 1933), Bk. 1, ch. XIII, p. 59: 'This has been taught to philosophers by reason, to barbarians by necessity, to the nations by custom, to wild animals by Nature itself. This law is not written but inborn.' F. Suarez, *De Triplici Virtute Theologica, Fide, Spe, et Charitate (1621)*, in J. B. Scott (ed.), *The Classics of International Law* (Oxford, Clarendon Press, 1933), 'Disputation XIII: On Charity', sec. 1, pp. 802–3, para. 4: 'Defensive war not only it is permitted but sometimes even commended. . . . The reason supporting it is that the right of self-defence is natural and necessary.'

origin directly and chiefly, in the fact that nature commits to each his own protection'.[3]

Self-defence then evolved from natural law to become a component of the just war theory which since its Aristotelian origins had admitted redress in the form of avenging a wrong.[4] According to Aquinas 'just as rulers rightly use the sword in awful defence against those who disturb the peace within the realm, when they punish criminals . . . so too they rightly use the sword of war to protect their polity from external enemies'.[5] It is important to note that self-defence in the medieval Christian tradition is also perceived as a form of punishment which restores the justice of the universal community.[6] Defence and punishment amalgamate in Vitoria for whom 'the defense of our neighbours is the rightful concern of each of us . . . even if it involves shedding blood'.[7] It thus corresponds conceptually with humanitarian intervention which takes place from a sense of universal solidarity against the malfeasants of the international society's morality.

The protection of nationals as self-defence implies an identification of interests between nationals and states which triggers the state's defensive action and coincides with the emergence of modern states.[8] It has its origins in the *lettres de marche* or *lettres de représailles* whereby individuals avenge and rectify any delict incurred with the acquiescence of the local ruler.[9]

---

[3] H. Grotius, *De Jure Belli ac Pacis Libri Tres*, in *The Classics of International Law*, J. B. Scott (ed.), vol. II (Buffalo, N.Y., W. S. Hein & Co. Inc., 1995), Bk. II, ch. I, s. iii, p. 172.

[4] J. von Elbe, 'The Evolution of the Concept of the Just War in International Law', 33 *AJIL* (1939), p. 665, at pp. 667–9.

[5] T. Aquinas, *Summa Theologia* (London, Blackfriars, 1964), II – II, q. 40a, 1c.

[6] A. J. Coates, *The Ethics of War* (Manchester, Manchester University Press, 1997), p. 157: 'Self-defence was justified not so much on its own grounds but as a vindication of the legal and moral community to which particular states or polities were thought to belong.' J. Finnis, 'The Ethics of War and Peace in the Catholic Natural Law Tradition', in T. Nardin (ed.), *The Ethics of War and Peace: Religious and Secular Perspectives* (Princeton, Princeton University Press, 1996), p. 15, at pp. 20–4.

[7] F. Vitoria, 'Lecture on the Evangelization of Unbelievers' in *Francisci de Vitoria: Political Writings*, A. Pagden, J. Lawrance (eds) (Cambridge, Cambridge University Press, 1991), p. 347, para. 3.

[8] *Deutsche Continental Gas-Gesellschaft*, *RTAM*, vol. IX, p. 336: 'Un Etat n'existe qu' à condition de posséder un territoire, une population habitant ce territoire et une puissance publique qui s'exerce sur la population et sur le territoire.' *Montevideo Convention on the Rights and Duties of States* (1933), Article 1, in 28 *AJIL* (1934 Suppl.), p. 75: 'A State as a person of international law should possess the following qualifications; (a) permanent population; (b) defined territory; (c) government and (d) capacity to enter into relations with other states.' J. Crawford, *The Creation of States in International Law* (Oxford, Clarendon Press, 1979), pp. 31–76.

[9] C. H. M. Waldock, 'The Regulation of the Use of Force by Individual States in International Law', 81 *RC* (1952 II), p. 455, at p. 459: 'in the absence of other means of redressing injuries to foreigners, it served a purpose and played an important part in the development of the modern right possessed by States of protecting their

Authorisation by the right authority belongs to the just war theory whose concept of self-defence, we should recall, also contained the notion of punishment. But this was not permitted to be meted by private individuals, hence the need for authorisation by the local ruler.[10] Later, the consolidation of state power, its political, military and economic predominance, caused the 'nationalisation de l'ancien système des représailles privées'.[11]

Hence, the bearer of an attack coalesces conceptually from the national to her or his state which consequently resorts to self-defence.[12] This reasoning can be explained by the social contract theory[13] according to which individuals relinquish certain rights such as the right to life and liberty which are now undertaken by the state which pursues their redemption.[14] As it was said in one case, 'in taking up the care of its nationals . . . a state is in reality asserting its own right'.[15] Social contract theories explain the relation between the people and their state but different views of such a link support either the defensive or the humanitarian character in these operations.

The self-defence character of the protective actions is supported by considering sovereignty as an inclusive notion. The state is viewed as an autonomous, closed entity enjoying a moral absolute. Accordingly, the state and its morality is not derivative because the people represented have achieved their highest

---

nationals abroad'. A. V. Freeman, *The International Responsibility of States for Denial of Justice* (London, Longmans, 1970), p. 54: 'an individual who was wronged in a strange land and who had there been unable to obtain reparation for his injury from the local sovereign, might with the permission of his own prince, initiate forceful measures to obtain that justice which had been refused to him'.

[10] Finnis, in Nardin, *The Ethics of War and Peace*, p. 21.

[11] P. de Visscher, 'Cours général de droit international public', 136 *RC* (1972 II), p. 1, at p. 155; G. Clark, 'English Practice with Regard to Reprisals by Private Persons', 27 *AJIL* (1927), p. 694, at pp. 704–5: 'As the English State through the 14th, 15th, and 17th centuries gradually became better organised and developed more effective authority within its own territory, it progressively encroached on the freedom of individual Englishmen to deal with outsiders as they chose. . . . Thus it would appear that as the English state approached a condition of governmental organisation comparable in inclusiveness to that of the English towns in the 13th century, it took away from private persons, as the towns have done more than five centuries earlier, the right to use force on their own account.'

[12] P. B. Porter, 'L'intervention en droit international modern', 32 *RC* (1930 II), p. 607, at pp. 647–50; R. Redslob, *Traité de Droit des Gens* (Paris, Recueil Sirey, 1950), p. 256; C. H. M. Waldock, 'The Regulation of the Use of Force by Individual States in International Law', 81 *RC* (1952 II), p. 455, at p. 459; Bowett, *Self-defence*, pp. 94–105; D. P. O'Connell, *International Law*, 2nd edn (London, Stevens & Sons, 1970), vol. I, pp. 303–4.

[13] Bowett, *Self-defence*, ch. V, p. 91.

[14] E. de Vattel, *Le Droit Des Gens ou Principes de la Loi Naturelle, appliqués à la Conduite et aux Affaires des Nations et des Souverains*, trans. C. G. Fenwick (Washington, D. C., Carnegie Institution of Washington, 1916), in *Classics of International Law*, Bk. II, ch. VI, sec. 71.

[15] *Panevezys – Saldutiskis Railway Case, PCIJ* (1939), Series A/B, No. 76, p. 16.

purpose by forming the state and have dissipated their individualities.[16] Thus, the state which resorts to self-defence measures to avenge an injury to its nationals in essence vindicates its sovereignty. Looked at from another angle, this approach also includes the outsiders' view on the relation between people and their states. If individuals are identified by outsiders with their state, the theory of state imputation is not otiose. For example, in Entebbe, the selective targeting of Israeli nationals was due to political animosity towards the state of Israel. Also in Iran, the occupation of the American Embassy which prompted the US abortive action was politically motivated. In both cases, the individual nationals were treated by their attackers as a compendium of their states and as a medium in achieving political objectives. They were caught in the middle, mute observers of actions which related to them but over which they have no control.

There is also a utilitarian perception of the individual's function in society which supports the self-defence position. If general happiness is the goal to be promoted and the primary duty of the government is the welfare of its citizens,[17] there is a reciprocal relation between the individual and her or his state which accentuates the protective function of the state. People are viewed as locomotives in the development of states. Their economic, cultural and political engagement contributes to the particularities a state acquires. The loss of a national is viewed as a material loss of the state because it diminishes the collective capability for progress. Consequently, the state in order to guarantee the welfare of its citizens can resort to protective actions, defending thus the essence of its sovereignty.[18] Again in Entebbe, it was also the interest in the general welfare of its nationals that urged Israel to resort to self-defence action.

The development of self-defence into an international legal proposition coincides with the emergence of the community of states and the organisation of its enforcement and sanctioning mechanisms. Article 51 of the UN Charter alludes to the origin of the right as a naturalist prescription but also contains a positivist description. Self-defence maintains its function as a natural law method of redress since even in elaborate and effective legal systems the centralised mechanisms for enforcement may fail or be delayed. The word 'inherent' in Article 51 gives substance to this claim. The underlying theme during the drafting of this Article is that the right to self-defence is self-evident, betraying its natural law origin.[19] As Gentili wrote, 'the right

---

[16] T. Hobbes, *Leviathan* (London, Dent, 1914); D. R. Mapel, 'Realism and the Ethics of War and Peace', in Nardin, *The Ethics of War and Peace* p. 54, at pp. 68–70.

[17] J. Bentham, *Introduction to the Principles of Morals and Legislation*, J. H. Burns, H. L. A. Hart (eds) (London, Methuen, [1789] 1970), Ch. I, para. V.

[18] F. S. Dunn, *The Protection of Nationals. A Study in the Application of International Law* (Baltimore, J. Hopkins Press, 1932), p. 38.

[19] 'The use of arms in legitimate self-defence remains admitted and unimpaired'. Report of the Rapporteur of Committee 1 to Commission I as adopted by Committee 1/I, 6 UNCIOD, p. 459.

of defence . . . is the most generally accepted of all rights. All laws and all codes allow the repelling of force by force.'[20] Likewise, Foreign Secretary Kellogg in his declaration concerning the Pact of Paris (1928)[21] said that the right of self-defence is 'inherent in every sovereign state and is implicit in every treaty'.[22]

On the other hand, Article 51 also contains the requirement of an armed attack for there to be a right to self-defence, thus betraying its positivist aspects. An inherent right broadens the opportunities for action beyond repelling an attack or protecting nationals abroad.[23] It thus frustrates the constituent elements of the international organisation characterised by the limitation of individual use of force and the co-ordination of collective use of force. It particularly alludes to a right of self-preservation which 'includes the protection of the State, its honour, and its possessions, and the lives and property of its citizens'.[24] Only Vattel has recognised such a wide right to use force 'for the defence and preservation of [men's] rights'.[25] Grotius on

[20] Gentili, *De Jure Belli Libri Tres*, Bk. 1, ch. XIII, p. 59.
[21] *Treaty Providing for the Renunciation of War as an Instrument of National Policy*, 94 *LNTS* 57.
[22] Note of 23 June 1928, in 22 *AJIL* (1928, Suppl.), p. 109. For South Africa it 'is not intended to deprive any party . . . of any of its natural right of legitimate self-defence'. Note of South Africa, 15 June 1928, in *Foreign Relations of the United States 1928-I*, note III.10, at pp. 89–90. For the British it was 'inalienable', *ibid.*, p. 67 and for Poland 'the pact does not affect in any way the right of legitimate defense inherent in each state', *ibid.*, p. 119.
[23] J. L. Kunz, 'Individual and Collective Self-defence in Article 51 of the Charter of the United Nations', 41 *AJIL* (1947), p. 877; N. Q. Dinh, 'La légitime défense d'après la Charte des Nations Unies', XIX *RGDIP* (1948), p. 223, at p. 240; H. Kelsen, *The Law of the United Nations* (London, Stevens & Sons, 1950), pp. 269, 797–8; I. Brownlie, *International Law and the Use of Force by States* (Oxford, Clarendon Press, 1963), pp. 271–5; J. Delivanis, *La légitime défense en droit international public moderne* (Paris, Librairie de Droit et de Jurisprudence, 1971), p. 49; J. Zourek, *L'interdiction de l émploi de la force en droit international* (Leiden, A.W. Sijhoff, 1974), p. 96; L. Henkin, *How Nations Behave. Law and Foreign Policy*, 2nd edn (New York, Columbia University Press, 1979), pp. 140–3.
[24] *Regulations for the Government of the Navy of the United States* (Washington, 1913), paras 1646–8 cited in M. Offutt, *The Protection of Citizens Abroad* (Baltimore, J. Hopkins Press, 1928), p. 6. W. F. Hall, *A Treatise on International Law*, P. Higgins (ed.), 8th edn (Oxford, Clarendon Press, 1924), pp. 331–2; H. Wheaton, *Elements of International Law*, in G. C. Wilson (ed.), *Classics of International Law* (Oxford, Clarendon Press, 1936), p. 106, para. 76.
[25] E. de Vattel, *Le Droit Des Gens ou Principes de la Loi Naturelle, appliqués à la Conduite et aux Affaires des Nations et des Souverains*, trans. C. G. Fenwick (Washington, Carnegie Institution of Washington, 1916), in *Classics of International Law*, Bk. III, Ch. I, para. 3, p. 233 and Bk. II, Ch. IV, para. 49, p. 130. See Judge Huber in the Spanish Moroccan Arbitration: 'However, it cannot be denied that at a certain point the interest of a state in exercising protection over its nationals and their property can take precedence over territorial sovereignty, despite the absence of any conventional provisions. This right of intervention has been claimed by all states:

the other hand admitted limitations on the right of self-defence which required an actual attack.[26]

Moreover, confining self-defence to a prior armed attack provides for international stability and security. As with Article 2(4), the underpinning assumption is peace which allows sovereignty to be reinstated only when there has been injury as the result of armed attack. Otherwise, if any instance deemed as threatening gave rise to self-defence, international order and stability would be jeopardised. The decision by the ICJ in the *Nicaragua* case illustrates the preferred values.[27] The Court there, pronouncing on the subject of self-defence, individual or collective, said that it should be preceded by an armed attack and that armed attack is a *sine qua non* condition of self-defence.[28] Hence, a narrow definition of self-defence limited to an armed attack coincides with a restrictive view of Article 2(4) because, according to the Court's President, the Court 'has to promote peace and cannot refrain from moving in that direction'.[29]

Having said that, state practice has firmly established the self-defence character of operations to protect nationals when their safety is jeopardised by the 'impotence or indisposition of the territorial sovereign'.[30] The USA in the pre-Charter period frequently afforded protection to their nationals when

---

only its limits are disputed.' *Claims of British Subjects and British Protected Persons against the Authorities of the Spanish Protectorate in Morocco*, Award of 1925, *RIAA* II, p. 616, at p. 641.

[26] Grotius, *De Jure Belli*, Bk. II, ch. I, sec. IV and V, pp. 173–5; F. de Victoria, *De Indis et de Jure Belli Relectiones*, in *The Classics of International Law*, ed. J. B. Scott (Buffalo, N.Y., W. S. Hein & Co., 1995), 'De Indis Relectio Posterior Sive De Jure Belli Hispanorum in Babados', p. 168, para. 424.5: 'But defence can be resorted to at the very moment of the danger . . . and so when the necessity of defence has passed there is an end to the lawfulness of war.'

[27] N. Tsagourias, 'The Nicaragua Case and the Use of Force: The Theoretical Construction of the Decision and Its Deconstruction', 1 *Journal of Armed Conflict Law* (1996), p. 81; H. W. Briggs, 'The International Court of Justice Lives Up to its Name', 81 *AJIL* (1987), p. 78; J. Verhoven, 'Le droit, le Juge et la violence. Les arrêts Nicaragua c. Etats-Unis', 91 *RGDIP* (1987), p. 1159. J. B. White, 'Law as Rhetoric, Rhetoric as Law: The Arts of Cultural and Communal Life', 52 *University of Chicago Law Review* (1985), p. 684, at p. 697: 'Similarly, the judicial opinion, often thought to be the paradigmatic form of legal expression might be far more accurately and richly understood if it were seen . . . as a statement by an individual mind or a group of individual minds exercising their responsibility to decide a case as well as they can and to determine what it shall mean in the language of the culture.'

[28] *Case Concerning Military and Paramilitary Activities in and against Nicaragua, ICJ Rep.* (1986), p. 14, at pp. 103, 122, paras 195, 237.

[29] Separate Opinion of the President of the Court Nagendra Singh, *Nicaragua* case, p. 153.

[30] C. Hyde, *International Law*, 2nd rev. edn, vol. I (Boston, Little, Brown, 1951), p. 647, para. 202; J. Westlake, *International Law*, 2nd edn, part I (Cambridge, Cambridge University Press, 1913), p. 299.

the local authorities were unable to do so.[31] During the deliberations in the American Senate of the Kellogg-Briand Pact, it was affirmed that any military or naval action purporting to protect nationals is in self-defence.[32] A decision of the French Cour de Cassation states similarly that 'pour la protection de ses nationaux, la France conserve toujours les droits qu'elle tient de la légitime défense'.[33] From the more recent practice, when Israeli commandos raided Entebbe airport in 1976 to release Israeli hostages, it was justified as an instance of self-defence.[34] The USA equivocally supported a well-established right, 'flowing from the right of self-defence, limited to such use of force as is necessary and appropriate to protect threatened nationals from injury'.[35] The legal justification for the Iranian action[36] as pronounced by President Carter in his message to the Congress[37] and in a letter to the Security Council was the 'inherent right to self-defence'.[38] The Grenada operation was also undertaken 'in accordance with well-established principles of international law regarding the protection of one's nationals'[39] which was supported by the British Foreign Secretary Sir Geoffrey Howe in the House of Commons.[40]

---

[31] 'No nation it would seem, has with more frequency than has this government used its military forces . . . in order to secure adequate safety and protection for its citizens and their property.' J. R. Clark, Jr., *Right to Protect Citizens in Foreign Countries by Landing Forces, Memorandum of the Solicitor for the Dept. of State, October 5, 1912*, 2nd rev. edn (Washington, US Government Printing Office, 1929), p. 32. M. Offutt, *The Protection of Citizens Abroad by the Armed Forces of the United States* (Baltimore, J. Hopkins Press, 1928).

[32] A. N. Mandelstam, 'L'interprètation du Pacte Briand-Kellogg par les Gouvernements et les Parlements des Etats Signataires', 40 *RGDIP* (1933), p. 537, at p. 596.

[33] Cour de Cassation, Ch. crim, arrêt du 17 mai 1839, in A. C. Kiss, *Repertoire de la Pratique Francaise en Matiere de Droit International Public*, tom. I (Paris, Editions du Centre National de la Recherche Scientifique, 1962), para. 10.

[34] UN SCOR, 1939th mtg, UN Doc. S/PV. 1939 (9 July 1976), p. 57, at pp. 59–60.

[35] UN SCOR, 1941st mtg, UN Doc. S/PV. 1941 (12 July 1976), pp. 31–2; M. L. Nash, 'Commentary: Practice of the United States Relating to International Law', 73 *AJIL* (1979), p. 122, at p. 123.

[36] J. R. D'Angelo, 'Resort to Force by States to Protect Nationals: The US Rescue Mission to Iran and its Legality under International Law', 21 *Va JIL* (1981), p. 485.

[37] 80 *Dep't State Bull.* (1980), No. 2039, pp. 42–3; *Case Concerning United States Diplomatic and Consular Staff in Tehran (United States of America v. Iran)*, *Pleadings*, pp. 484–9.

[38] UN Doc. S/13908, 25 April 1980.

[39] Testimony before the Senate by Deputy Secretary of State Kenneth W. Dam in M. Nash Leigh, 'Commentary: Practice of the United States Relating to International Law', 78 *AJIL* (1984), p. 200, at p. 203. See letter by D. R. Robinson, The Legal Adviser, United States Department of State, 18 *International Lawyer* (1984), p. 381, at p. 385.

[40] 'We would not dispute that a state has the right in international law to take appropriate action to safeguard the lives of its citizens where there has been a breakdown of law and order. . . .' 47 *Hansard*, HC Deb. (1983), col. 332.

When the United States invaded Panama in 1989 in order to protect American lives, it was the 'inherent right of self-defence . . . in accordance with Article 51 of the United Nations Charter'.[41]

In the self-defence argument, one can trace a state-conscious concept, an attempt to buttress legal discourse against de-legitimisation and destabilisation.[42] Since protection of nationals raises similar moral and legal questions as humanitarian intervention, this may jeopardise the clarity and efficiency of legal rules to order state interaction. Humanitarian intervention has always been fraught with the suspicion of threatening the order imposed by the notion of sovereignty and non-intervention. Protection of nationals as humanitarian intervention would revive similar objections whereas self-defence is more amenable to order.

However, within this reasoning, individuals are viewed as objects of an omnipotent and omnipresent state. If the injury to a national is by legal fiction attributed to her or his national state, then individuals are presented as depsychologised, unemotional and impotent creatures who submit their existence to the will of their own state. Equally, state discretion within the domestic jurisdiction is also justified. It is evident then that the self-defence justification for rescue operations is indifferent to the individual identity obliterated within the notion of state.[43]

The humanitarian character of the actions

When individual humanity intrudes into the area of protection, it alters the basis for such actions, from the correspondence of offences to feelings of sympathy for the violations of human rights. Hence, the essence of rescue operations becomes humanitarian.

This reasoning views the corporate notion of the state as corresponding to the moral perspectives of its people. The state does not have an autonomous moral standing but its morality or rights are derivative, based on the morality

[41] Statement by the US Representative to the Security Council, Jeane Kirkpatrick. UN SCOR, 44th Sess., 2899th mtg., UN Doc. S/PV.2899 (1989). Also statement by President Bush in M. Nash Leigh, 'Commentary: Practice of the United States Relating to International Law', 84 *AJIL* (1990), p. 536, pp. 546–8; 'Agora: US Forces in Panama: Defenders, Aggressors or Human Rights Activists?', 84 *AJIL* (1990), pp. 494–524; J. Quigley, 'The Legality of the United States Invasion of Panama', 15 *Yale JIL* (1990), p. 276; A. D. Sofaer, 'The Legality of the United States Action in Panama", 29 *Columbia J. Trans L* (1991), p. 281; L. Henkin, 'The Invasion of Panama Under International Law: A Gross Violation', *ibid.*, p. 293.
[42] D. W. Bowett, 'The Use of Force for the Protection of Nationals Abroad', in A. Cassese, *The Current Legal Regulation of the Use of Force* (Dordrecht/Boston/Lancaster, Martinus Nijhoff, 1986), p. 39, at pp. 49–51.
[43] T. Schweisfurth, 'Operations to Rescue Nationals in Third States Involving the Use of Force in Relation to the Protection of Human Rights', 23 *German YBIL* (1980), p. 159.

of the individuals it represents. Hence, the protective action by the state vindicates those individual rights and moralities it has come to protect. It can also be motivated by a feeling of revulsion towards the maltreatment of people including the state nationals. The feeling of human solidarity and compassion in these instances has a double foundation. There are the intrinsic, sentimental bonds between members of the same group which create an interest in their welfare and there is also a general feeling of human compassion for the predicament of the people whose rights are endangered. Consequently, the conceptual basis for rescue operations is modified from a sense of injured statist pride to approximating humanitarian intervention proper whose permanent characteristic since Grotius has been a feeling of human solidarity and revulsion for crimes committed against people. This approach attaches importance to and promotes the human values of societies and persons. It springs from a notion of self-defence residing in the just war theory according to which, as we will remember, a defensive war can also be offensive in its nature if it is for the restoration of the vestiges of the universal society. Again, as in the medieval tradition, it can imply a sanctioning process of what is considered to be the law and the foundations of justice. As was said by Pradier-Fodéré, the state has the right to protect its nationals abroad 'lorsque l'État étranger a procédé contre eux en violant les principes du droit inernational'.[44]

Moreover, rescue operations have frequently afforded protection to people not exclusively nationals of the intervening state, thus betraying the humanitarian character of such operations. Hence, the US operation in Liberia in 1990 and 1996 rescued American but mostly foreign nationals.[45] In relation to the intervention in the Dominican Republic, the US Administration emphasised the fact that protection was afforded not only to Americans but also to 'people from 46 nations'.[46] This is not incidental but is prompted by considerations of humanity because a purely self-defence reasoning would confine the operation to the nationals of the intervening state.

---

[44] P. Pradier-Fodéré, *Traité de droit international public*, tom. 1 (Paris, G. Pedone-Laurel, 1885), p. 614, para. 402; J. C. Bluntschli, *Le droit international codifié*, trans. C. Lardy, 5th edn, vol. I (Paris, Alcan, 1895), p. 273, sec. 474; H. Bonfils, *Manuel de droit international public*, vol. I (Paris, A. Rousseau, 1905), p. 160; Hyde, *International Law*, 2nd rev. edn, vol. I, p. 252.

[45] *Keesing's* (1990), p. 37644; R. B. Lillich, 'Forcible Protection of Nationals Abroad: The Liberian 'Incident' of 1990', 35 *German YBIL* (1992), p. 205, at p. 209. *The Economist*, 13–19 April 1996, pp. 58–9; *Keesing's* (1996), p. 41031.

[46] See President Johnson's statement 'to preserve the lives of American citizens and the citizens of a good many other nations . . . We removed 5,600 people from 46 nations, and we didn't sprain an ankle doing it.' 53 *Dep't State Bull.* (5 July 1965), pp. 19, 20. See also Senator Fulbright: 'If the United States had really been intervening to save American lives, as it had a moral if not strictly legal right to do, it could have done so promptly and then withdrawn and the incident would soon have been forgotten'. 111 *Congress Records* (15 September 1965), p. 23001.

Moreover, there exist other common grounds with humanitarian intervention proper. It was argued above that humanitarian intervention takes place when state authority breaks down and is unable to bring about the realisation of those values which bind together its citizens. Rescue operations take place in similar circumstances. A recurrent pattern is for the state to protect its citizens 'whenever menaced by lawless acts, which the general or local authority is unwilling or impotent to prevent'.[47] For instance, President Carter invoked the right to protect the American nationals in Iran 'where the government of the territory in which they are located is unable or unwilling to protect them'.[48] The US operation in Liberia took place amid civil strife and lawlessness which reached savage dimensions with indiscriminate killings, burnings of villages and looting.[49] Foreign nationals were threatened and targeted by the rebels.[50] Likewise, according to the rationale for the US action in the Dominican Republic,[51] 'the situation was completely out of control' and only US forces 'could safeguard and protect the lives of thousands of Americans and thousands of citizens of some thirty other counties'.[52] The gist of this position is that sovereignty and non-intervention protect the authoritative function of the state only when it accomplishes the reasons for its existence, that is, internal order and legitimacy.

As with humanitarian intervention, the motive behind such operations is also crucial. Thus, the American action in Iran had a prominent humanitarian aspect. As spelt out by President Carter, 'the mission was a humanitarian mission' to 'safeguard American lives'.[53] According to Ambassador Bunker, US forces were sent to the Dominican Republic in 1965 'purely and solely for humanitarian purposes, for the protection of the lives not only of the United States citizens but the lives of citizens of other countries as well'.[54] As for Liberia, the aim of the US action was 'to make sure that the American lives are protected'. [55]

Even if self-defence appears to be the central argument, the humanitarian element should not be overlooked. In fact, it is present and decisive, although discounted in the political hubbub. For instance, in Entebbe, the Israeli

[47] Statement by Acting Secretary of State Hill in J. B. Moore, *A Digest of International Law*, vol. II (Washington, Government Printing Office, 1906), pp. 401–2.

[48] 80 *Dep't State Bull.* (1980), No. 2039, pp. 42–3.

[49] 36 *Keesing's* (1990), p. 37174; The situation was described as a 'slaughterhouse'. 3852 *West Africa* (8–4 July 1991), p. 1123.

[50] O'Neill, 'Liberia – An Avoidable Tragedy, Current History', 113 *US News and World Report*, No. 20 (23 November 1992), p. 216; 36 *Keesing's* (1990), p. 37601.

[51] A. J. Thomas, A. V. W. Thomas, *The Dominican Republic Crisis 1965* (Dobbs Ferry, N.Y., Oceana Pub. Inc., 1967).

[52] 20 UN SCOR, 1196th mtg (3 May 1965), para. 67, p. 14.

[53] 80 *Dep't State Bull.* (1980), No. 2039, p. 38.

[54] 52 *Dep't State Bull.* (1965), p. 854.

[55] *US Policy and the Crisis in Liberia, Hearing Before the Subcomm. on Africa of the House Comm. on Foreign Affairs*, 101st Congress, 2nd Sess. 1990, p. 24.

nationals were targeted because they were identified with their government but the life-threatening circumstances were genuine and the rescue operation also addressed this element. In fact, the two aspects – defensive and humanitarian – intermingle because it is the threat of annihilation which makes the demands imperative and compelling, impinging upon the state's sovereignty and triggering the defensive action. We should recall that the traditional criteria for self-defence as formulated in the *Caroline* case are 'a necessity of self-defence, instant, overwhelming, leaving no choice of means, and no moment for deliberation.'[56] Thus the protection of nationals and humanitarian intervention *stricto sensu* share a common denominator. They describe attempts to save the lives of people or to protect their personal dignity. The self-defence reasoning is unconvincing because it is discriminatory. It involves only the nationals of the intervening state in circumstances where the danger is indiscriminate. Having said that, one may invoke a reticent utilitarian argument that in circumstances of chaos or great and imminent danger it is better to save some people than none at all. This does not address the issue. Discrimination resides in the sheer foundation of the notion: it is conceptual not circumstantial. Protection in this case concerns *ab initio* the safety only of nationals and not that of people in general. The situation in Liberia, for example, warranted a comprehensive humanitarian action[57] which the protection of foreign nationals partially achieved and provides the most compelling arguments for enlarging the factual and legal basis of such actions. The reports of the airlifting from the US Embassy's compound in Liberia refer to the frustration and agony of the remaining Liberian civilians.[58]

In conclusion, we have treated the protection of nationals as humanitarian intervention *lato sensu* because both instances share common properties and, moreover, the notion of self-defence includes a sense of solidarity towards threatened individuals. The debate presented above revealed the inherent tensions within the legal argument, its prevalent assumptions and the underlying ideological foundations. Legal argument contains ambiguities which afflict humanitarian intervention with indeterminacy and incommensurability. However, this should not generate a fatalistic and retreating mood which will eventually misspend human mind and nature. In the next chapter we shall present a redescription through the dialogic framework of human dignity.

[56] 29 *British and Foreign State Papers* (1840–1841), p. 1129, at p. 1138. *Nicaragua* case, p. 94, para. 176.
[57] *Le Monde diplomatique* (September 1990), p. 24.
[58] *Newsweek*, 29 April 1996, pp. 18–19; *The Economist*, 13–19 April, 1996, pp. 58–9; *The Sunday Times,* 14 April 1996, A.15.

7

Redescription: humanitarian intervention in a discursive model of human dignity

Redescription through a discursive model

The analysis of the theoretical and legal constituents of humanitarian intervention revealed their immanent controversies and contradictions and their intrinsic conception of societal organisation. Legal reasoning with its asseverated tendency of generating objective solutions leads towards hermetic modes of interpretation in the style of 'either/or'. It frustrates any attempt to enfranchise ourselves from the deductive patterns of the received form of doctrine.

Hence, legal discourse exhibits a property reminiscent of the hero's tragic persona in ancient Greek tragedies who experiences trepidation in making choices between human order and divine justice. *Antigone*, the play, exerts a therapeutic function because it reconciles *psyche* with reason. It satisfies our sense of justice but also our sense of order. Whereas order and formality prevails, the reader associates himself with the catharsis which the interplay of justice achieves.[1]

In international law, practitioners or theorists agonise like the tragic hero to choose from among incommensurable and competing 'goods'. These goods have been simplified as peace, order, justice and human dignity. Knowing that making choices and facing their repercussions is an anguishing process, international law is presented as formal rules which form a complete system and which provide objective answers, thus reducing the subjectivity of values. As Descartes exhorted, 'I am happy enough to discover one thing only which is certain and indubitable.'[2] Distancing law from values also has, surprisingly,

[1] A. MacIntyre, *After Virtue: A Study in Moral Theory* (London, Duckworth, 1981), pp. 223–5; J. Finnis, *Natural Law and Natural Rights* (Oxford, Clarendon Press, 1980), pp. 92–5.
[2] R. Descartes, 'Meditations on First Philosophy', in *The Philosophical Works of Descartes*, trans. E. S. Haldane, G. R. T. Ross, vol. I (Cambridge, Cambridge University Press, 1931), p. 144.

an emotional appeal. It signifies the human need to avoid the turmoil which the lack of referents may cause.[3] But in order to avoid rigidity and to serve order, a modicum of *ad hoc* justice is permitted. Humanitarian intervention is a prime example of an eclectic process of reformulation, recombination and reconciliation of opposing values and rules since legal discourse, as we have seen in the previous chapters, remains squeezed between the Scylla of ideas and the Charybdis of facts.[4] If rules relating to intervention distance themselves from morality, they may become irrelevant, whereas 'the less it is possible to distinguish law from ideas of moral obligation or propriety . . . the less importance do positive rules have in law'.[5]

The peregrination of values and rules, facts and ideas is, however, incessant. It is claimed that legal rules attain normativity only by ostracising ideas because the latter are 'open-textured' and subjectively verified.[6] Against this it is maintained that ideas are external to the observing person, hence objective. This may refer to God, nature, *recta ratio*, *Grundnorm* or rule of recognition. Again, the issue of how an external idea is apprehended introduces subjective evaluations.[7] It is also claimed that empirical research can identify those uniformities which produce 'value clarification'.[8] Thus, ideas are concretised but normativity may be threatened because practice may inflate law. Moreover, appreciation of the consolidated feeling hidden in practice requires interpretation[9] which poses afresh the problem of subjectiveness.[10] However judicious, this process entails questions in the field of both *sein*

---

[3] 'I can neither make certain of setting my feet on the bottom, nor can I swim and so support myself on the surface . . .'. Descartes, 'Meditations on First Philosophy', p. 149.

[4] R. Dworkin, *Taking Rights Seriously* (London, Duckworth, 1977), chs 2, 3.

[5] R. M. Unger, *Law in Modern Society. Toward a Criticism of Social Theory* (New York, The Free Press, 1976), p. 214.

[6] T. Hobbes, *Leviathan*, ed. C. B. Macpherson (Harmondsworth, Penguin Books, 1968), ch. 4, pp. 109–10: 'For one man callethe *Wisdome*, what another calleth *feare*; and one *cruelty*, what another *justice*; one *prodigality*, what another *magnanimity*; . . . And therefore such names can never be true grounds of any ratiocination.'

[7] R. J. Bernstein, *Beyond Objectivism and Relativism* (Oxford, Blackwell, 1983), p. 9: 'What is "out there" (objective) is presumed to be independent of us (subjects), and knowledge is achieved when a subject correctly mirrors or represents objective reality.'

[8] R. Pound, 'Philosophical Theory and International Law', I *Bibliotheca Visseriana* (1923), p. 71; N. Politis, *The New Aspects of International Law* (Washington, Carnegie Endowment for International Peace, 1928); C. de Visscher, 'Cour général de principes de droit international public', 86 *RC* (1954 II), p. 445, at p. 451. M. S. McDougal, 'International Law, Power and Policy: A Contemporary Perspective', 82 *RC* (1953 I), p. 133.

[9] S. Sur, *L'interprétation en droit international public* (Paris, L.G.D.J., 1974), p. 32: 'on y considère davantage les choses comme on voudrait qu'elles soient plutôt que telles qu'elles sont'.

[10] P. Allott, 'Language, Method and the Nature of International Law', 45 *BYBIL* (1971), p. 79, at pp. 123–5.

and *sollen*. Ideas and facts inter-combine because ideas categorise and characterise the facts[11] whereas these concepts are 'internalised' through the practices we observe.[12] Only through this process can a particular act be factually substantiated and legally characterised. For instance, in the *Nicaragua* case, only by starting from the premises of non-intervention was the Court able to dismiss and pronounce illegal any contrary practice. Law preserved its normativity but not its relevance when facts are understood as modifying the rule or crystallising a new rule.

Another argument is that a framework for deliberation may overcome the subjective–objective division. However, the corpus of the method is not hermetically sealed against ideology. Kelsen's *Grundnorm* in international law as customary behaviour presupposes a shared 'form of life' contrary to the objectivity which its penumbra of deduced logicality may imply.[13] Likewise, as we have observed for the policy school, it requires a certain conception of the social matrix in order to be disentangled and appreciated which depends on pre-existing convictions. Another method which can neutralise legal rules is 'the right process'[14] such as the process within the UN Security Council. However, the latter has managed only a 'checkerboard' approach explained not only by the political configuration of each case and the constellation of power within the Security Council but also by the internal interplay of standards such as justice, human rights and sovereignty which mould legal discourse in their reformulations and recombinations evidenced in individual cases. Not all human rights crisis have met with the same response. For instance, the Kosovo crisis has defied the 'right process' approach. The humanitarian crisis amounted to a threat to peace but the Security Council was kept effectively at the sidelines. Thus, 'right process' fulfils the role of objectivity and concreteness only if approached superficially, that is, technically and not substantially.

[11] N. MacCormick, O. Weinberger, *An Institutional Theory of Law* (Dordrecht, D. Reidel, 1986), pp. 13–16, 49–67.

[12] P. Winch, *The Idea of a Social Science and Its Relation to Philosophy* (London, Henley, 1947), pp. 14–15, 83–91.

[13] With certain scepticism, Kelsen has admitted that on this matter there exists resemblance between his *Grundnorm* and natural law. H. Kelsen, 'Justice et droit naturel' (trad. E. Mazingue), in *Annales de philosophie politique*, vol. III, 'Droit Naturel' (Paris, PUF, 1959), p. 1, at p. 121. L. Wittgenstein, *On Certainty* (Oxford, Blackwell, 1969), pp. 15–16, 28, 35–6, paras 102, 105, 144, 274, 298.

[14] T. M. Franck, 'Legitimacy in the International System', 82 *AJIL*, p. 705, at p. 706: 'Legitimacy is used here to mean that quality of a rule which derives from a perception on the part of those to whom it is addressed that it has come into being in accordance with right process.' T. M. Franck, 'Why a Quest for Legitimacy?', 21 *University of California Davis Law Review* (1988), p. 535. T. M. Franck, *The Power of Legitimacy Among Nations* (New York, Oxford University Press, 1990), chs 1–4, 9–11 and *Fairness in International Law and Institutions* (Oxford, Clarendon Press, 1995), ch. 2. Dworkin, *Taking Rights Seriously*, p. 17.

Professing that objectivity is elusive provokes the fear that 'there really is no middle ground between matters of taste and matters capable of being settled by a previously stable algorithm'.[15] Objectivity and its companion, certainty, are presumed to neutralise the propensity for abuse and predatory practices.[16] What has been coined as objectification mistake[17] instals itself between the agent and the social action and transforms subjective elements into neutralised components. On the other hand, subjectivity is insidious because it can reify power when constraints are non-existent.[18] If everyone is left to pursue her or his preferences, eventually the mightiest will prevail.[19] More specifically, if law's restraining power is based on a rational foundation, what could constrain conduct if we dismantle such foundation? Therefore, critical reflection is always suspected of destroying the knowledge and the certainty which accompanies it.[20] The situation is surmised in the question posed by Ludwig Wittgenstein: 'Why should it be possible to have grounds for *believing* anything if it isn't possible to be certain?'[21]

Human beings, however, are both described and describing objects[22] and this works against reducing descriptions to monolithic constructions. Thus, beliefs and concepts may be followed or adhered to without attempting to present them as objective.[23]

In order to escape this quandary, we should embrace a new conversation which combines the theory, the practice but also our *phronesis*. This envision

[15] R. Rorty, *Philosophy and the Mirror of Nature* (Oxford, Blackwell, 1979), p. 336.

[16] F. Boyle, 'Ideals and Things: International Legal Scholarship and the Prison – House of Language', 26 *Harvard JIL* (1985), p. 327, at pp. 347–9. S. Sur, *L'interprétation en droit international public* (Paris, L.G.D.J., 1974), discussing natural law and sociological theories affirms that 'n'établit nullement un fondement assuré du droit, pas plus qu'il n'en fournit clairement une détermination objective', p. 32.

[17] R. Geuss, *The Idea of a Critical Theory: Habermas and the Frankfurt School* (Cambridge, Cambridge University Press, 1981), p. 14.

[18] E. A. Percell, Jr., *The Crisis of Democratic Theory. Scientific Naturalism and the Problem of Value* (Lexington, University Press of Kentucky, 1973), p. 163.

[19] Plato, *Gorgias*, trans. W. Hammilton (Harmondsworth, Penguin Books, 1960), p. 78, para. 483. Thusydides, *The Peloponnesian War*, trans. Rex Warner (Harmondsworth, Penguin Books, 1954), Bk. 5, p. 402, para. 89: 'The standard of justice depends on the equality of power to compel and that in fact the strong do what they have the power to do and the weak accept what they have to accept.' 'Every man is enemy of every man'. Hobbes, *Leviathan*, ed. C. B. Macpherson, ch. 13, p. 186. M. Wight, 'Western Values in International Relations', in H. Butterfield, M. Wight (eds), *Diplomatic Investigations: Essays in the Theory of International Politics* (London, Allen & Unwin, 1966), p. 89, at p. 122.

[20] J. W. Singer, 'The Player and the Cards: Nihilism and Legal Theory', 94 *Yale LJ* (1984), p. 1, at p. 48.

[21] L. Wittgenstein, *On Certainty* (Oxford, Blackwell, 1969), p. 48e, para. 373.

[22] Rorty, *Philosophy and the Mirror*, p. 378; T. W. Adorno, M. Horkheimer, *Dialectic of Enlightenment* (London, Verso, 1979), pp. 3–80.

[23] Rorty, *Philosophy and the Mirror*, pp. 333–4; J. Fiskin, 'Liberal Theory and the Problem of Justification', *Nomos XXVIII*, p. 207, at p. 216.

is a conversation of understudying, reflection, choice and imagination which projects the individual as the focus and bearer of description.[24] It reclaims our conflictual humanity and the manifold forms of human reality against those who nullify conversation through hypostatisation. However, we do not become agnostics, just aware that our views can only be justified instead of being grounded on some true source.[25]

The embraced dialectical culture entails certain processes: we need to identify situations and the concurring set of alternative reactions, contemplate the consequences of each alternative and appraise their inherent values. We also need to inform ourselves of the relevant lego-jurisprudential arguments. We have already pursued and accomplished these stages in the previous chapters. We have dealt with the different perspectives, ideals, arguments of either the legal or the theoretical tradition and realised that they do not achieve unanimity and that reality is still flawed. But instead of being withdrawn into a state of pessimism or perpetual deconstruction we attempt a redescription which is the result of reflection upon human conditions and of the belief that we can reshape our ephemeral reality only through judicious thinking and understanding of our humanity. Dismissing previous algorithms as grounds for our knowledge or values relocates their source in the individuals who are now empowered to appreciate, contemplate and decide.[26] Having said that, we shall redescribe our actualisation under the discursive framework of human dignity which describes a process but also a human achievement. Human dignity encompasses our sense of humanity which transgresses the particular individual and reveals the solidarity established by acknowledging our humanity and our empowerment to share it.[27]

---

[24] 'We need to unfreeze the world as it appears to common sense as a bunch of more or less objectively determined social relations and to make it appear as (we believe) it really is: people acting, imagining, rationalizing, justifying.' R. W. Gordon, 'New Developments in Legal Theory', in D. Kairys (ed.), *The Politics of Law: A Progressive Critique* (New York, Pantheon Books, 1982), p. 281, at p. 289; *and see* R. Rorty, 'Pragmatism, Relativism and Irrationalism', p. 727: 'Our identification with our community – our society, our political tradition, our intellectual heritage –, is heightened when we see this community as ours rather than nature's, shaped rather than found, one among many which men have made. In the end, the pragmatists tell us, what matters is our loyalty to other human beings clinging together against the dark, not our hope of getting things right.'

[25] Rorty, *Philosophy and the Mirror*, pp. 333–4.

[26] R. M. Unger, *Knowledge and Politics* (New York, The Free Press, 1975), pp. 3–25; R. M. Unger, 'The Critical Legal Studies Movement', 96 *Harvard L Rev* (1983), p. 561, at pp. 579–80. Unger in a later work describes 'passion' as the 'brio and panche, the sheer vibrant life, of a personality' which enhances our 'sense of experiences of human power'. R. M. Unger, *Passion: An Essay on Personality* (New York, The Free Press, 1984), pp. 260–1.

[27] Solidarity is described as 'our feeling of responsibility for those whose lives touch in some way upon our own and our greater or lesser willingness to share their fate'. Unger, *Law in Modern Society*, p. 206.

The process described here reveals the possibility of discourse since it elucidates the constitutive perspectives of humanitarian actions, also deciphering their merits. Moving away from compartmentalised legal arguments raises the prospect of capturing the essence of the problem. Otherwise the capacity of understanding is forfeited. Humanitarian actions should not be impersonal, insouciant debates on their effects on rules. We need to see their essentiality, the human tragedy and its effects on human dignity which would eventually redirect our thinking and action. Concerning legal argumentation, its insularity is transgressed and its dialectic enhanced.[28] The debater can now imagine a revisionary programme and stimulate transformation and revision of legal concepts.[29] By abandoning foundational theories, the prospects for introspection of the character of our life and our world loom.[30] People live in a social, cultural, ideological context and form opinions, creatively, from within.[31] Consensus between conflicting opinions is not found 'but created by the same people. They form within their shared living a community of understanding.'[32]

Consequently, this mode of reasoning is not foundational, although it exhorts the ideal of human dignity and evaluates state actions accordingly. The projection of human dignity may provoke accusations of reverting to the previously criticised attitude of anchoring. It may also provoke the suspicion of ideological domination as it aspires to apply in fields or subjects which may not share the same 'false consciousness'. Against such criticisms, we say that human dignity describes the mundane modes of human existence and our solidarity. Conversing between possibilities and alternatives confronts the introverted, silent discourse of existing legal argument. It is amenable to revision because it is cognisant of new dynamics. Our project does not depend on commensuration but only on its argumentative value,

[28] Boyle, 'Ideals and Things', p. 358: 'Yet the fetishism of essences, the belief that this is how one showed oneself to be correct, actually subverts the commitment to enlightened rationality and replaces it with reified ideas, thus ruling out the possibility of real discussion.'

[29] R. M. Unger, *The Critical Legal Studies Movement* (Cambridge, Mass., Harvard University Press, 1983), pp. 25–42, 91–117.

[30] G. Frug, 'The Ideology of Bureaucracy in American Law', 97 *Harvard L Rev* (1984), p. 1276, at p. 1386: 'The alternative to foundations is not chaos but the joint reconstruction of social life, the quest for participatory democracy.'

[31] Bernstein, *Beyond Objectivism*, pp. xiv, 37: 'We should be comfortable viewing both rationality and social life as historically and culturally situated.' L. Wittgenstein, *On Certainty*, p. 16e, para. 105: 'All testing, all confirmation and disconfirmation of a hypothesis takes place already within a system. And this system is not a more or less arbitrary and doubtful point of departure for all our arguments: no, it belongs to the essence of what we call an argument. The system is not so much the point of departure, as the element in which arguments have their life.'

[32] Bernstein, *Beyond Objectivism*, pp. 203–4, 215–16, 223–9; M. V. Tushnet, 'Following the Rules Laid Down: A Critique of Interpretivism and Neutral Principles', 96 *Harvard L Rev* (1983), p. 781, at pp. 826–7.

its ability to see what is significant in the particular case and to make adjustments. The conversation should not assume that, eventually, there should be an agreement but it should focus on the criteria for good arguments and evaluate the propositions presented for the attainment of human dignity. What is pursued here is a 'search for new and better solutions' through critical examination.[33]

Human dignity[34] in a discursive model

Human dignity cannot be the subject of a definite statement because in a discursive culture its content will be the subject of debate and the prospect of revision unleashes dynamics that are better served through an open concept. This may provoke the suspicion of arbitrariness; if human dignity connotes different things to different classes of people, it may justify any action under its rubric. However, uniformity is not required because the participants in the discussion about human dignity are informed of its facets, and creativity and diversity are not considered detrimental. The referents which assist our perception contain a minimum but also an optimum mandate. Thus, we speak of a dignified human existence and delineate its content by referring to the protection of life. This is only the beginning as the optative *telos* of human dignity contains quantitative and qualitative indices which dignify human life, achieving the flourishing of human beings.

Human dignity as dignified human existence refers to the Greek words for life: *zoe*, the biological life, and *bios*, the life as lived. Life has natural and human aspects but its biological aspect is a prerequisite. The human aspect refers to the interests people have invested in the character of their lives, the entitlement of human beings to pursue their dignified life. Hence, we have made three distinctions: life as *zoe* (existence); dignity as critical interest; dignified life as valuable *bios*. The three of them are interconnected and dignified life cannot be attained if people are denied the possibility of pursuing their interests and, above all, if they are exterminated biologically.

Human dignity as dignified existence becomes then the guiding ideal in our redescription which transforms the legal argument concerning humanitarian intervention. We shall relate human dignity to actuation, arguments or consequences and link the private and the public domain of human discourse. How we act publicly relies on our private reasons, otherwise how can we

[33] H. Albert, 'Science and the Search for Truth', in G. Radnitzky, G. Andersson (eds), *Progress and Rationality in Science* (Dordrecht, D. Reidel, 1978), p. 204. A. MacIntyre, *After Virtue: A Study in Moral Theory* (London, Duckworth, 1981), p. 244; T. A. Sprangens, Jr., 'Justification, Practical Reason, and Political Theory', *Nomos* XXVIII, p. 336.
[34] Some of the ideas concerning the definition of human dignity, although in a different context, are taken from R. Dworkin, *Life's Dominion: An Argument about Abortion and Euthanasia* (London, HarperCollins, 1993).

justify our public shows of inhumanity? For instance, if a massacre takes place, any explanation would be superficial unless we ask why those involved did such an act – be they laymen or officials. The disjunction between private and public relies on external truths and grounds which serve to impose uniformity and stability, with the cost, however, of dehumanisation and depersonalisation. Therefore, the distinction cannot be sustained within a culture of self-reflection and expression, investigation and solidarity but their interweaving will eventually reformulate the public domain through a redescription.[35] Additionally, human dignity is not presented as an *ad hoc* criterion. It is comprehensive, disconnected from instantaneous emotive reactions because it relates to our inner humanity. Above all, admitting the possibility of transformation, it justifies our ability for revision through discussion, instead of unquestioned adherence to stringent doctrines.

In the following section, the argument for humanitarian intervention will be presented in a discursive model of human dignity. Prior to this we need to discount the position that, dispensing with the need to verify human dignity against an external form, everything becomes relative.[36] Human dignity as our premise cannot be objectively grounded[37] but enjoys a contingency which our 'context-bound character' exhibits.[38] It is argued that between competing ideals and the lack of objective basis for privileging some at the expense of others, we can only anticipate respect and tolerance. This argument echoes the nineteenth-century Italian theorist, Fiore, for whom 'la loi de la sociabilité nous oblige à la tolérance'[39] which is raised then to a normative concept against relativism's instincts.[40] Consequently, humanitarian action is impeded because it is accused of being ideologically motivated. A century ago, Pradier-Fodéré considered humanitarian intervention illegal because it relates to *la justice subjective* and not *la justice objective*.[41] It is presumed that a certain

---

[35] R. M. Unger, *Politics, a Work in Constructive Social Theory*, vol. 1 (Cambridge, Cambridge University Press, 1987), pp. 18–35, 135–7; R. M. Unger, *What Should Legal Analysis Become?* (London, Verso, 1996).

[36] F. R. Tesón, 'International Human Rights and Cultural Relativity', 25 *Va. JIL* (1985), p. 869; A. D. Rentlen, 'The Unanswered Challenge of Relativism and the Consequences for Human Rights', 7 *Hum. RQ* (1984), p. 514.

[37] R. Descartes, 'Meditations on First Philosophy', in *The Philosophical Works of Descartes*, trans. E. S. Haldane, G. R. T. Ross, vol. I (Cambridge, Cambridge University Press, 1931), p. 144.

[38] A. MacIntyre, *Whose Justice? Which Rationality?* (London, Duckworth, 1988), p. 4.

[39] P. Fiore, *Nouveau droit international public*, P. Pradier-Fodéré (trad.) (Paris, A. Durand and Pedone-Lauriel, 1868), p. 226.

[40] R. B. Brandt, *Ethical Theory: The Problems of Normative and Critical Ethics* (Englewood Cliffs, N.J., Prentice-Hall, 1959), p. 289: 'the value of intolerance is as justified (or unjustified) as that of tolerance'.

[41] P. Pradier-Fodéré, *Traité de droit international public: Européen et Americain*, tom. I (Paris, G. Pedone-Lauriel, 1885), pp. 656–7, para. 427: 'La justice objective se révèle graduellement et après de longues et penibles luttes par l'opinion publique. Quand elle entre dans la conscience générale, c'est à dire, quant elle devient généralement

communal character exists within such community prescribed by an observation of the legal and social context. Interference is prohibited because it does
not only impinge upon this supposed cohesion but may additionally impose
'foreign' ideas. For instance, Walzer allows for intervention only on the
basis of promoting those inherent values in a community which have tempor-
arily been obstructed. Later Rawls approximates Walzer since both pursue
to different degrees 'pluralistic' legitimacy.[42] Diversity does not preclude dialectic
agreement unless disagreement is presupposed which in its turn abrogates
the potentiality for action. On the other hand, even relativism requires assessment and understanding[43] between cultures in order to demarcate 'our' and
'their' limits. Otherwise, how can we say that a certain practice represents
a particular culture? For instance, following the ousting of Idi Amin, the
President of Tanzania, Julius Nyerere, condemned the OAU's inaction in
relation to the human rights violations in Africa by saying: 'There is a
strange habit in Africa: an African leader, as long as he is African, can kill
Africans just as he pleases'[44] and adding: 'Blackness has become a certificate
to kill with immunity.'[45] But this understanding should be profound not
superficial and its point of departure should be the bearers of ideas, not the
ab initio incompatibility of ideas. Hence, we can rediscover the commonalities
or differences between cultures. It should also entail conversation in order
to find the objects of human desire. The prospect of change is nullified if we
have no idea of how our reality should be transformed. It is obvious then
that the demarcation between particular traditions is not insular but involves
inquiry, interaction and communication. As MacIntyre wrote, the problem
of diversity requires 'a prior understanding' which does not abolish the problem but 'render[s] it amenable to solution'.[46] This makes explicit the recon-
figuration between traditions and the idea of solidarity which forms part of
human dignity. It stems from an understanding of our mundane humanity
and its exigencies and works through self-exploration and exploration to
human empowerment.[47] It may initially have a shrinking locality but by
keeping up the inquiry, by not terminating the conversation, it can extend to
other people or humanity as a whole.[48]

---

subjective, elle est réalisée sans aucune intervention, et sous la seule impulsion de la
civilisation.'

[42] J. Rawls, 'The Law of Peoples', 20 *Critical Inquiry* (1993), p. 36.

[43] R. Rorty, 'Pragmatism, Relativism, and Irrationalism', 53 *Proceedings &
Addresses of the American Philosophical Association* (1980), p. 719, at pp. 727–30.

[44] 11 *Africa Contemporary Records* (1978–79), p. 394.

[45] *Keesing's* (1979), p. 29670A.

[46] MacIntyre, *Whose Justice?*, p. 10.

[47] R. M. Unger, *Passion: An Essay on Personality* (New York, The Free Press,
1984), pp. 8–15.

[48] R. Rorty, *Contingency, Irony and Solidarity* (Cambridge, Cambridge University
Press, 1989), p. 190.

Finally, we do not claim unanimity but rather dialogical understanding and inter-subjectivity because human dignity is not a mere indicator of a certain aspect of life or, in particular, of legal-political achievement. It is the constituent of such an achievement. Humans retain their individuality and they are appreciated as units who face the future with the same fear and anxiety and who experience the same conflictual reality, questioning the way of human living. Reflection upon and appreciation of these conditions reaches the nucleus of our individualities but also of our humanity which grows through incorporation and overcomes the distinction between individuality and society and the need for grounding.[49] Thus, the conversing argumentation purports to produce an inter-subjective sense of community and solidarity whilst the participants are liberated from the constrains of 'their' approach and expand their concept of 'we'.[50] Eventually, human dignity would redirect state or human activities because it presents the prospect of a redescription. As such it has *universal* application and shows *impartiality* among people. In a discursive culture, choice is included but it should be *effective* in bringing about human dignity. The person making the choice amongst the alternative ways of approaching human dignity should choose those practices which are fit to achieve this imperative and which are proportional. These limitations, however, are not superimposed but self-imposed because there exists communication between people, self-reflection on situations and possibilities and because our shared humanity also shares a feeling of pain in connection with impropriety or happiness in connection with success.

Redescription of practice

The promotion of human dignity as dignified existence

Re-exploring the instances where humanitarian intervention took place will, it is hoped, be recapitulating conceptually because they contain the germane ingredients which have become the substance of our inquiries. The dialectical

[49] R. M. Unger, *Knowledge and Politics* (New York, The Free Press, 1975), pp. 220–1: 'Community is held together by an allegiance to common purposes. The more these shared ends express the nature of humanity, rather than simply the preferences of particular individuals and groups, the more would one's acceptance of them become and affirmation of one's own nature; the less would it have to represent the abandonment of individuality in favour of assent and recognition. Thus, it would be possible to view others a complementary rather than opposing wills; furtherance of their ends would mean the advancement of one's own. The conflict between the demands of individuality and of sociability would disappear. Each person, secure in his individuality, would be able to recognise his own humanity in other persons.'

[50] R. Rorty, 'Solidarity or Objectivity', in J. Rajchman, C. West (eds), *Post-Analytic Philosophy* (New York, Columbia University Press, 1985), p. 3, at p. 5.

process we have articulated above becomes evident when we consider cases such as the Rwandan genocide. The situation in Rwanda was characterised by genocidal events, indiscriminate and heinous killings, uprooting of populations, coupled with the apathy of states and the inadequacy or unwillingness of international institutions to respond. The contrasting legal positions which characterise this case betray an aura of disorientation, entangled as they are in antagonistic interests and principles. When finally the French operation was launched, the international community reacted in a lukewarm fashion.[51] The reasons for such a hesitant approach are obvious and reside in the strong grip of such principles as non-intervention and sovereignty and the fear that values such as humanitarian ones are not only thin disguises for imperialist policies but may also destabilise the existing order.[52] It is also apparent that such reasoning fails to offer satisfactory answers beyond the prospect of prolonging the massacres. If we rethink the situation in terms of the people who were massacred and denied their right of existence we approach the situation differently and see the operation as providing sanctuary to persecuted, intimidated and demoralised people and also assisting international agencies in the provision of aid.[53] The operation also proceeded impartially and did not influence the internal political struggle.[54] As it was stated in the Security Council, the operation was 'exclusively humanitarian' and the objective was 'to rescue endangered civilians and put an end to the massacres, and to do so in an impartial manner'.[55] Consequently, the operation had an overall humanitarian character amid international inaction and domestic massacres.[56]

Similar genocidal events took place in Bangladesh when the Pakistani army tried to quell the nationalistic sentiment. The result was thousands of

[51] SC Res. 929, UN SCOR, 3393rd mtg, UN Doc. S/RES/929 (1994). China, Brazil, New Zealand, Pakistan and Nigeria abstained.

[52] UN SCOR, 49th Sess., 3392d mtg, UN Doc. S/PV.3392 (1994), pp. 6–7.

[53] 'Il s'agit d'une opération où il peut etre fait usage de la force, mais avec un objectif uniquement humanitaire, à savoir sauver des vies humaines et mettre à l'abri des enfants, des malades, des populations terrorisées.' Press Conference of the French Foreign Minister (5 July 1994), *PEF*, July–August, p. 30.

[54] The Security Council, through its President, reaffirmed: 'le caractère humanitaire de la zone sure au sud – ouest du Rwanda et exige que tous ceux que cela concerne respectent ce caractère'. Declaration of the President of the Security Council, S/PRST/1994/34 (14 July 1994). With the victory of the F.P.R., France declared in the Security Council that 'les autorités rwandaises sont par définition souveraines sur l'ensemble du territoire rwandais'. Letter by the French Permanent Mission to the United Nations, 8 September 1994, S/1994/944.

[55] UN SCOR, 49th Sess., 3392d mtg, UN Doc. S/PV.3392 (1994), pp. 5–6.

[56] 'L'opération Turquoise a été dictée par les événements. A vocation strictement humanitaire, elle a rempli ses objectifs: sauver des dizaines de milliers de vies; faire cesser les massacres; sécuriser les populations; mobiliser la communauté internationale pour qu'elle apporte son aide'. Interview by the French Foreign Minister, 14 September 1994, *PEF*, Septembre–October, p. 91.

deaths and millions of refugees. When India intervened, the official justification was self-defence, whereas for the international community humanitarian intervention was an option 'in view of the inability of international organisations to take any effective action to bring to an end the massive violations of human rights in East Pakistan'.[57] This ambiguity is relieved under the perspective of human dignity where the essence of the action becomes primordial. It saved people when their lives where endangered and when there was no intention in any quarter to do so. The cases of Uganda and Kampuchea should be evaluated in the same way, not according to their effects on the governmental structures but according to how they secured human dignity. Kampuchea was not totally propitious in this regard. Humanitarian intervention stopped widespread massacres at a genocidal level and in this way secured human dignity, but the ensuing situation did not correspond to the standards of human dignity.

Following the position developed here, cases such as Entebbe and Liberia are included within the concept of humanitarian intervention. The traditional legal reasoning of self-defence misrepresents the essence of the case because it shows indifference to the plight of threatened people and avows respect for a sense of statist pride. It is discriminatory and selfish and therefore we have reclassified these incidents as humanitarian intervention *lato sensu*. Our redescription then becomes crucial because it involves not only securing human dignity in its periphery as the attributes of a dignified life but also in its essence, which is the preservation of life. The only reservation concerns the invocation of impartiality or universality. The Entebbe incident, as it progressed, involved Israeli nationals only and the rescue operation was strictly confined to them. On the other hand, the Liberian operation by rescuing only foreigners was discriminatory although it cannot be entirely discarded from the purview of human dignity. Under our perspective, the essence of the situation is recognised and the solidarity which stems from understanding our human fate includes also nationals of the target state. This has been recognised later when ECOWAS forces entered Liberia as a Peace-Keeping Force. It was admitted that 'for an African government to have the right to kill its citizens or let its citizens be killed, I believe there is no clause in the [OAU] Charter that allows this. To tell the truth, the Charter was created to preserve the humanity, dignity, and the rights of the African.'[58]

---

[57] *The Events in East Pakistan, 1971*, A Legal Study by the Secretariat of the International Commission of Jurists (Geneva, 1972), p. 96.
[58] 'Africa's Destiny', *West-Africa Magazine*, 22–28 October 1990, p. 2690. The Nigerian Head of State declared: 'We are in Liberia because events in that country have led to massive destruction of property, the massacre by all parties of thousands of innocent civilians including foreign nationals, women and children . . . contrary to all standards of civilised behaviour and international ethics and decorum.' *West-Africa Magazine*, 1–7 February 1993, p. 146.

In a consideration of operations in a wider context of protecting human dignity and its attributes, the French operation in the Central African Republic (April–May 1996) provides an example. Initially it involved the protection of nationals[59] during civil disturbances and violence.[60] The wider dimensions of the operation were also acknowledged and those involved the establishment of institutions and practices which would facilitate the democratic process and respect the 'droit de l'homme, qui serait en danger'.[61] Hence, the operation was endowed with a wider mandate: it transgressed the traditional 'extraction' of citizens and assisted the democratic institutions.[62]

This case brings to the forum the relationship between democracy[63] and human dignity. Although it is beyond the scope of this book, according to our understanding the two notions interweave. Human dignity containing a hard core of preserving life and a soft core of political and social flourishing empowers the people, and democracy can be realised through this empowerment. In Panama, for example, the American action cannot be justified on the basis of its short-term purpose of protecting nationals.[64] It was prompted by the killing of one off-duty American soldier and the detention of a US Navy lieutenant and his wife.[65] Although the humanitarian element of the

[59] According to the French Defence Ministry, the French troops 'ont été déployées dans plusieurs quartiers de Bangui afin d'assurer la sécurité des ressortissants français et étrangers'. *Le Monde*, 22 June 1996, p. 3.

[60] *Le Monde*, 21 June 1996, p. 4. *Le Monde*, 23 June 1996, p. 4: 'Les gens vivent tellement dans la misère que tout ce qu'ils trouvent dans les maisons [des étrangers], ils le volent'. The EU noted with 'satisfaction les mesures prises pour la protection des populations et, en particulier les actions enterprises par la France pour assurer la sécurité des ressortissants étrangers, notamment européens, et aider à ce que s'engage une négociation'. 100 *RGDIP* (1996), p. 813.

[61] *Le Monde*, 22 June 1996, p. 3. According to the French Foreign Minister, France condemns 'toute atteinte à la légalité en République Centrafricaine et entend aider les institutions démocratiquement élues à défendre l'ordre constitutionnel et favoriser l'apaisement'. 100 *RGDIP* (1996), p. 812.

[62] The French Minister for Co-operation declared that: 'La mission, c'est de maintenir un Etat démocratique, . . . avec tous ses attributs' and 'Les chefs d'Etats africains . . . sont très solidaires d'un de leurs collègues élu au suffrage universel. Donc il y a . . . un fort appui à ce que fait la France.' *Le Monde*, 24 June 1996, p. 2.

[63] T. M. Franck, 'The Emerging Right to Democratic Governance', 86 *AJIL* (1992), p. 46; A. A. D'Amato, *International Law Anthology* (Anderson Publishing Co., 1994), ch. 15. W. M. Reisman, 'Coercion and Self-Determination: Construing Charter Article 2(4)', 78 *AJIL* (1984), p. 642; O. Schachter, 'The Legality of Pro-Democratic Invasion', 78 *AJIL* (1984), p. 645, at p. 659.

[64] 'The deployment of US forces is an exercise of the right of self-defence recognised in Article 51 of the United Nations Charter and was necessary to protect American lives in imminent danger . . .' See Letter from President Bush to Congress, HR Doc. No. 127, 101st Cong., 2nd Sess. (1990). Also speech to the United Nations by Ambassador Thomas R. Pickering, UN Doc. S/PV.2899 (1989), p. 31.

[65] President Bush characterised the attack against the American soldier as an attack on the United States. See 'Fighting in Panama: Text of Statement by Fitzwater', *NY Times*, 21 December 1989, at A19, col. 2; 'Excerpts from Statement by Baker on

action could not be discounted, its significance was minimal and the operation exceeded the bounds of proportionality.[66] The long-term effect of the
action which was the restoration of democracy has assisted in fulfilling the
soft core of human dignity. Similarly in Haiti, following the *coup* against
Jean-Bertrand Aristide, the democratically-elected president,[67] the situation
concerning human rights quickly degenerated.[68] The international community concentrated its efforts on re-establishing the democratically-elected
government[69] through an agreement in 1993[70] which was not implemented.[71]
Responding to the gravity of the situation, the United Nations passed Resolution 940[72] which authorised the dispatch of a multilateral force with the
critical participation of the United States.[73] Eventually, the transfer of power
was achieved peacefully by agreement between the junta and the US nego-
tiators. In this case, human rights violations have been characterised as a
'threat to peace' which justify forcible responses as is the current perspective
in international law.[74] There is hence an *ad hoc* evaluation of state benevolence or opportunism. Contrary to this, according to our approach, the

---

US Policy', *ibid.*, col. 3. R. Wedgwood, 'The Use of Armed Force in International
Affairs: Self-Defense and the Panama Invasion', 29 *Col. J Trans. L* (1991), p. 609.

[66] G. A. Res. 240, 44 UN GAOR Supp. (No. 49) p. 52, UN Doc. A/RES/44/240
(1989).

[67] Inter-American Commission on Human Rights, *Annual Report* (1990–91), OEA/
Ser.L/V/II.79, rev. 1 (1991), p. 468.

[68] House Comm. on Foreign Affairs, Senate Comm. on Foreign Relations, 102nd
Cong., 2nd Sess., Country Reports on Human Rights Practices for 1992 (1992);
Lawyers' Committee for Human Rights, *Haiti: A Human Rights Nightmare* (1992).

[69] GA Res. 46/7, UN GAOR, 46th Sess., UN Doc. A/RES/46/7 (1992); OAS Res.
MRE/RES. 1/91 OEA/SER. F/V.1 (3 October 1991) (*Ad hoc* Meeting of Ministers of
Foreign Affairs, Washington, D.C.); OAS Res. MRE/RES. 2/91 OEA/SER. F/V.1
(8 October 1991) (*Ad hoc* Meeting of Ministers of Foreign Affairs, Washington, D.C.);
Y. Daudet, 'L'ONU et l'OEA en Haïti et le droit international', 38 *AFDI* (1992), p. 89.

[70] *Governor's Island Accord*, OEA/Ser. G CP/INF. 3480/93 (3 July 1993). *United
Nations, The Situation of Democracy and Human Rights in Haiti: Report of the
Secretary-General*, UN Doc. A/47/975-S/26063 (1993).

[71] SC Res. 875, UN SCOR, 3293nd mtg, UN Doc. S/RES/875 (1993).

[72] SC Res. 940, UN SCOR, 49th Sess., 3413th mtg, UN Doc. S/RES/940 (1994).

[73] The multilateral force consisted of 15,000 Americans and 266 soldiers from
different Caribbean countries. France has welcomed Resolution 940 which 'manifeste
la détermination à mener à bien, par tous les moyens nécessaires, la tâche que le
Conseil s'est fixée'. *PEF*, July–August 1994, p. 165. France did not participate in the
multilateral force, although 'approuvant l'intervention américaine', Point de presse
du MAE du 15 septembre 1994, *PEF*, September–October, 1994, p. 100.

[74] According to Resolution 940, the 'significant deterioration of the humanitarian
situation' and 'systematic violation of civil liberties' constitutes a 'threat to peace
and security' under the margin of Chapter VII. SC Res. 940, UN SCOR, 49th Sess.,
3413th mtg, UN Doc. S/RES/940 (1994). W. M. Reisman, 'Haiti and the Validity of
International Action', 89 *AJIL* (1995), p. 82; F. Tesón, 'Collective Humanitarian
Intervention', 17 *Michigan Journal of International Law* (1996), p. 323, at p. 358.

Haitian case is an example of action where the constituent channels for effectuating the value of human dignity in its soft or hard core have been sustained. The amelioration and realisation of their substance is beyond the scope of this study.

Before we proceed with our next case, the evaluation pursued here has drawn to our attention wider issues than would be achieved by a search into legality. One can count as positive aspects the protection offered to endangered individuals and the empowerment of the wider population to realise the values of human dignity. Some actions have been derailed and attained results which can be included synoptically in the devaluation of human dignity. The cases of Somalia and Kosovo which will be discussed immediately below illustrate not only the contradictions of the legal arguments but also the labours in connection with the value of human dignity.

The promotion of human dignity and its 'disvalue': Somalia and Kosovo

As has been argued here, in order to redescribe a situation, we need first to identify the situation and also its legal and theoretical underpinnings. In Somalia, the governmental void and inter-clan war created a humanitarian crisis with refugees fleeing the country and the distribution of humanitarian assistance being impeded. The other parameters of the crisis were the endemic famine, the disastrous economy and the collapse of the state apparatus.[75] In Kosovo, we witnessed the persecution of an ethnic population by their government which had reversed the previous autonomous status for the province. The situation is not characterised by a governmental void but by repression, denial of civil and political rights, the struggle between ethnic militias and governmental forces and the flow of refugees. Other elements which add to the complexity of the situation are the hostile relations between the populations, the injustices which each group claimed it suffered and the manipulation of these tensions by politicians and war-lords who persistently galvanised nationalistic feelings. Reclaiming national myths and ethnic ideologies resulted in the two main groups, the Serbs and the Kosovars, dehumanising and discrediting themselves. Internationally though, with the precedent of Bosnia still fresh in the memory, there were specific recipients of moral approbation.[76]

[75] *Letter Dated 24 November 1992 from the Secretary-General to the President of the Security Council*, UN Doc. S/24859 (1992); *Letter Dated 29 November 1992 from the Secretary-General to the President of the Security Council*, UN Doc. S/24868 (1992); G. Prunier, 'La dimension historique de la crise somalienne', 9 *Relations internationales et strategiques* (1993), p. 89.

[76] For instance it was claimed that 'any people that commits such deeds . . . clearly consists of individuals with damaged faculties of moral judgement and has sunk into a moral abyss from which it is unlikely . . . to emerge unaided'. D. Goldhagen, 'A New Serbia', *The New Republic* (17 May 1999), p. 16, at p. 17.

The reaction by the United Nations in connection with Somalia, the first of the two cases mentioned above, was to adopt Resolutions[77] characterising the situation in Somalia as 'a threat to international peace and security' and authorising humanitarian assistance which culminated with Resolution 794 allowing an international presence.[78] In connection with Kosovo, Resolutions 1203 and 1199[79] characterised the situation in Kosovo as a 'threat to the peace' but did not authorise any intervention.[80] The evaluation of the events by the UN seems to fit squarely the interpretation of its enforcement capabilities which address human rights by legal fiat, by an act of capitulation. Peace, a monipolar objective, also undergirds the aspirations for justice and human rights although in both cases it was the internal situation that amounted to a threat to peace.[81] The ensuing operations are also fraught with disagreement on their legal merits. They can lead to different constructions since these actions had their own configuration which can be revealed and appreciated only after understanding their constituents.

Operation 'Restore Hope' for Somalia is marked by the disagreements between the United Nations and the participant states concerning its purposes and means.[82] The Secretary-General pursued a comprehensive plan of nation-

[77] SC Res. 733, UN SCOR, 47th Sess., 3039th mtg, UN Doc. 737 (1992); SC Res. 767, UN SCOR, 47th Sess., 3101st mtg, UN Doc. 767 (1992); SC Res. 775, UN SCOR, 47th Sess., 3110th mtg, UN Doc. 775 (1992). See also *Letter Dated 20 January 1992 from the Chargé D'Affaires A.I. of the Permanent Mission of Somalia to the United Nations Addressed to the President of the Security Council*, UN SCOR, 47th Sess., UN Doc. S/23445 (1992).

[78] SC Res. 794, UN SCOR, 47th Sess., 3145th mtg, UN Doc. S/RES/794 (1992): '*Recognising* the unique character of the present situation in Somalia and mindful of its deteriorating complex and extraordinary nature . . . *Determining* that the magnitude of the human tragedy caused by the conflict in Somalia, further exacerbated by the obstacles being created to the distribution of humanitarian assistance, constitutes a threat to international peace and security . . .'

[79] *Letter Dated 29 November 1992 from the Secretary-General to the President of the Security Council*, UN SCOR, 47th Sess., UN Doc. S/24868 (1992).

[80] F. L. Kirgis, 'The Kosovo Situation and NATO Military Action', *ASIL Insight*, March 1999. Madeleine Albright claimed that NATO's actions were taken within the framework of Chapter VII of the UN Charter. This is disputed by Professor Arend who says that 'the Security Council has never had any difficulty authorising the use of force if that's what it wants to do'. (26 March 1999) http://www.latimes.com. National Security Council spokesman Mike Hammer claimed that when the United Nations 'passed these resolutions clearly indicat[ed] that if force were necessary to prevent this, that it would be justified'. (29 March 1999) http://www.boston.com/.

[81] According to the Secretary-General, 'le Conseil de sécurité a créé un précédént dans l'histoire de l'ONU: il a décidé pour la première fois d'intervenir militairement à des fins strictement humanitaires'. A/48/1, para. 431. M.-C. Djiena Wembou, 'Validité et portée de la résolution 794 (1992) du Conseil de Sécurité', 5 *African JI & Comp. L* (1993), p. 340.

[82] According to Mr. J. Sills, spokesman for the Secretary-General: 'Bien que cette opération soit hautement appréciée par le Secrétaire général de l'ONU, M. Boutros-Ghali, et qu'elle ait été autorisée par le Conseil de securité, la force militaire unifiée

building involving economic reconstruction, political and social rebuilding and national reconciliation.[83] This transformed its mandate to peace enforcement.[84] The UNOSOM II forces started to pursue a more aggressive policy, gradually appearing to be less the 'Good Samaritans'.[85] Hence, they interfered in a partisan manner in the civil war, causing much havoc and distraction. The Somalis soon became hostile and fights erupted between local people and UN forces.[86] Gradually, the operation was reduced to an obsessive pursuit of General Aideed who was vilified for the ills of the situation.[87] This caused disquiet among the participating Italians, French and the Islamic countries who saw that the mission was losing its purpose.[88] Eventually, after much confusion and with its mandate substantially unfulfilled, the US contingent withdrew, followed by the United Nations contingent. The operation was finally moderated to a traditional peace-keeping one with the caveat that it will only assist the political process in Somalia.[89]

---

n'est pas sous commandement des Nations Unies, et, par conséquent, le drapeau de l'ONU ne sera pas utilisé par la force.' *Le Monde*, 10 December 1992; The French Foreign Minister M. Dumas stated: 'Il ne faut pas qu'une nation, sous prétexte qu'elle est plus forte qu'une autre, s'arroge le droit d'aller faire le gendarme, de remettre de l'ordre.' *Le Monde*, 8 December 1992.

[83] *Report of the Secretary-General submitted in pursuance of paragraphs 18 and 19 of Security Council Resolution 794 (1992)*, S/24992 (19 December 1992); *Supplement to An Agenda for Peace: Position Paper of the Secretary-General on the Occasion of the Fiftieth Anniversary of the United Nations*, UN GAOR, 50th Sess., UN Doc. A/50/60 (1995).

[84] SC Res. 814, UN SCOR, 48th Sess., 3188th mtg, UN Doc. S/RES/814 (1993); *Further Report of the Secretary-General submitted in pursuance of paragraphs 18 and 19 of resolution 794 (1992), proposing that the mandate of UNOSOM II cover the whole country and include enforcement powers under Chapter VII of the Charter*, S/25354, 3 March 1993, and addenda: S/25354/Add. 1, 11 March 1993 and S/25354/Add. 2, 22 March 1993. The US Representative to the Security Council characterised UNOSOM II 'an unprecedented enterprise', S/PV. 3188.

[85] See *Further Report of the Secretary-General*, UN Doc. S/26317 (1993).

[86] The gravest incident took place on 5 June 1993, when 24 Pakistani peacekeepers were ambushed, 56 wounded and 20 Somalis killed. *Executive Summary of the report prepared by Professor Tom Farer of American University, Washington, D.C., on the 5 June 1993 attack on United Nations forces in Somalia*, UN SCOR, 48th Sess., UN Doc. S/26351 (24 August 1993).

[87] SC Res. 837, UN SCOR, 48th Sess., 3229th mtg, UN Doc. S/RES/837 (1993).

[88] Resolution 865 attempts to re-emphasise the aims of the mission which are national reconciliation and the rebuilding of institutions. SC Res. 865, UN SCOR, 48th Sess., 3280th mtg, UN Doc. S/RES/837 (1993).

[89] SC Res. 897, UN SCOR, 49th Sess., 3334th mtg, UN Doc. S/RES/897 (1994); *Further Report of the Secretary-General submitted in pursuance of paragraph 19 of resolution 814 (1993) and paragraph 5 of resolution 865 (1993) on the situation in Somalia, including the 3 October 1993 incident in Mogadishu, and presenting three options for the continuation of UNOSOM II*, S/26738, 12 November 1993; *Further Report of the Secretary-General submitted in pursuance of resolution 886 (1993), reviewing the options for the future mandate of UNOSOM II*, S/1994/12, 6 January 1994.

In Kosovo, on the other hand, the operation was controlled by NATO and the Security Council was held at bay. There was no authorisation for the military operation whose beginning, objectives and termination was determined by NATO.[90] The Security Council has only confirmed the end of hostilities negotiated previously by NATO.[91] The operation was preceded by political negotiations between the Contact Group and Serb and Kosovar representatives. The Rambouillet agreement[92] provided for wide autonomy for the province within the FRY. Its final status would have been decided at the end of a three-year period by a referendum. In order to secure the agreement NATO forces would have been deployed, having access to the whole of the FRY's territory. The negotiation of the agreement was conducted under immense pressure on the parties and the occasional threat of force if they failed to accept it. When it was rejected by the FRY authorities, the military operation started and covered the whole Yugoslav territory. The reasons offered were primarily humanitarian, to avert the humanitarian disaster in Kosovo. As Tony Blair wrote: 'this was a moral cause . . . we now have a chance to build a new internationalism based on values and the rule of law'. The operation was also militated by other geopolitical and strategic factors such as NATO's credibility and identity or the fear of destabilising a volatile region.[93]

After the operation started, a large number of refugees sought refuge in neighbouring countries, fleeing the persecution of the Yugoslav authorities, or became internally displaced. It is questioned whether the human rights nightmare which followed the operation and the refugee problem are evidence

[90] See Statement by NATO Secretary-General, Javier Solana on 23 March 1999: 'failure to meet these demands would lead NATO to take whatever measures were necessary to avert a humanitarian catastrophe. This military action is intended to support the political aims of the international community.' *Keesing's* (1999), p. 42847. The air campaign ended on 10 June 1999. It was announced by NATO Secretary-General Javier Solana following the Military-Technical Agreement between NATO and the FRY signed on 9 June 1999. *Keesing's* (1999), pp. 43006–18.

[91] NATO's Secretary-General informed the UN Secretary-General and the President of the Security Councuil of the cessation of hostilities. The Security Council passed Resolution 1244 on 10 June, welcoming the end of hostilities and the search of a political solution based on the general principles adopted by the G8 on 6 May 1999 and the principles contained in the paper presented by the President of Finland and the Special Representative of the Russian Federation. It also authorised member states and international organisations to establish an international security presence. *Keesing's* (1999), pp. 43006–18.

[92] Interim Agreement for Peace and Self-Government in Kosovo (23 February 1999). http://kosovainfo.com/. *Keesing's* (1999), pp. 42805–67.

[93] T. Blair, 'A New Moral Crusade', *Newsweek* (14 June 1999), p. 38; see also *Hansard* (23 March 1999). Z. Brzezinski, 'Guerre totale contre Milosevic', *Le Monde*, 17 April 1999; Professor M. T. Klare, 'The Clinton Doctrine', *The Nation*, 19 April 1999. I. H. Daalder, 'NATO, the UN, and the Use of Force', Brookings Institution, March 1999, http://www.unausa.org/.

of a predetermined policy by the Yugoslav authorities which justified NATO's action to reverse it or whether they were provoked by the action. The operation was terminated when the Yugoslav authorities accepted NATO's demands of withdrawal, international policing and autonomy. NATO and UN forces entered the province which is divided into sectors. Kosovar refugees are returning (at the time of writing) but a large number of Serbs who lived in the province have fled. There is a new circle of refugees and a number of acts of vengeance which NATO forces are struggling to contain.

In trying to assess the Somali and Kosovo operations, one cannot overlook the fact that there was a human catastrophe developing but also that the operations exacerbated passions and caused much destruction. Political stabilisation and propitiation of democratic institutions which the Somali operation aimed for have not materialised whereas in Kosovo the second stage of the operation is still in progress and its results remain to be analysed at a later date.

It is also important to emphasise the fact that in both cases there is a general feeling of compassion and sympathy for the victims of starvation or persecution which propelled the actions. The international community was initially hesitant to respond, encumbered as it is with such concepts as sovereignty or non-intervention. Reports and images of human agony though have re-sensitised our humanity and precipitated the impetus for international action. Secondary motives can always be invented. However, the fact that those who participated in the action and the people who felt their inner humanity to be affected by the perpetuated savageries belong presumably to different religions or cultures or continents is evidence that our human contextualities within the discursive culture of human dignity can have a universal appeal and reformulate our actions.

The far-fetched mandate of the operations of installing democratic institutions, creating a civic society and setting up national reconciliation coincides with or are prerequisites for the enjoyment of human dignity. However, their implementation was deficient in Somalia. I believe the operation floundered in this respect because the requirements of universality, impartiality and effectiveness which demarcate human dignity were ignored. It should be acknowledged that the building of a secure order may require a certain confrontation with recalcitrant participants. There exists a line to be crossed between a purely facilitative and a facultative operation. The confrontation though, if it has to be, should entail those issues which aspire towards securing human dignity. In Somalia, the operation started from a misconception and a misunderstanding of the society's tribal structure. It then proceeded towards an obsessive vilification and exclusion of a particular powerholder and his clan. It is difficult to imagine how a viable political environment could have been established while exclusion, monomaniac persecution and polarisation were taking place. Consequently, the action lost its impartiality.[94] At this point, it should be pointed out that by 'impartiality' we do not mean indifference and insensitivity; we mean definition of aims and understanding of ground realities and means to pursue these aims. The Somali action had defined the ends of the operation but had been lacking in the assessment of the situation. In a nutshell, it promoted both the value of human dignity in its hard core as protection of life but also its devaluation by creating conditions in its operative phase which were life-threatening. Concerning the soft core of human dignity, it should be said that it failed.

The Kosovo operation should be divided into its military and its civilian phase. Although the conduct of the military operation is not within the purview of this book, it is our belief that it was not the most effective means of protecting lives and it was not impartial. On the contrary, it seemed to punish the Serb people in order to 'degrade' the capabilities of the Serb regime; it created, intentionally or not, thousands of refugees; and it exacerbated the hatred among the ethnic communities which will complicate further any attempt at reconciliation. The civilian phase is still unravelling (at the time of writing) and has the potential of attaining human dignity if it proves to work impartially and restores the confidence of the communities. The creation of a civil society with democratic institution is also its priority. As we have argued, human dignity is in harmony with democracy because the latter assists people through empowerment, self-refection and expression to understand that the society they form is their 'artefact', not a structure superimposed either by religion or politics. Hence, they can realise their humanities through the solidarity which they create and which has become a trait of human dignity.[95]

[94] I. Lewis, J. Mayall, 'Somalia', in J. Mayall (ed.), *The New Interventionism 1991–1994: United Nations Experience in Cambodia, former Yugoslavia and Somalia* (Cambridge, Cambridge University Press, 1996), p. 94; *Report of the Commission of Enquiry established pursuant to resolution 885 (1993) to investigate armed attacks on UNOSOM II personnel*, S/1994/653, 1 June 1994.
[95] R. M. Unger, *Politics, a Work in Constructive Social Theory*, vol. 1 (Cambridge, Cambridge University Press, 1987); Rorty, *Contingency, Irony and Solidarity*, pp. xiii–xvi.

Epilogue

In this book we have dealt with humanitarian intervention *lato sensu* by exploring the interface of facts, rules and ideas, assessing their significance and elucidating the interrelations between the theory and the *praxis* of humanitarian intervention. We have finally opted for a reflective perspective under the discursive model of human dignity which performed a central role in redescribing and redirecting our approach to humanitarian actions. Being a reflective standpoint it succeeds in unveiling the essence of the pursued good, assists in distinguishing from among the mass of information what is relevant and important,[1] accepts modifications and finally allows for reconceptualisation.

Our motivation has been the status of legal reasoning. It oscillates between objectivity, relativism and nihilism[2] by appealing to superseded ontologies or objective procedures, to pluralistic exhortation of tolerance or to a pessimistic view of the world as being incurably unstable. Legal argument adopts certain 'legal technology' in order to decipher and legalise phenomena. Hence, the legal position which considers humanitarian intervention as illegal *per se* is mainly rule-oriented and exhorts the benefits of peace and order. This creates a sense of complacency because it seems successful in containing a situation within the legal matrix. However, it does not address the essential issues which a situation of human catastrophe gives rise to. Such a situation is not an arithmetic condition where the outcome is an objective and determined extrapolation. Hence, a situation involving a human tragedy puts pressure on the norms which lose their rigidity and, thus, grow cracks in their interpretative orthodoxy. Any proffered answer though is only hinted at, dressed in a legalistic language. Consequently, a residue for humanitarian

[1] A. MacIntyre, 'The Indispensability of Political Theory', in D. Miller, L. Siedentop (eds), *The Nature of Political Theory* (Oxford, Clarendon Press, 1983), p. 17.
[2] O. Korhonen, 'New International Law: Silence, Defence or Deliverance?', 7 *EJIL* (1996), p. 1.

actions is acknowledged by expanding the letter of the law. Human tragedies such as those in Rwanda, Somalia or Kosovo are eventually tamed within legal structures but they are presented as distant issues because the *phronesis* of the theorising or 'lawyerising' person is obliterated by the legal structure.

Such an approach is unreflective because by legalising the different aspects of any action, the legal arguments which are produced do not correspond to the essence of the action.[3] It rather reveals the fact that international lawyers disagree and lack understanding of what principles or which of their constituents should apply in a particular case. The cases we have examined show that the offered justifications vary and illustrate the fact that the principles of the legal traditions we have studied illuminate which issues are at stake in each case, how the analysis of the incident should be pursued, what outcomes are desired and what goals should be preserved. Hence, natural law, positivism, realism and their values such as sovereignty, peace or human rights moderate legal reasoning and explain actions through various combinations.

In order to avoid the perpetuation of this dilemma, we have adopted a discursive framework where alternatives are considered by appraising the different variables and policies and their interrelations and weight in certain contexts. Thus, we have tried to discover the conformity of events with the realities of life, detect areas of discord between actual and ideational social life and transform the format of that theoretical matrix by proposing the perspective of human dignity. By looking at the whole action, one can trace the tendencies and value elements linked therein. This comprehensive evaluation is different from the opportunistic interest in 'hard cases' where important values are at stake and also from the automation of the legal argument which cannot travel beyond the legal context.

Human dignity does not depend on any ultimate reason for its validity but this does not mean that reasons which support this ideal for societal and legal development do not exist. Human dignity is based on self-reflection and assessment and creates a sense of solidarity which extends to other human beings. Hence we can recognise our common and shared humanity and realise the essence of any humanitarian action as such rather than as a legal proposition which evades reality. Moreover, human dignity is prospective and perspective, overcoming the sterile and unreflective evaluation and moving towards a more comprehensive approach. Hence, there have been illustrations of the immediate effects of the action which is the protection of life or the long-term effects which is the promotion of a dignified life.

The discursive model of human dignity opens the horizon towards a more human-centred and comprehensive encounter which connects our mind and effective nature with the situation and exposes what is significant in each

[3] A. Carty, 'Introduction: Post-Modern Law', in A. Carty (ed.), *Post-Modern Law* (Edinburgh, Edinburgh University Press, 1990), p. 1.

case. This is the only method for producing meaningful arguments and influencing reality. A reflective attitude towards conditions of human indignity can influence the situation because it entails personal responsibility and through reflective argumentation we can try to reach optimum ends. It instils awareness and direct responsibility which differentiates it from the distant and *ex cathedra* legal discourse that is self-indulgent in the legal world but is eventually alienated. Situations such those in Rwanda, Burundi, Liberia, Kampuchea and Kosovo do not need a 'technological' approach of legality or illegality. This is inadequate and, above all, it hides the personal responsibility of the international lawyer. Personal responsibility and meaningful influence is achieved only through reflection on what is significant and how to achieve it. In order to achieve this, it would be necessary to include in our thinking the whole cadre of indices and also the modes of influencing practice. Consequently, the approach of human dignity pursued in this study contains responsibility, reflection, openness and accountability for the results, but above all a belief in the strength of the theorising person to stand above the thrust of tradition.

Select bibliography

Books

Alexandrov, S. A., *Self-Defence Against the Use of Force in International Law*, The Hague/London/Boston, Kluwer, 1996.

Allott, P., *Eunomia: New Order for a New World*, Oxford, Oxford University Press, 1990.

Allott, P., Carty, T., Koskenniemi, M., Warbrick, C., *Theory and International Law: An Introduction*, London, The British Institute of International and Comparative Law, 1991.

Aquinas, T., *Summa Theologia*, London, Blackfriars, 1964.

Arend, A. C. and Beck, R. J., *International Law and the Use of Force*, London, Routledge, 1993.

Asrat, B., *Prohibition of Force Under the UN Charter: A Study of Art. 2(4)*, Uppsala, Iustus förlag, 1991.

Austin, J., *The Province of Jurisprudence Determined*, London, Weidenfeld & Nicolson, 1954.

Barry, B., *The Liberal Theory of Justice: A Critical Examination of the Principal Doctrines in 'A Theory of Justice' by John Rawls*, Oxford, Clarendon Press, 1973.

Barry, J. A., *The Sword of Justice: Ethics and Coercion in International Politics*, Westport, Connecticut, Praeger, 1998.

Beitz, C. R., *International Ethics*, Princeton, Princeton University Press, 1985.

Bentham, J., *A Fragment on Government*, Oxford, Blackwell, 1967.

Bernstein, R., *Beyond Objectivism and Relativism*, Oxford, Blackwell, 1983.

Bettati, M., *Le droit d'ingérence: mutation de l'ordre international*, Paris, O. Jacob, 1996.

Bluntschli, J. C., *Le droit international codifié*, trans. C. Lardy, 5th edn., Paris, Alcan, 1895.

Bonfils, H., *Manuel de droit international public*, Paris, A. Rousseau, 1905.

Borchard, E., *The Diplomatic Protection of Citizens Abroad or the Law of International Claims*, New York, The Banks Law Publ. Co., 1915.

114

Select bibliography

Bowett, D. W., *Self-Defence in International Law*, Manchester, Manchester University Press, 1958.

Brierly, J. L., *The Law of Nations*, 6th edn. rev. by C. H. M. Waldock, Oxford, Clarendon Press, 1963.

Brownlie, I., *International Law and the Use of Force by States*, Oxford, Clarendon Press, 1963.

Bull, H., *The Anarchical Society: A Study of Order in World Politics*, 2nd edn, London, Macmillan, 1997.

Carlyle, R. W., Carlyle, A. J., *A History of Medieval Political Theory in the West*, Edinburgh, W. Blackwood & Sons, 1903.

Carty, A., *The Decay of International Law? A Reappraisal of the Limits of Legal Imagination in International Affairs*, Manchester, Manchester University Press, 1986.

Cassese, A., *International Law in a Divided World*, Oxford, Clarendon Press, 1986.

Chemiller-Gendreau, M., *Humanité et souverainetés: essai sur la fonction du droit international*, Paris, Editions la Découverte, 1995.

Chen, Lung-Chu, *An Introduction to Contemporary International Law: A Policy Oriented Perspective*, New Haven, Yale University Press, 1989.

Chimni, B., *International Law and World Order: A Critique of Contemporary Approaches*, London, Sage Publications, 1993.

Clark, Jr., J. R., *Right to Protect Citizens in Foreign Countries by Landing Forces, Memorandum of the Solicitor for the Dept. of State, 5 October 1912*, 2nd rev. edn, Washington, US Government Printing Office, 1929.

Claude Jr., I., *Swords into Plowshares*, 4th edn, New York, Random House, 1971.

Coates, A. J., *The Ethics of War*, Manchester, Manchester University Press, 1997.

Corbett, P. E., *Law and Society in the Relations of States*, New York, Harcourt, Brace & Co., 1951.

Corten, O., Klein, P., *Droit d'ingérence ou obligation de réaction*, Bruxelles, Bruylant, 1992.

D'Amato, A. A., *The Concept of Custom in International Law*, Ithaca, Cornell University Press, 1971.

D'Amato, A. A., *Jurisprudence: A Descriptive and Normative Analysis of Law*, Dordrecht, Martinus Nijhoff, 1984.

D'Amato, A. A., *International Law: Process and Prospect*, New York, Transnational Pub., 1987.

Davidson, S., *Grenada: A Study in Politics and the Limits of International Law*, Aldershot, Avebury, 1987.

Damrosch, L. F., Scheffer, D. J., *Law and Force in the New International Order*, Boulder, Westview Press, 1991.

Delivanis, J., *La légitime défense en droit international public moderne*, Paris, Librairie de droit et de jurisprudence, 1971.

D'Entrèves, A. P., *Natural Law: An Introduction to Legal Philosophy*, London, Hutchinson University Library, 1970.

Destexhe, A., *Rwanda and Genocide in the Twentieth Century*, London, Pluto Press, 1994.

Deutsch, K. W. and Hoffmann, S. (eds), *The Relevance of International Law: Essays in Honor of Leo Gross*, Cambridge, Mass., Schenkman Publ., 1968.

de Vattel, E., *Le Droit Des Gens ou Principes de la Loi Naturelle, appliqués à la Conduite et aux Affaires des Nations et des Souverains*, trans. C. G. Fenwick, in J. B. Scott (ed.), *Classics of International Law*, Washington, D. C., Carnegie Institution of Washington, 1916.

de Visscher, C., *Theory and Reality in Public International Law*, 2nd rev. edn, Princeton, Princeton University Press, 1968.

Dewey, J., *The Public and its Problems*, New York, Holt & Co., 1927.

Dinstein, Y., *War, Aggression and Self-defence*, 2nd edn, Cambridge, Grotius Publications, 1994.

Dunn, F. S., *The Protection of Nationals. A Study in the Application of International Law*, Baltimore, J. Hopkins Press, 1932.

Duxbury, N., *Patterns of American Jurisprudence*, Oxford, Clarendon Press, 1995.

Dworkin, R., *Taking Rights Seriously*, London, Duckworth, 1977.

Dworkin, R., *Life's Dominion: An Argument about Abortion and Euthanasia*, London, HarperCollins, 1993.

Falk, R. A., *Legal Order in a Violent World*, Princeton, Princeton University Press, 1968.

Falk, R. A., *Revitalising International Law*, Ames, Iowa University Press, 1989.

Fenwick, C. G., *International Law*, New York, Century Co., 1924.

Finnis, J., *Natural Law and Natural Rights*, Oxford, Clarendon Press, 1980.

Fiore, P., *Nouveau droit international public*, trad. P. Pradier-Fodéré, Paris, A. Durand et Pedone-Lauriel, 1868.

Fiskin, J. S., *Beyond Subjective Morality*, New Haven, Yale University Press, 1984.

Forbes, I. and Hoffmann, M. (eds), *International Relations, Political Theory and the Ethics of Intervention*, London, Macmillan, 1993.

Forsythe, D., *The Politics of International Law*, Boulder, L. Rienner, 1990.

Frank, J., *Law and the Modern Mind*, Gloucester, Mass., Peter Smith, [1930] 1970.

Franck, T. M., *The Power of Legitimacy Among Nations*, New York, Oxford University Press, 1990.

Franck, T. M., *Fairness in International Law and Institutions*, Oxford, Clarendon Press, 1995.

Freeman, M. D. A. (ed.), *Lloyd's Introduction to Jurisprudence*, 6th edn, London, Sweet & Maxwell, 1994.

Friedman, W., *The Changing Structure of International Law*, London, Stevens & Sons, 1964.

Friedmann, W., *Legal Theory*, 5th edn, New York, Columbia University Press, 1967.

Fukuyama, F., *The End of History and the Last Man*, London, Hamish Hamilton, 1992.

Fuller, L. L., *The Morality of Law*, New Haven, Yale University Press, 1969.

Gadamer, H. G., *Philosophical Hermeneutics*, Berkeley, University of California Press, 1976.

Galston, W. A., *Liberal Purposes: Goods, Virtues, and Diversity in the Liberal State*, Cambridge, Cambridge University Press, 1991.

Ganji, M., *International Protection of Human Rights*, Geneva, Librairie E. Droz, 1962.

George, R. P. (ed.), *Natural Law Theory*, Oxford, Clarendon Press, 1992.

Geus, R., *The Idea of a Critical Theory. Habermas and the Frankfurt School*, Cambridge, Cambridge University Press, 1981.

Gilmore, W. C., *The Grenada Intervention: Analysis and Documentation*, London, Mansell Publishing, 1984.

Goodrich, L. M., Hambro, E., Simons, A. P., *Charter of the United Nations*, New York, Columbia University Press, 1969.

Grotius, H., *De Jure Belli ac Pacis Libri Tres*, in *The Classics of International Law*, ed. J. B. Scott, Washington, Carnegie Endowment for International Peace, 1995.

Guéhenno, J.-M., *The End of the Nation-State*, Minneapolis, London, University of Minneapolis Press, 1995.

Guthrie, W. K. C., *A History of Greek Philosophy*, vols I–III, Cambridge, Cambridge University Press, 1969.

Hall, W. E., *A Treatise on International Law*, 8th edn, Oxford, Clarendon Press, 1924.

Harris, J. W., *Law and Legal Science*, Oxford, Oxford University Press, 1979.

Hart, H. L. A., *Essays on Bentham*, Oxford, Clarendon Press, 1982.

Hart, H. L. A., *Essays in Jurisprudence and Philosophy*, Oxford, Clarendon Press, 1983.

Hart, H. L. A., *The Concept of Law*, 2nd rev. edn, Oxford, Clarendon Press, 1994.

Henkin, L., *How Nations Behave: Law and Foreign Policy*, New York, Columbia University Press, 1979.

Henkin, L., *International Law: Politics and Values*, Dordrecht, Martinus Nijhoff, 1995.

Higgins, R., *Problems and Process: International Law and How We Use It*, Oxford, Clarendon Press, 1994.

Hilaire, M., *International Law and the United States Military Intervention in the Western Hemisphere*, The Hague/London/Boston, Kluwer Law International, 1997.

Hinsley, F. H., *Sovereignty*, 2nd edn, Cambridge, Cambridge University Press, 1986.

Hobbes, T., *Leviathan*, R. Tuck (ed.), Cambridge, Cambridge University Press, 1991.

Hoffmann, S., *The Ethics and Politics of Humanitarian Intervention*, Notre Dame, Ind., University of Notre Dame Press, 1996.

Holmes, O. W., *The Common Law*, Boston, Little, Brown, 1881.

Honoré, A. M., *Making Law Bind: Essays Legal and Philosophical*, Oxford, Oxford University Press, 1987.

Jessup, P. C., *A Modern Law of Nations: An Introduction*, New York, Macmillan, 1949.

Kahn, C. H., *Anaximander and the Origins of Greek Cosmology*, New York, Columbia University Press, 1960.

Keeton, G. W., Schwarzenberger, G., *Jeremy Bentham and the Law*, London, Stevens & Sons, 1948.

Kelman, M., *A Guide to Critical Legal Studies*, Cambridge, Mass., Harvard University Press, 1987.

Kelsen, H., *General Theory of Law and State*, trans. Wedberg, A., Cambridge, Mass., Harvard University Press, 1949.

Kelsen, H., *What is Justice?*, Berkeley, University of California Press, 1957.

Kelsen, H., *Théorie pure du droit*, trad. E. Eisemann, Paris, Dalloz, 1962.

Kelsen, H., *The Law of the United Nations*, New York, Praeger, 1964.

Kelsen, H., *The Pure Theory of Law*, trans. Max Knight, Berkeley, Calif., University of California Press, 1967.

Kelsen, H., *Principles of International Law*, 2nd rev. edn, R. W. Tucker (ed.), New York, Holt, Rinehart and Winston, 1968.

Kelsen, H., *Introduction to the Problems of Legal Theory. A Translation of the First Edition of the Reine Rechtslehre or Pure Theory of Law*, trans. B. L. Paulson, S. L. Paulson, Oxford, Clarendon Press, 1992.

Kennedy, D., *International Legal Structures*, Baden-Baden, Nomos Verlagsgesellschaft, 1987.

Kerferd, G. B., *The Sophistic Movement*, Cambridge, Cambridge University Press, 1981.

Koskenniemi, M., *From Apology to Utopia: The Structure of International Legal Argument*, Helsinki, Finnish Lawyers' Publishing Company, 1989.

Kouchner, B., *Le malheur des autres*, Paris, O. Jacob, 1991.

Kuhn, T., *The Structure of Scientific Revolutions*, 2nd edn, Chicago, University Press of Chicago, 1970.

Lauterpacht, H., *The Function of Law in the International Community*, Oxford, Clarendon Press, 1933.

Lauterpacht, H., *International Law and Human Rights*, London, Stevens & Sons, 1950.

Lawrence, T. J., *The Principles of International Law*, 3rd rev. edn, Boston, D. C., Heaton & Co., 1909.

Lillich, R. B., *Humanitarian Intervention and the United Nations*, Charlottesville, University Press of Virginia, 1973.

Llewellyn, K. N., *Jurisprudence: Realism in Theory and Practice*, Chicago, University of Chicago Press, 1962.

Long, A. A., *Hellenistic Philosophy: Stoics, Epicureans, Skeptics*, 2nd edn, London, Duckworth, 1986.

Mackie, J. L., *Ethics. Inventing Right and Wrong*, Harmondsworth, Penguin, 1977.

MacCormick, N., *H. L. A. Hart*, Stanford, Stanford University Press, 1981.

MacCormick, N., Weinberger, O., *An Institutional Theory of Law*, Dordrecht, D. Reidel, 1986.

MacIntyre, A., *After Virtue: A Study in Moral Theory*, London, Duckworth, 1981.

MacIntyre, A., *Whose Justice? Which Rationality?*, London, Duckworth, 1988.

McCoubrey, H., White, N. D., *International Law and Armed Conflict*, Aldershot, Dartmouth, 1992.

McDougal, M. S., Feliciano, F., *Law and Minimum World Public Order: The Legal Regulation of International Coercion*, New Haven, Yale University Press, 1961.

McDougal, M. S., Lasswell, H. D., Chen, Lung-Chu, *Human Rights and World Public Order: The Basic Policies of an International Law of Human Dignity*, New Haven, Yale University Press, 1980.

Miller, D., Siedentop, L., *The Nature of Political Theory*, Oxford, Clarendon Press, 1983.

Morgenthau, H., *Scientific Man Vs. Power Politics*, Chicago, University of Chicago Press, 1946.

Murphy, S. D., *Humanitarian Intervention: The United Nations in an Evolving World Order*, Philadelphia, University of Pennsylvania Press, 1996.

Nardin, T., Mapel, D. R., *Traditions of International Ethics*, Cambridge, Cambridge University Press, 1992.

Nino, C. S., *The Ethics of Human Rights*, Oxford, Clarendon Press, 1991.

Nussbaum, A., *A Concise History of the Law of Nations*, New York, Macmillan, 1947.

Offutt, M., *The Protection of Citizens Abroad*, Baltimore, J. Hopkins Press, 1928.

Oppenheim, L., *International Law: A Treatise*, vol. I, 'Peace', 9th edn, Jennings, Sir R. Y., Watts, Sir A. (eds), London, Longmans, 1992.

Oppenheim, L., *International Law: A Treatise*, vol. II, 'Disputes, War and Neutrality', 7th edn, Lauterpacht, H. (ed.), London, Longmans, 1958.

Plato, *Gorgias*, trans. W. Hammilton, Harmondsworth, Penguin Books, 1960.

Pogge, T. W., *Realising Rawls*, Ithaca, Cornell University Press, 1989.

Pollock, Sir F., *A First Book of Jurisprudence*, 2nd. edn, London, Macmillan, 1904.

Pradier-Fodéré, P., *Traité de droit international public: Européen et Americain*, Paris, G. Pedone-Lauriel, 1885.

Pufendorf, S., *On the Duty of Man and Citizen According to Natural Law*, J. Tully (ed.), trans. M. Silverthorne, Cambridge, Cambridge University Press, 1991.

Rajchman, J., West, C., *Post-Analytic Philosophy*, New York, Columbia University Press, 1985.

Rawls, J., *A Theory of Justice*, Cambridge, Mass., Harvard University Press, 1971.

Raz, J., *The Authority of Law*, Oxford, Clarendon Press, 1979.

Redslob, R., *Traité de droit des gens*, Paris, Recueil Sirey, 1950.

Reisman, W. M., *Nullity and Revision*, New Haven, Yale University Press, 1971.

Roberts, A., Kingsbury, B., *United Nations, Divided World*, Oxford, Clarendon Press, 1993.

Rodley, N. S., *To Lose the Bands of Wickedness*, London, Brassey's, 1992.

Ronzitti, N., *Rescuing Nationals Abroad Through Military Coercion and Intervention on Grounds of Humanity*, Dordrecht/Boston/Lancaster, Martinus Nijjoff, 1985.

Rorty, R., *Philosophy and the Mirror of Nature*, Oxford, Blackwell, 1979.

Rorty, R., *Contingency, Irony and Solidarity*, Cambridge, Cambridge University Press, 1989.

Rosenthal, B., *Étude de l'oeuvre de Myres Smith McDougal en matière de droit international public*, Paris, Librairie générale de droit et de jurisprudence, 1970.

Rubin, A. D., *Ethics and Authority in International Law*, Cambridge, Cambridge University Press, 1997.

Rumble, W. E., *American Legal Realism: Scepticism, Reform, and the Judicial Process*, Ithaca, New York, Cornell University Press, 1968.

Russell, R., Muther, J. E., *A History of the United Nations Charter: The Role of the United States*, Washington, D. C., The Brookings Institution, 1958.

Salmond, J. W., *Jurisprudence*, 6th edn, London, Sweet & Maxwell, 1920.

Sandel, M., *Liberalism and the Limits of Justice*, Cambridge, Cambridge University Press, 1982.

Schachter, O., *International Law in Theory and Practice*, Dordrecht/Boston/London, Martinus Nijhoff, 1991.

Sicilianos, L.-A., *Les réactions décentralisées à l'illicite. Des contre-mesures à la légitime défense*, Paris, L.G.D.J., 1990.

Sophocles, *Antigone*, Grene, D. and Lattimore, R. (eds), *The Complete Greek Tragedies*, Chicago, University of Chicago Press, 1959.

Stone, J., *Legal Controls of International Conflict*, London, Stevens & Sons, 1954.

Stone, J., *Aggression and World Order: A Critique of the United Nations Theories of Aggression*, London, Stevens & Sons, 1958.

Stowell, E., *Intervention in International Law*, Washington, Byrne, 1921.

Lévi-Strauss, C., *Structural Anthropology*, Harmondsworth, Penguin, 1979.

Suarez, F., *De Triplici Virtute Theologica, Fide, Spe, et Charitate 1621*, in J. B. Scott (ed.), *The Classics of International Law*, Oxford, Clarendon Press, 1933.

Sur, S., *L'interprétation en droit international public*, Paris, L.G.D.J., 1974.

Taylor, C., *Philosophy and the Human Sciences: Philosophical Papers 2*, Cambridge, Cambridge University Press, 1985.

Tesón, F. R., *Humanitarian Intervention: An Inquiry Into Law And Morality*, 2nd edn, Dobbs Ferry, N.Y., Transnational Pub., 1996.

Tesón, F. R., *A Philosophy of International Law*, Boulder, Westview Press, 1998.

Thusydides, *The Peloponnesian War*, trans. Rex Warner, Harmondsworth, Penguin Books, 1954.

Unger, R. M., *Knowledge and Politics*, New York, The Free Press, 1975.

Unger, R. M., *Law in Modern Society. Toward a Criticism of Social Theory*, New York, The Free Press, 1976.

Unger, R. M., *The Critical Legal Studies Movement*, Cambridge, Mass., Harvard University Press, 1983.

Unger, R. M., *Social Theory: Its Situation and Its Task. A Critical Introduction to Politics, A Work in Constructive Social Theory*, Cambridge, Cambridge University Press, 1987.

Victoria, F. de, *De Indis et de Jure Belli Relictiones*, in *The Classics of International Law*, ed. J. B. Scott, Buffalo, N.Y., W. S. Hein & Co., 1995.

Vincent, R. J., *Nonintervention and International Order*, Princeton, Princeton University Press, 1974.

von Jehring, R., *Law as a Means to an End*, trans. I. Husic, Boston, Boston Book Comp., 1913.

Walker, T. A., *The Science of International Law*, London, Stevens & Sons, 1893.

Walzer, M., *Just and Unjust Wars: A Moral Argument with Historical Illustrations*, New York, Basic Books, 1977.

Walzer, M., *Thick and Thin: Moral Argument at Home and Abroad*, Notre Dame, Ind., University of Notre Dame Press, 1995.

Weston, B. H., Falk, R. A., D'Amato, A. A., *International Law and World Order*, St. Paul, Minn., West Publishing Co., 1990.

Weinreb, L. L., *Natural Law and Justice*, Cambridge, Mass., Harvard University Press, 1987.

White, N. D., *Keeping the Peace: The United Nations and the Maintenance of International Peace and Security*, Manchester, Manchester University Press, 1993.

Wild, J., *Plato's Modern Enemies and the Theory of Natural Law*, Chicago, University of Chicago Press, 1953.

Williams, B., *Ethics and the Limits of Philosophy*, London, Fontana Press/Collins, 1985.

Winch, P., *The Idea of a Social Science and its Relation to Philosophy*, London, Routledge, 1958.

Wittgenstein, L., *On Certainty*, Oxford, Blackwell, 1969.

Wolff, C., *Jus Gentium Methodo Scientifica Pertractatum*, 1741, trans. J. H. Drake, Oxford, Clarendon Press, 1934.

Select bibliography

Collected essays and papers

Al-Nauimi, N., Meese, R. (eds), *International Legal Issues Arising under the United Nations Decade of International Law*, The Hague/London/Boston, Martinus Nijhoff, 1995.

Beck, R. J., Arend, A. C., Vander Lugt, R. D. (eds), *International Rules: Approaches from International Law and International Relations*, New York, Oxford University Press, 1996.

Bedjaoui, M. (réd. gén.), *Droit International: Bilan et perspectives*, tom. 1–2, Paris, Editions Pedone, 1991.

Blackschield, A. (ed.), *Legal Change: Essays in Honour of Julius Stone*, Sydney, Butterworths, 1983.

Boyle, J. (ed.), *Critical Legal Studies*, Aldershot, Dartmouth, 1992.

Bull, H. (ed.), *Intervention in World Politics*, Oxford, Clarendon Press, 1984.

Butler, W. E. (ed.), *The Non-Use of Force in International Law*, Dordrecht/Boston/London, Martinus Nijhoff, 1989.

Butterfield, H., Wight, M. (eds), *Diplomatic Investigations: Essays in the Theory of International Politics*, London, Allen & Unwin, 1966.

Carty, A. (ed.), *Post-Modern Law*, Edinburgh, Edinburgh University Press, 1990.

Cassese, A. (ed.), *The Current Legal Regulation of the Use of Force*, Dordrecht/Boston/Lancaster, Martinus Nijhoff, 1986.

Cot, J.-P., Pellet, A. (eds), *La Charte des Nations Unies*, 2nd edn, Paris, Economica, 1991.

Falk, R. A., Black, C. E. (eds), *The Future of the International Legal Order*, vols I–IV, Princeton, Princeton University Press, 1969–72.

Falk, R. A., Kratoschwil, F., Medlovitz, S. (eds), *International Law: A Contemporary Perspective*, Boulder, Westview Press, 1985.

Henkin, L. (ed.), *Right v. Might: International Law and the Use of Force*, New York, Council on Foreign Relations Press, 1991.

Jennings, W. I. (ed.), *Modern Theories of Law*, London, Oxford University Press, 1933.

Kairys, D. (ed.), *The Politics of Law: A Progressive Critique*, New York, Pantheon Books, 1982.

Kelsen, H., 'Collective Security under International Law', in *International Law Studies*, Naval War College, Navpapers 15031, Vol. XLIX, Washington, Government Printing Office, 1957.

Koskenniemi, M. (ed.), *International Law*, Aldershot, Dartmouth, 1992.

Lowe, V., Warbrick, C. (eds), *The United Nations and the Principles of International Law*, London, Routledge, 1994.

Luper-Foy, S. (ed.), *Problems of International Justice*, Boulder, Westview Press, 1988.

Lyons, G. M., Mastanduno M. (eds), *Beyond Westphalia? State Sovereignty and International Intervention*, Baltimore, J. Hopkins University Press, 1995.

Makarczyk, J. (ed.), *Essays in International Law in Honour of Judge Manfred Lachs*, The Hague/Boston/Lancaster, Martinus Nijhoff, 1984.

Makarczyk, J. (ed.), *Theory of International Law at the Threshold of the 21st Century. Essays in Honour of Krzysztof Skubiszewski*, The Hague-London-Boston, Kluwer Law International, 1996.

MacDonald, R. St. J., Johnston D. M. (eds), *The Structure and Process of International Law: Essays in Legal Philosophy, Doctrine and Theory*, Dordrecht/Boston/ Lancaster, Martinus Nijhoff, 1983.
Mayall, J. (ed.), *The New Interventionism 1991–1994*, Cambridge, Cambridge University Press, 1996.
Moore, J. N. (ed.), *Law and Civil War in the Modern World*, Princeton, Princeton University Press, 1974.
Nardin, T. (ed.), *The Ethics of War and Peace: Religious and Secular Perspectives*, Princeton, Princeton University Press, 1996.
Pieterse Nederveen, J. (ed.), *World Orders in the Making: Humanitarian Intervention and Beyond*, London, Macmillan, 1998.
Reisman, W. M., Weston B. H. (eds), *Toward World Order and Human Dignity. Essays in Honor of M. S. McDougal*, New York, The Free Press, 1976.
Simma, B. (ed.), *The Charter of the United Nations*, Oxford, Oxford University Press, 1994.
Tur, R., Twining W. (eds), *Essays on Kelsen*, Oxford, Clarendon Press, 1986.
Yasuaki, Onuma (ed.), *A Normative Approach to War. Peace, War, and Justice in Hugo Grotius*, Oxford, Clarendon Press, 1993.

Articles

'Agora: US Forces in Panama: Defenders, Aggressors or Human Rights Activists?', 84 *AJIL* (1990), pp. 494–524.
Akehurst, M., 'The Use of Force to Protect Nationals Abroad', 5 *International Relations* (1977), p. 3.
Allott, P., 'Language, Method and the Nature of International Law', 45 *BYBIL* (1971), p. 79.
Allott, P., 'Reconstituting Humanity – New International Law', 3 *EJIL* (1992), p. 219.
Allott, P., 'The Concept of International Law', 10 *EJIL* (1999), p. 31.
Anand, R. P., 'Sovereign Equality of States in International Law', 197 *RC* (1986 II), p. 9.
Arangio-Ruiz, G., 'The Normative Role of the General Assembly of the United Nations and the Declaration of Principles of Friendly Relations', 137 *RC* (1972 III), p. 418.
Arbour, J., 'Aspects juridiques de la crise americano-iranienne', 21 *Les cahiers de droit* (1980), p. 367.
Arend, A. C., 'International Law and the Recourse to Force: A Shift in Paradigms', 27 *Stanford Journal of International Law* (1990), p. 1.
Ashley, R., Walker, R. B. J., 'Reading Dissidence/Writing the Discipline: Crisis and the Question of Sovereignty in International Studies', 34 *International Studies Quarterly* (1990), p. 367.
Bart, J., 'Le droit, la loi, les moeurs', *Droit et Société* (1990), p. 45.
Basdevant, J., 'Règles générales du droit de la paix', 58 *RC* (1936 IV), p. 471.
Bazyler, M. J., 'Re-examining the Doctrine of Humanitarian Intervention in Light of the Atrocities in Kampuchea and Ethiopia', 23 *Stanford Journal of International Law* (1987), p. 547.

Select bibliography

Behuniak, T. E., 'The Law of Unilateral Humanitarian Intervention by Armed Force', 79 *Military Law Review* (1978), p. 157.

Beitz, C. R., 'Nonintervention and Communal Integrity', 9 *Philosophy & Public Affairs* (1979–80), p. 354.

Berman, A., 'In Mitigation of Illegality: The US Invasion of Panama', 79 *Kentucky Law Journal* (1990–91), p. 735.

Bettati, M., 'Un droit d'ingérence?', *RGDIP* (1991), p. 640.

Bidschelder, R. L., 'La délimitation des competences des Nations Unies', 108 *RC* (1963 I), p. 307.

Bobbio, N., '"Sein" and "Sollen" in Legal Science', LVI *Archiv für Rechts- und Sozialphilosophie* (1970), p. 7.

Bogen, D. S., 'The Law of Humanitarian Intervention: United States Policy in Cuba 1898 and in the Dominican Republic 1966', 7 *Harvard International Law Club Journal* (1966), p. 296.

Bolton, J. R., 'Wrong Turn in Somalia', 73 *Foreign Affairs* (1994), p. 61.

Boutin, M., 'Somalia: The Legality of U.N. Forcible Humanitarian Intervention', 17 *Suffolk Transnational Law Review* (1994), p. 138.

Bowett, D. W., 'The Use of Force in the Protection of Nationals', 43 *Transanctions of Grotius Society of International Law* (1957), p. 111.

Boyle, F. A., 'The Entebbe Hostage Crisis', 22 *Indian Journal of International Law* (1982), p. 199.

Boyle, J., 'Towards Understanding the Principle of Double Effect', 90 *Ethics* (1980), p. 527.

Boyle, J., 'Ideals and Things: International Legal Scholarship and the Prison-house of Language', 26 *Harvard ILJ* (1985), p. 327.

Boyle, J., '*Just and Unjust Wars*: Casuistry and the Boundaries of the Moral World', 11 *Ethics & International Affairs* (1997), p. 83.

Brierly, J. L., 'International Law and Resort to Armed Force', 4 *Cambridge Law Journal* (1932), p. 308.

Briggs, H. W., 'The International Court of Justice Lives Up to its Name', 81 *AJIL* (1987), p. 78.

Brilmayer, L., 'The Odd Advantage of Reliable Enemies', 32 *Harvard ILJ* (1991), p. 331.

Brownlie, I., 'The Use of Force in Self-Defence', 37 *BYBIL* (1961), p. 183.

Bula-Bula, S., 'La doctrine d'ingérence humanitaire revisitée' 9 *African JI & Comp. L* (1997), p. 600.

Burmester, B., 'On Humanitarian Intervention: The New World Order', 1 *Utah Law Review* (1994), p. 269.

Carty, A., 'Critical International Law: Recent Trends in the Theory of International Law', 2 *EJIL* (1991), p. 66.

Carty, A., 'The Continuing Influence of Kelsen on the General Perception of the Discipline of International Law', 9 *EJIL* (1998), p. 344.

Cassese, A., 'Ex iniuria ius oritur: Are We Moving Towards International Legitimation of Forcible Humanitarian Countermeasures in the World Community?', 10 *EJIL* (1999), p. 23.

Cass, D. Z., 'Navigating the Newstream: Recent Critical Scholarship in International Law', 65 *Nordic Journal of International Law* (1996), p. 341.

Charlesworth, H., 'Customary International Law and the Nicaragua Case', 11 *Australian YBIL* (1987), p. 1.

123

Charney, J. I., 'Anticipatory Humanitarian Intervention in Kosovo', 93 *AJIL* (1999), p. 834.

Chilstrom, R. M., 'Humanitarian Intervention under Contemporary International Law: A Policy-Oriented Approach', 1 *Yale Studies of World Public Order* (1974), p. 93.

Chinkin, C. M., 'Kosovo: A "Good" or "Bad" War', 93 *AJIL* (1999), p. 841.

Christenson, G. A., 'The World Court and Jus Cogens', 81 *AJIL* (1987), p. 101.

Chroust, A. H., 'The Philosophy of Law of St Thomas Aquinas: His Fundamental Ideas and Some of his Historical Precursors', 19 *American Journal of Jurisprudence* (1974), p. 1.

Clark, G., 'English Practice with Regard to Reprisals by Private Persons', 27 *AJIL* (1927), p. 694.

Cohen, J., 'The Political Element in Legal Theory: A Look at Kelsen's Pure Theory', 88 *Yale LJ* (1978), p. 1.

Corten, O., Klein, P., 'Droit d'ingerence ou obligation de réaction non armée', 23 *Revue belge de droit international* (1990), p. 368.

Corten, O., Klein, P., 'Devoir d'ingerence ou droit de réaction armée collective?', 24 *Revue belge de droit international* (1991), p. 46.

Corten, O., Klein, P., 'L'autorisation de recourir à la force à des fins humanitaires: droit d'ingérence ou retour aux sources?', 4 *EJIL* (1993), p. 506.

Corten, O., 'La résolution 940 du conseil de sécurité autorisant une intervention militaire en Haïti: L'emergence d'un principe de légitimité démocratique en droit international?', 6 *EJIL* (1995), p. 116.

Cossman, B., 'Reform, Revolution, or Retrenchment? International Human Rights in the Post Cold War Era', 32 *Harvard ILJ* (1991), p. 339.

Coussirat-Coustère, V., 'L'arrêt de la Cour internationale de Justice sur le personnel diplomatique et consulaire américain à Téhéran', 26 *AFDI* (1980), p. 201.

Cowan, T. A., 'Law Without Force', 59 *California Law Review* (1971), p. 683.

D'Amato, A. A., 'Is International Law Really Law', 72 *Northwestern University Law Review* (1984–85), p. 1293.

D'Amato, A. A., 'Trashing Customary International Law', 81 *AJIL* (1987), p. 101.

D'Angelo, J. R., 'Resort to Force by States to Protect Nationals: The US Rescue Mission to Iran and its Legality under International Law', 21 *Va JIL* (1981), p. 485.

Daudet, Y., 'L'ONU et l'OEA en Haïti et le droit international', 38 *Annuaire Français de droit international* (1992), p. 89.

David, E., 'Portée et limite du principe de non intervention', 23 *Revue belge de droit international* (1990), p. 350.

Delbrück, J., 'A Fresh Look at Humanitarian Intervention Under the Authority of the United Nations', 67 *Indiana Law Journal* (1992), p. 887.

De Schutter, B., 'Humanitarian Intervention: A United Nations Task', 3 *California Western International Law Journal* (1972), p. 21.

De Schutter, B., 'Les CLS au pays du droit international public', *Droit et Societé* (1992), p. 585.

de Visscher, C., 'Cour général de principes de droit international public', 86 *RC* (1954 II), p. 445.

de Visscher, P., 'Cours général de droit international public', 136 *RC* (1972 II), p. 7.

Dieguez, R. P., 'The Grenada Intervention: "Illegal" in Form, Sound as Policy', *NYUJ Int'l L & Pol.* (1984), p. 1167.

Select bibliography

Dinh, N. Q., 'La légitime défense d'après la Charte de Nations Unies', XIX *RGDIP* (1948), p. 783.

Djiena Wembou, M.-C., 'Validité et portée de la résolution 794 1992 du Conseil de Sécurité', 5 *African JI & Comp. L* (1993), p. 340.

Domestici-Met, M.-J., 'Aspects juridiques récentes de l'assistance humanitaire', *AFDI* (1989), p. 117.

Donnelly, J., 'Human Rights, Humanitarian Intervention and American Foreign Policy', 37 *Journal of International Affairs* (1984), p. 311.

Doppelt, G., 'Walzer's Theory of International Relations', 8 *Philosophy & Public Affairs* (1978–79), p. 3.

Doppelt, G., 'Statism without Foundations', 9 *Philosophy & Public Affairs* (1980), p. 398.

Doswald-Beck, L., 'The Legality of the United States Intervention in Grenada', 31 *Neth. ILR* (1984), p. 355.

Duke, S., 'The State and Human Rights: Sovereignty Versus Humanitarian Intervention', 12 *International Relations* (1994), p. 25.

Dupuy, P.-M., 'Sécurité collective et organisation de la paix', 97 *RGDIP* (1993), p. 617.

Dworkin, R., 'What is Equality? Part 3: The Place of Liberty', 73 *Iowa Law Review* (1987), p. 1.

Eisemann, P., 'L'arrêt de la C.I.J. du 27 juin 1986 (fond), dans l'affaire des activités militaires et paramilitaires au Nicaragua et contre celui-ci', 32 *AFDI* (1986), p. 153.

Ellerman, C., 'Command of Sovereignty Gives Way to Concern for Humanity', 26 *Vanderbilt J Tran. L* (1993), p. 341.

Falk, R. A., 'International Jurisdiction; Horizontal and Vertical Conceptions of Legal Order', 32 *Temple Law Quarterly* (1959), p. 295.

Falk, R. A., 'Kosovo, World Order, and the Future of International Law', 93 AJIL (1999), p. 847.

Fawcett, J. E. S., 'Intervention in International Law, A Study of Some Recent Cases', 103 *RC* (1961 II), p. 347.

Fairley, H. S., 'State Actors, Humanitarian Intervention', 10 *Ga. JI & Comp. L* (1980), p. 29.

Farer, T. J., 'The Regulation of Foreign Intervention in Civil Armed Conflict', 142 *RC* (1974 II), p. 291.

Fenwick, C. G., 'The Dominican Republic: Intervention or Collective Self-defence', 60 *AJIL* (1966), p. 64.

Finnis, J., 'Liberalism and Natural Law Theory', 45 *Mercer Law Review* (1994), p. 687.

Fisher, R., 'Bringing Law to Bear on Governments', 74 *Harvard L Rev.* (1961).

Fiskin, J., 'Liberal Theory and the Problem of Justification', *Nomos* XXVIII, p. 207.

Fitzmaurice, G. G., 'The Foundations of the Authority of International Law and the Problem of Enforcement', 19 *Modern L Rev.* (1966), p. 1.

Fonteyne, J.-P. L., 'The Customary International Law Doctrine of Humanitarian Intervention: Its Current Validity Under the United Nations Charter', 4 *California Western International Law Journal* (1973–74), p. 203.

Forsythe, D., 'Human Rights in a Post Cold War World', 15 *Fletcher Forum* (1991), p. 54.

Franck, T. M., 'Who Killed Article 2(4)? or the Changing Norms Governing the Use of Force by States', 64 *AJIL* (1970), p. 809.

Franck, T. M., Rodley, N. S., 'The Law, the United Nations and Bangladesh', 2 *Israel YBHR* (1972), p. 142.

Franck, T. M., Rodley, N. S., 'After Bangladesh: The Law of Humanitarian Intervention by Military Force', 67 *AJIL* (1973), p. 245.

Franck, T. M., 'United Nations Based Prospects for a New Global Order', 22 *New York University Journal of International Law & Policy* (1990), p. 601.

Franck, T. M., 'The Emerging Right to Democratic Governance', 86 *AJIL* (1992), p. 46.

Franck, T. M., 'Break It, Don't Fake It', 78 *Foreign Affairs* (1999), p. 116.

Franck, T. M., 'Lessons from Kosovo', 93 *AJIL* (1999), p. 857.

Gardot, A., 'Jean Bodin. Sa place parmi les fondateurs du droit international', 50 *RC* (1934 IV), p. 545.

Gaus, G., 'Subjective Value and Justificatory Political Theory', *Nomos* XXVIII, p. 241.

Georgiev, D., 'Politics or Rule of Law: Deconstruction and Legitimacy in International Law', 4 *EJIL* (1993), p. 1.

Gill, T., 'The Law of Armed Attack in the Context of the Nicaragua Case', 1 *Hague YBIL* (1988), p. 30.

Giraud, E., 'La théorie de la legitime défense', 49 *RC* (1934), p. 687.

Giraud, E., 'L'interdiction du recours à la force. La théorie et la pratique des Nations Unies', 67 *RGDIP* (1963), p. 501.

Giraud, E., 'Le droit international public et la politique', 110 *RC* (1963 III), p. 419.

Glennon, M. J., 'The New Interventionism: The Search of a Just International Law', 78 *Foreign Affairs* (1999), p. 2.

Gordon, E., 'Use of Force for the Protection of Nationals Abroad; The Entebbe Incident', 9 *Case Western Reserve Journal of International Law* (1977), p. 177.

Gordon, E., 'Article 2(4) in Historical Context', 10 *Yale JIL* (1984–85), p. 271.

Green, L. C., 'Armed Conflict, War and Self-Defence', 6 *Archiv des Völkerrechts* (1956–57), p. 387.

Green, L. C., 'Rescue at Entebbe', 6 *Israel YBHR* (1976), p. 312.

Green, L. C., 'The Teheran Embassy Incident', 18 *Archiv des Völkerrechts* (1980), p. 1.

Greig, D., 'Self-Defence and the Security Council', 40 *ICLQ* (1991), p. 366.

Grisez, G., Boyle, J., Finnis, J., 'Practical Principles, Moral Truth, and Ultimate Ends', 32 *American Journal of Jurisprudence* (1987), p. 99.

Gross, L., 'The Peace of Westphalia 1648–1948', 42 *AJIL* (1948), p. 20.

Haggenmacher, P., 'La doctrine des deux éléments du droit coutumier dans la pratique et la Cour Internationale', 90 *RGDIP* (1986), p. 5.

Hargrove, J. L., 'The Nicaragua Judgment and the Future of the Law of Force and Self-Defence', 81 *AJIL* (1987), p. 135.

Hart, H. L. A., 'Kelsen Visited', *UCLA Law Review* (1963), p. 709.

Hart, H. L. A., 'Bentham on Sovereignty', 2 *Irish Jurist* (1967), p. 327.

Hasnas, J., 'Back to the Future: From Critical Legal Studies Forward to Legal Realism, or How Not to Miss the Point of the Indeterminacy Argument', 45 *Duke Law Journal* (1995), p. 84.

Hassan, F., 'Realpolitik in International Law: After the Tanzanian-Ugandan Conflict', 17 *Willammette Law Review* (1981), p. 859.

Henkin, L., 'The Reports of the Death of Article 2(4) are Greatly Exaggerated', 65 *AJIL* (1971), p. 544.

Henkin, L., 'General Course in Public International Law', 216 *RC* (1989 IV), p. 148.

Henkin, L., 'The Invasion of Panama Under International Law: A Dangerous Precedent', 29 *Col. J Trans. L* (1991), p. 293.

Henkin, L., 'Kosovo and the Law of "Humanitarian Intervention"', 93 *AJIL* (1999), p. 824.

Hoffmann, M., 'Critical Theory and the Inter-Paradigm Debate', 16 *Millennium: Journal of International Studies* (1987), p. 231.

Hunt, A., 'The Ideology of Law', 19 *Law & Society Review* (1985), p. 11.

Hurrell, A., 'Collective Security and International Order Revisited', XI *International Relations* (1992), p. 37.

Hutchison, A. C., Monaham, P. J., 'Law, Politics and the Critical Legal Scholars: The Unfolding Drama of American Legal Thought', 36 *Stanford Law Review* (1984), p. 199.

Hyde, A., 'The Concept of Legitimation in the Sociology of Law', *Wisconsin Law Review* (1983), p. 379.

'International Law and The United States Action in Grenada: A Report', 18 *Int'l Law*, 1984, p. 331.

Jeffrey, A., 'The American Hostages in Teheran', 30 *ICLQ* (1981), p. 717.

Jennings, R. Y., 'General Course on Principles of International Law', 121 *RC* (1967 II), p. 325.

Jones, T., 'The Haitian Refugee Crisis', 15 *Michigan Journal of International Law* (1993), p. 77.

Joyner, C. C., 'The United States Action in Grenada: Reflections on the Lawfulness of Invasion', 78 *AJIL* (1984), p. 131.

Kairys, D., 'Law and Politics', 52 *Georgia Law Review* (1984), p. 243.

Kaufmann, E., 'Règles générales du droit de la paix', 54 *RC* (1935 IV), p. 309.

Kelsen, H., 'The Pure Theory of Law and Analytical Jurisprudence', 55 *Harvard L Rev* (1941), p. 44.

Kelsen, H., 'Collective Security and Collective Self-Defence under the Charter of the United Nations', 42 *AJIL* (1948), p. 783.

Kelsen, H., 'Théorie du Droit International Public', 84 *RC* (1953 III), p. 1.

Kelsen, H., 'Professor Stone and the Pure Theory of Law', 17 *Stanford Law Review* (1965), p. 1130.

Kennedy, D., 'Form and Substance in Private Law Adjudication', 89 *Harvard L Rev* (1976), p. 1685.

Kennedy, D., 'The Structure of Blackstone's Commentaries', 18 *Buffalo Law Review*, (1979), p. 205.

Kennedy, D., 'Theses about International Legal Discourse', 23 *German YBIL* (1980), p. 353.

Kennedy, D., 'Critical Theory, Structuralism and Contemporary Legal Scholarship', 21 *New England Law Review* (1985–86), p. 209.

Kennedy, D., 'International Legal Education', 26 *Harvard ILJ* (1985), p. 361.

Kennedy, D., 'A New Stream of International Law Scholarship', 7 *Wisconsin International Law Journal* (1988), p. 1.

Kirkpatrick, J., 'Review Essay: The Use of Force in the Law of Nations', 16 *Yale JIL* (1991), p. 583.

Kirgis, F. L., Jr., 'Custom on a Sliding Scale', 81 *AJIL* (1987), p. 146.

Kiwanuka, R., 'The International Human Rights Implications of the ICJ's Decision in Nicaragua', 57 *Nordic Journal of International Law* (1988), p. 470.

Knisbacher, M., 'The Entebbe Operation: A Legal Analysis of Israel's Rescue Action', 12 *Journal of International Law & Economics* (1977), p. 57.

Korhonen, O., 'New International Law: Silence, Defence or Deliverance?', 7 *EJIL* (1996), p. 1.

Korhonen, O., 'Liberalism and International Law: A Centre Projecting a Periphery', 65 *Nordic Journal of International Law* (1996), p. 481.

Koskenniemi, M., 'The Politics of International Law', 1 *EJIL* (1990), p. 4.

Koskenniemi, M., 'The Future of Statehood', 32 *Harvard ILJ* (1991), p. 392.

Koskenniemi, M., 'The Police in the Temple, Order, Justice and the UN: A Dialectical View', 6 *EJIL* (1995), p. 325.

Kranz, J., 'Notion de souveraineté et de droit international', 30 *Archiv des Völkerrechts* (1992), p. 411.

Kratoschwil, F., 'Thrasymachos Revisited', 37 *Journal of International Affairs* (1984), p. 343.

Kratoschwil, F., 'Is International Law Proper Law', 69 *Archives of the Philosophy of Law & Socical Philosophy* (1983), p. 13.

Krift, T., 'Self-Defence and Self-Help: The Israeli Raid on Entebbe', 4 *Brooklyn Journal of International Law* (1977), p. 43.

Krygier, M., 'The Concept of Law and Social Theory', 2 *Oxford Journal of Legal Studies* (1982), p. 155.

Kunz, J. L., 'Individual and Collective Self-Defence in Article 51 of the Charter of the United Nations', 41 *AJIL* (1947), p. 877.

Lachs, M., 'General Course in Public International Law', 169 *RC* (1980 IV), p. 9.

Lasswell, H. D., McDougal, M. S., 'Legal Education and Public Policy: Professional Training in the Public Interest', 52 *Yale LJ* (1943), p. 203.

Lasswell, H. D., McDougal, M. S., 'Criteria for a Theory About Law', 44 *South California Law Review* (1971), p. 362.

Lauterpacht, H., 'The Grotian Tradition in International Law', 23 *BYBIL* (1946), p. 1.

Lauterpacht, E., 'The Development of the Law of International Organizations by the Decisions of International Tribunals', 152 *RC* (1976 IV), p. 380.

Leben, C., 'Hans Kelsen and the Advancement of International Law', 9 *EJIL* (1998), p. 287.

Le Fur, L., 'La théorie du droit naturel depuis le XVIIe siècle et la doctrine moderne', 18 *RC* (1927 III), p. 471.

Levitin, M. J., 'The Law of Force and the Force of Law. Grenada, the Falklands and Humanitarian Intervention', 27 *Harvard ILJ* (1986), p. 621.

Lillich, R. B., 'Forcible Self-Help by States to Protect Human Rights', 53 *Iowa Law Review* (1967), p. 325.

Lillich, R. B., 'Intervention to Protect Human Rights', 15 *McGill Law Journal* (1969), p. 205.

Lillich, R. B., 'Forcible Self-Help under International Law', 22 *Naval War College Review* (1970), p. 61.

Lillich, R. B., 'Duties of States Regarding the Civil Rights of Aliens', 161 *RC* (1978 III), p. 329.

Select bibliography

Lillich, R. B., 'Forcible Protection of Nationals Abroad. The Liberian Incident of 1990', 35 *German YBIL* (1992), p. 205.

Lillich, R. B., 'Humanitarian Intervention through the United Nations', 53 *ZaöRV* (1993), p. 557.

Livingston, D., 'Note: Round and Round the Bramble Bush: From Legal Realism to Critical Legal Studies', 95 *Harvard L Rev* (1982), p. 1669.

Luban, D., 'Just War and Human Rights', 9 *Philosophy & Public Affairs* (1979–80), p. 160.

MacCormick, N., 'Natural Law Reconsidered', 1 *Oxford Journal of Legal Studies* (1981), p. 99.

Macdonald, R. St. J., 'The Nicaragua Case', 24 *Canadian YBIL* (1986), p. 127.

Maguire, J. P., 'Plato's Theory of Natural Law', 10 *Yale Classical Studies* (1947), p. 151.

Marcus-Helmons, S., 'Le droit d'intervention, un corollaire des droits de l'homme?', 12 *Revue Trimestrielle des Droits de l'Homme* (1992), p. 471.

Margo, R., 'The Legality of the Entebbe Raid', 94 *South African Law Journal* (1977), p. 306.

Itsouhou Mbadinga, M., 'Considérations sur la légalité des interventions militaires étatiques dans la crise du Rwanda (1990–1994)', 10 *African JI & Comp. L* (1998), p. 1.

McBride, W. L., 'The Essential Role of Models and Analogies in the Philosophy of Law', 43 *New York University Law Review* (1968), p. 53.

McDougal, M. S., 'The Law School of the Future: From Legal Realism to Policy Science in the World Community', 56 *Yale LJ* (1946–47), p. 1345.

McDougal, M. S., 'International Law, Power and Policy: A Contemporary Conception', 82 *RC* (1953 I), p. 133.

McDougal, M. S., 'Remarks on International Concern versus Domestic Jurisdiction', 48 *Proc. ASIL* (1954), p. 120.

McDougal, M. S., Feliciano, F. P., 'The Legal Regulation of Resort to International Coercion: Aggression and Self-Defence in Policy Perspective', 68 *Yale LJ* (1958–59), p. 1057.

McDougal, M. S., 'Perspectives for an International Law of Human Dignity', 53 *Proc. ASIL* (1959), p. 107.

McDougal, M. S., 'Authority to Use Force on the High Seas', 20 *Naval War College Review* (1967), p. 19.

McDougal, M. S., Lasswell, H. D., Reisman, M. W., 'Theories about International Law: Prologue to a Configurative Jurisprudence', 8 *Va JIL* (1968), p. 188.

McDougal, M. S., Lasswell, H. D., Chen, Lung-Chu, 'Human Rights and World Public Order: A Framework for Policy-Oriented Inquiry', 63 *AJIL* (1969), p. 237.

McDougal, M. S., 'International Law and Social Science: A Mild Plea in Avoidance', 66 *AJIL* (1972), p. 77.

McDougal, M., 'Law and Minimum World Public Order', 3 *UCLA Pacific Basin Law Journal* (1984), p. 21.

Mirvahabi, F., 'Entebbe: Validity of Claims in International Law', *Philippine Yearbook of International Law* (1977), p. 58.

Montague, F., 'Two Concepts of Rights', 9 *Philosophy & Public Affairs* (1980), p. 372.

Moore, J. N., 'Prolegomenon to the Jurisprudence of Myres McDougal and Harold Lasswell', 54 *Va LR* (1968), p. 662.

Moore, J. N., 'The Control of Foreign Intervention in Internal Conflict', 9 *Va JIL* (1969), p. 205.

Moore, J. N., 'Grenada and the International Double Standard', 78 *AJIL* (1984), p. 145.

Moore, M., 'Moral Reality', *Wisconsin Law Review* (1982), p. 1061.

Morgenthau, H. J., 'Positivism, Functionalism, and International Law', 34 *AJIL* (1940), p. 260.

Morrison, F. L., 'Legal Issues in the Nicaragua Opinion', 81 *AJIL* (1987), p. 160.

Mouton, J.-D., 'La notion d'état et le droit international public', 16 *Droits: Rev française de théorie juridique* (1992), p. 45.

Mouton, J.-D., 'La crise Rwandaise de 1994 et les Nations Unies', *AFDI* (1994), p. 214.

Nanda, V. P., 'The United States' Action in the 1965 Dominican Crisis: Impact on World Order – Part I', 43 *Denver Law Journal* (1966), p. 439.

Nanda, V. P., 'The United States Action in the 1965 Dominican Crisis: Impact on World Order – Part II', 44 *Denver Law Journal* (1967), p. 225.

Nanda, V. P., 'A Critique of the UN Inaction in Bangladesh', 49 *Denver Law Journal* (1972), p. 53.

Nanda, V. P., 'The United States' Armed Intervention in Grenada – Impact on World Order', 14 *California Western International Law Journal* (1984), p. 395.

Nanda, V. P., 'The Use of Force in the Post Cold War Era', 20 *Denver Journal of International Law & Policy* (1991), p. 1.

Nino, C. S., 'Positivism and Communitarism between Human Rights and Democracy', 7 *Ration Juris* (1994), p. 14.

Nolte, G., 'Restoring Peace by Regional Action: International Legal Aspects of the Liberian Conflict', 53 *ZaöRV* (1993), p. 603.

Onuf, N. G., 'The International Legal Order as an Idea', 73 *AJIL* (1979), p. 244.

Onuf, N. G., 'Sovereignty: Outline of a Conceptual History', 16 *Alternatives* (1991), p. 425.

Onuf, N. G., 'Civitas Maxima: Wolff, Vattel and the Fate of Republicanism', 88 *AJIL* (1994), p. 280.

Ouguergouz, F., 'La tragédie Rwandaise du printemps 1994: quelques considérations sur les premiéres réactions de l'organisation des Nations Unies', 100 *RGDIP* (1996), p. 149.

Paden, R., 'Reconstructing Rawls's Law of Peoples', 11 *Ethics & International Affairs* (1997), p. 215.

Paulson, S. L., 'The Neo-Kantian Dimension of Kelsen's Pure Theory of Law', 12 *Oxford Journal Legal Studies* (1992), p. 311.

Paulson, S. L., 'Kelsen's Legal Theory: The Final Round', 12 *Oxford Journal Legal Studies* (1992), p. 265.

Paust, J. J., 'Entebbe and Self-help: The Israeli Response to Terrorism', 2 *The Fletcher Forum* (1978), p. 86.

Paust, J. J., 'The Concept of Norm: A Consideration of the Jurisprudential Views of Hart, Kelsen and McDougal – Lasswell', 52 *Temple Law Quarterly* (1979), p. 9.

Pearse, K., Forsythe, D., 'Humanitarian Intervention and International Law', 45 *Austrian Journal of Public International Law* (1993), p. 1.

Perez, V., 'La protection d'humanité en droit international', 5 *Revue belge de droit international public* (1969), p. 401.

Plofchan, T., 'Article 51 Limits on Self Defence', 13 *Michigan Journal of International Law* (1992), p. 336.

Porter, P. B., 'L'intervention en droit international modern', 32 *RC* (1930 II), p. 607.

Pound, R., 'Philosophical Theory and International Law', I *Bibliotheca Visseriana* (1923), p. 71.

Purvis, N., 'Critical Legal Studies in International Law', 32 *Harvard ILJ* (1991), p. 32.

Quigley, J., 'The Legality of the United States Invasion of Panama', 15 *Yale JIL* (1990), p. 276.

Raby, J., 'The State of Necessity and the Use of Force to Protect Nationals', 26 *Canadian YBIL* (1988), p. 253.

Rawls, J., 'Justice as Fairness: Political not Metaphysical:, 14 *Philosophy & Public Affairs* (1985), p. 223.

Rawls, J., 'The Idea of an Overlapping Consensus', 7 *Oxford Journal of Legal Studies* (1987), p. 1.

Rawls, J., 'The Priority of Right and Ideas of the Good', 17 *Philosophy & Public Affairs* (1988), p. 251.

Rawls, J., 'The Domain of the Political and Overlapping Consensus', 64 *New York University Law Review* (1989), p. 233.

Rawls, J., 'The Law of Peoples', 20 *Critical Inquiry* (1993), p. 36.

Raz, J., 'Kelsen's Theory of the Basic Norm', 19 *American Journal of Jurisprudence* (1974), p. 94.

Raz, J., 'The Purity of the Pure Theory', *Revue Internationale de Philosophie* (1983), p. 442.

Raz, J., 'Facing Diversity: The Case of Epistemic Diversity', 19 *Philosophy & Public Affairs* (1990), p. 3.

Reisman, W. M., 'Coercion and Self-Determination: Construing Charter Article 2(4)', 78 *AJIL* (1984), p. 642.

Reisman, W. M., 'Article 2(4): The Use of Force in Contemporary International Law', *Proceedings of the American Society of International Law* (1984), p. 74.

Reisman, W. M., 'International Incidents: An Introduction to a New Genre in the Study of International Law', 10 *Yale JIL* (1984), p. 1.

Reisman, W. M., 'Criteria for the Lawful Use of Force in International Law', 10 *Yale JIL* (1985), p. 279.

Reisman, W. M., 'International Law after the Cold War', 84 *AJIL* (1990), p. 859.

Reisman, W. M., 'Haiti and the Validity of International Action', 89 *AJIL* (1995), p. 82.

Reisman, W. M., 'Kosovo's Antimonies', 93 *AJIL* (1999), p. 860.

Rigaux, F., 'Hans Kelsen on International Law', 9 *EJIL* (1998), p. 325.

Rijkema, P., 'Customary International Law in the Nicaragua Cases', 20 *Netherlands Yearbook of International Law* (1989), p. 91.

Rodley, N. S., 'Human Rights and Humanitarian Intervention: The Case law of the World Court', 38 *ICLQ* (1989), p. 321.

Rorty, R., 'Pragmatism, Relativism and Irrationalism', 53 *Proceedings & Addresses of the American Philosophical Association* (1980), p. 719.

Rentlen, A. D., 'The Unanswered Challenge of Relativism and the Consequences for Human Rights', 7 *Hum. RQ* (1984), p. 514.

Rostow, E. V., 'The Politics of Force: Analysis and Prognosis', 36 *Yearbook of World Affairs* (1982), p. 38.

Rostow, E. V., 'The Legality of the International Use of Force by and from States', 10 *Yale JIL* (1985), p. 286.

Rougier, A., 'La théorie d'intervention d'humanité', 17 *RGDIP* (1910), p. 468.

Rubin, A., 'The Hostages Incident', 36 *Yearbook of World Affairs* (1982), p. 213.

Salmon, J. J. A., 'Le fait dans l'application du droit international', 175 *RC* (1982 II), p. 257.

Scelle, G., 'Règles générales du droit de la paix', 46 *RC* (1933 IV), p. 331.

Schachter, O., 'Towards a Theory of International Obligation', 8 *Va JIL* (1967–68), p. 300.

Schachter, O., 'Human Dignity as a Normative Concept', 77 *AJIL* (1983), p. 848.

Schachter, O., 'The Right of States to Use Armed Force', 82 *Michigan Law Review* (1984), p. 1620.

Schachter, O., 'The Legality of Pro-Democratic Intervention', 78 *AJIL* (1984), p. 645.

Schachter, O., 'In Defence of the International Rules on the Use of Force', 53 *University of Chicago Law Review* (1986), p. 113.

Schachter, O., 'Self-Judging Self-Defence', 19 *Case Western Reserve Journal of International Law* (1987), p. 121.

Schachter, O., 'Self-Defence and the Rule of Law', 83 *AJIL* (1989), p. 259.

Scheffer, D., 'Toward a Modern Doctrine of Humanitarian Intervention', 23 *University of Toledo Law Review* (1992), p. 253.

Schwarzenberger, G., 'The Fundamental Principles of International Law', 87 *RC* (1955 I), p. 190.

Schwebel, S. M., 'Aggression, Intervention and Self Defence', 136 *RC* (1972 II), p. 411.

Schweisfurth, T., 'Operations to Rescue Nationals in Third States Involving the Use of Force', 23 *German YIL* (1980), p. 159.

Scott, J. B., 'The Legal Nature of International Law', 1 *AJIL* (1907), p. 831.

Sheeban, J. A., 'The Principle of Self-Help in International Law as Justification for State Use of Armed Force', 1 *The Fletcher Forum* (1977), p. 135.

Sicilianos, L.-A., 'L'invocation de la légitime défense', 2 *Hague YBIL* (1989), p. 147.

Simma, B., 'NATO, the UN and the Use of Force: Legal Aspects', 10 *EJIL* (1999), p. 12.

Singer, J. W., 'Catcher in the Rye Jurisprudence', 35 *Rutgers Law Review* (1983), p. 275.

Singer, J. W., 'The Player and the Cards. Nihilism and Legal Theory', 94 *Yale LJ* (1984), p. 1.

Slater, J., Nardin, T., 'Nonintervention and Human Rights', 48 *Journal of Politics* (1986), p. 86.

Slaughter, A.-M., 'International Law in a World of Liberal States', 6 *EJIL* (1995), p. 503.

Slaughter, A.-M., 'Liberal International Relations Theory and International Economic Law', 10 *American University Journal of International Law & Policy* (1995), p. 717.

Sofaer, A. D., 'The Legality of the United States Action in Panama', 29 *Columbia Journal of Transnational Law* (1991), p. 282.

Sparer, E., 'Fundamental Human Rights, Legal Entitlements: A Friendly Critique of CLS', 36 *Stanford Law Review* (1984), p. 509.

Spragens, T., 'Justification, Practical Reason and Political Theory', *Nomos* XXVIII, p. 335.

Stewart, I., 'The Basic Norm as Fiction', *Juridical Review* (1980), p. 199.

Stone, J., 'Mystery and Mystique in the Basic Norm', 26 *Modern LRev.* (1963), p. 34.

Suzuki, E., 'The New Haven School of International Law: An Invitation to A Policy-Oriented Jurisprudence', 1 *Yale Studies in Public Order* (1974), p. 1.

Tasioulas, J., 'In Defence of Relative Normativity: Communitarian Values and the Nicaragua Case', 16 *Oxford Journal of Legal Studies* (1996), p. 85.

Tesón, F. R., 'International Human Rights and Cultural Relativity', 25 *Va JIL* (1985), p. 869.

Tesón, F. R., 'Le peuple, c'est moi! The World Court and Human Rights', 81 *AJIL* (1987), p. 173.

Tesón, F. R., 'The Kantian Theory of International Law', 92 *Columbia Law Review* (1992), p. 53.

Tesón, F. R., 'The Rawlsian Theory of International Law', 9 *Ethics & International Affairs* (1995), p. 79.

Tesón, F. R., 'Collective Humanitarian Intervention', 17 *Michigan Journal of International Law* (1996), p. 323.

Tipson, F. S., 'The Lasswell – McDougal Enterprise', 14 *Va JIL* (1974), p. 535.

Trimble, P., 'International Law, World Order and CLS', 42 *Stanford Law Review* (1990), p. 811.

Tsagourias, N., 'The Lost Innocence of Humanity: The Tragedy of Rwanda and the Doctrine of Humanitarian Intervention', 2 *International Law and Armed Conflict Commentary* (1995), p. 19.

Tsagourias, N., 'The Nicaragua Case and the Use of Force: The Theoretical Construction of the Decision and Its Deconstruction', 1 *Journal Armed Conflict Law* (1996), p. 81.

Tushnet, M. V., 'Following the Rules Laid Down: A Critique of Interpretivism and Neutral Principles', 96 *Harvard Law Review* (1983), p. 781.

Tushnet, M. V., 'An Essay on Rights', 62 *Texas Law Review* (1984), p. 1363.

Tushnet, M. V., 'Critical Legal Studies: A Political History', 100 *Yale LJ* (1991), p. 1515.

Unger, R. M., 'The Critical Legal Studies Movement', 96 *Harvard Law Review* (1983), p. 561.

von Verdross, A., 'Le fondement du droit international', 16 *Recueil des Cours* (1927 I), p. 245.

von Verdross, A., 'Idées directrices de l' Organisation des Nations Unies', 83 *RC* (1953 II), p. 1.

Verhoeven, J., 'Le droit, le juge et la violence. Les arrêts Nicaragua c. Etats-Unis', 91 *RGDIP* (1987), p. 1159.

Verwey, W., 'Humanitarian Intervention in International Law', 32 *Netherlands International Law Review* (1985), p. 357.

Waldock, C. H. M., 'The Regulation of the Use of Force', 81 *RC* (1952 II), p. 451.

Waldock, C. H. M., 'General Course on Public International Law', 106 *RC* (1962 II), p. 1.

Walzer, M., 'The Moral Standing of States: A Response to Four Critics', 9 *Philosophy & Public Affairs* (1980), p. 209.

Walzer, M., 'The Politics of Rescue', *Dissent* (1995), p. 35.

Wani, I. J., 'Humanitarian Intervention and the Tanzania-Uganda War', 3 *Horn of Africa* (1980), p. 18.

Wedgwood, R., 'The Use of Armed Force in International Affairs: Self-Defense and the Panama Invasion', 29 *Columbia Journal of Transnational Law* (1991), p. 609.

Wedgwood, R., 'NATO's Campaign in Yugoslavia', 93 *AJIL* (1999), p. 828.

Wehberg, H., 'L'interdiction du recours à la force; le principe et les problèmes qui se posent', 78 *RC* (1951 I), p. 1.

Weil, P., 'Towards Relative Normativity in International Law', 77 *AJIL* (1983), p. 413.

Wellens, K. C., 'Diversity in Secondary Rules and the Unity of International Law: Some Reflections on Current Trends', 25 *Netherlands Yearbook of International Law* (1994), p. 3.

Wengler, W., 'L'interdiction de recourir à la force. Problèmes et tendances', 7 *Revue belge de droit international* (1971), p. 401.

White, N. D., 'Humanitarian Intervention', 1 *International Law and Armed Conflict Commentary* (1994), p. 13.

Winfield, P. H., 'The History of Intervention in International Law', 3 *BYBIL* (1922–23), p. 130.

Williams, G. L., 'International Law and the Controversy Concerning the Word "Law"', 22 *BYBIL* (1945), p. 146.

Wolf, D., 'Humanitarian Intervention', 9 *Michigan Yearbook of International Legal Studies* (1988), p. 333.

Wright, Q., 'The Meaning of the Pact of Paris', 27 *AJIL* (1933), p. 39.

Wright, Q., 'The Legality of Intervention under the UN Charter', 51 *Proc. ASIL* (1957), p. 79.

Wright, G., 'A Contemporary Theory of Humanitarian Intervention', 4 *Florida International Law Journal* (1989), p. 435.

Zedalis, R. J., 'Protection of Nationals Abroad: Is Consent the Basis of Legal Obligation?', 25 *Texas International Law Journal* (1990), p. 209.

Index